21/-

TEACHER'S GUIDE
FOR BOOK 3
[METRIC]

THE SCHOOL MATHEMATICS PROJECT

TEACHER'S GUIDE
FOR BOOK 3
[METRIC]

CAMBRIDGE
AT THE UNIVERSITY PRESS
1970

Published by the Syndics of the Cambridge University Press
Bentley House, 200 Euston Road, London, N.W.1
American Branch: 32 East 57th Street, New York, N.Y. 10022

Library of Congress Catalogue Card Number: 66–73798

International Standard Book Number: 0 521 08121 1

First edition 1967
Metricated 1970

Printed in Great Britain
at the University Printing House, Cambridge
(Brooke Crutchley, University Printer)

THE
SCHOOL MATHEMATICS
PROJECT

When the S.M.P. was founded in 1961, its objective was to devise radically new mathematics courses, with accompanying G.C.E. syllabuses and examinations, which would reflect, more adequately than did the traditional syllabuses, the up-to-date nature and usages of mathematics.

The first stage of this objective is now more or less complete. *Books 1–5* form the main series of pupil's texts, starting at the age of 11+ and leading to the O-level examination in 'S.M.P. Mathematics', while *Books 3T, 4* and *5* give a three-year course to the same O-level examination. (*Books T* and *T4*, together with their Supplement, represent the first attempt at this three-year course, but they may be regarded as obsolete.) *Advanced Mathematics Books 1–4* cover the syllabus for the A-level examination in 'S.M.P. Mathematics' and in preparation are five (or more) shorter texts covering the material of various sections of the A-level examination in 'S.M.P. Further Mathematics'. There are two books for 'S.M.P. Additional Mathematics' at O-level Every Book is accompanied by a Teacher's Guide.

For the convenience of Schools, the S.M.P. has an arrangement whereby its examinations are made available by every G.C.E. Examining Board, and it is most grateful to the Secretaries of the eight Boards for their cooperation in this. At the same time, most Boards now offer their own syllabuses in 'modern mathematics' for which the S.M.P. texts are suitable.

By 1967, it had become clear from experience in comprehensive schools that the mathematical content of the S.M.P. texts was suitable for a much wider range of pupil than had been originally anticipated, but that the presentation needed adaptation. Thus it was decided to produce a new series, *Books A–H*, which could serve as a secondary school course starting at the age of 11+. These books are specially suitable for pupils aiming at a C.S.E. examination; however, the framework of the C.S.E. examinations is such that it is inappropriate for the S.M.P. to offer its own examination as it does for the G.C.E.

The completion of all these books does not mean that the S.M.P. has no more to offer to the cause of curriculum research. The team of S.M.P. writers, now numbering some thirty school and university mathematicians, is continually testing and revising old work, and preparing for new. At the same time, the effectiveness of the S.M.P.'s work depends, as it always has done, on obtaining reactions from active teachers—and also from pupils—in the classroom. Readers of the texts can therefore send their comments to the S.M.P. in the knowledge that they will be warmly welcomed.

Finally, the year-by-year activity of the S.M.P. is recorded in the annual Director's Reports which readers are encouraged to obtain on request to the S.M.P. Office at Westfield College, University of London, London, N.W. 3.

ACKNOWLEDGEMENTS

We are much indebted to the Cambridge University Press for their cooperation and help at all times in the preparation of this book.

The Project owes a great debt to its secretary, Miss Anne Freeman, and to Miss M. Z. Andrews and Mrs C. Young for their typing work in connection with this book.

CONTENTS

A NOTE ON METRICATION

With the 1970 reprint of this book, some changes have been made in the notation and units used.

(i) All quantities of money have been expressed in pounds (£) and new pence (p).

(ii) All measures have been expressed in metric units. The fundamental units of the Système International (that is the metric system to be used in Great Britain) are the metre, the kilogram and the second. These units have been used in the book except where practical classroom considerations or an estimation of everyday practice in the years to come have suggested otherwise.

(iii) The notation used for the abbreviations of units and on some other occasions conforms to that suggested in the British Standard publications PD 5686: 1967 and BS 1991: Part 1: 1967.

Where units and numbers have been changed in the texts, the corresponding changes in the Teacher's Guides have been listed in a small leaflet which will be available with the present Guides. Changes involving notation only will not be so listed. The contents of the leaflet will be incorporated into the Teacher's Guides when they are next reprinted.

1

PROBABILITY

1. PROBABILITY

Probability is a topic that always goes down well in the classroom. Starting as it does with games of chance, it makes an immediate appeal to students. Moreover, probability is an important branch of applied mathematics which is of increasing use in science, economics and sociology. Its inclusion at this stage of the school course can be further justified by the way in which it encourages the pupil to think clearly and logically.

Probability began through gambling: in 1654 a Frenchman, the Chevalier de Méré, sought help from Blaise Pascal (of Pascal's Triangle fame) to ask why he was not winning on the wager that he would get at least one double six in 24 throws of two dice. In this country Samuel Pepys and Isaac Newton were corresponding in 1693 on a similar topic. (See *The Gentle Art of Mathematics*, by Dan Pedoe.) But probability is no longer limited to such trivia, interesting though they are. In 1865 Mendel was able to account for results of experiments in the cross-breeding of plants by using probability, and thereby began the study of genetics. A later application concerned the motion of molecules. It is not possible to predict exactly how a particular molecule will move, just as it is impossible to say exactly what the result of tossing a coin will be. However, using probabilities one can predict the overall effect of the motion, in the same way as one can more accurately predict the results when a large number of coins are tossed. At the subatomic level it is not possible to give both the position and velocity of an electron; the best that can be done is to give the probability that an electron is in a certain position with a certain velocity.

This chapter begins with the pupil's experience of the qualitative notion of chance: 'the chances are that we shall win on Saturday'. This is then made quantitative through an example such as counting the frequency of letters in sentences. This leads to the idea of experimental probability or relative frequency. For example, if a die has

1

been thrown 100 times and there have been 15 sixes, then the experimental probability of a six being thrown is $\frac{15}{100}$. $\frac{3}{20}$

In some cases it is possible to predict purely on the grounds of symmetry; for example, when throwing a symmetrical die there is a set $\mathscr{E}$ of possible outcomes each of which is regarded as equally likely $$\mathscr{E} = \{1, 2, 3, 4, 5, 6\}.$$

If we require to score an even number, then the set S in which we are interested is $$S = \{2, 4, 6\}.$$

The expected probability $p(S)$ is

$$p(S) = \frac{n(S)}{n(\mathscr{E})} = \frac{3}{6} = \frac{1}{2}.$$

In terms of an experiment, if the die were thrown a large number of times we would expect the fraction of outcomes producing an even number, that is, the experimental probability, to tend to $\frac{1}{2}$, the expected probability. In general, if N is the number of trials,

$$\text{expected probability} = \lim_{N \to \infty} (\text{experimental probability}).$$

It is interesting to see how this works out in practice (see Exercise B, Question 12).

The definitions of probability are still argued about by philosophers. For example, our definition of expected probability involves 'equally likely'. Is this begging the question? For an interesting discussion of the problem see *Mathematical Ideas*, by Jagjit Singh.

There is no mention of odds until the end of Exercise C. There is a danger that probability and odds will be confused. Mathematically, probability is the more important. It must be emphasized that the probability associated with an event is a number and not a ratio as in the case of odds. 'Probability' and 'chance' are taken to be synonymous.

The chapter then goes on to discuss randomness (this has been implied in, for example, Questions 7 and 11 of Exercise B). The acquisition of a critical outlook is valuable, especially where advertisements are concerned. This is something which we hope will be remembered long after the detailed mathematics is forgotten. It is an interesting class activity to collect examples from the press and to display prize specimens on the noticeboard. Election times are fruitful periods for such projects.

2

It is possible to develop probability from an axiomatic point of view. See, for example, *Mathematics, A New Approach*, Vol. 4, Mansfield and Bruckheimer, and also *Mathematical Gazette*, October 1966.

However, while it is important that the teacher should be familiar with the axiomatic treatment, we do not believe that this is the best way to introduce probability to pupils of 13 and 14. Consequently, the chapter is built on the experience of the pupils, and is treated in a practical way. It is important that the experiments in the text should be carried out. In the classroom this requires organization and planning. It is best in most cases to have the pupils working in pairs, one to toss, for example, and the other to record. In some cases results can be pooled.

The use of ordered pairs and graphical representation is worth encouraging. The set $\mathscr{E}$ of possible outcomes is often referred to as the sample *space*: when throwing two dice the outcomes can be represented in a two-dimensional space; for three dice, the outcomes can be represented by ordered triples in three-dimensional space. The graphical approach brings out the Venn diagram representation—this will be taken up in Book 4. As an example, suppose two dice are thrown and the results are recorded as ordered pairs. Consider the set of outcomes, A and B, where

$$A = \{(x, y): x+y = 7\} \quad \text{and} \quad B = \{(x, y): x+y = 11\}.$$

Then $p(A) = \frac{6}{36}$ and $p(B) = \frac{2}{36}$ (see Figure A). The probability of *A or B* is

$$p(A \cup B) = p(A)+p(B) = \tfrac{6}{36}+\tfrac{2}{36} = \tfrac{8}{36} = \tfrac{2}{9}.$$

But if

$$C = \{(x, y): x+y = 6\} \quad \text{and} \quad D = \{(x, y): x = y\},$$

then

$$p(C \cup D) \neq p(C)+p(D).$$

It is clear from Figure A that

$$p(C \cup D) = p(C)+p(D)-p(C \cap D).$$

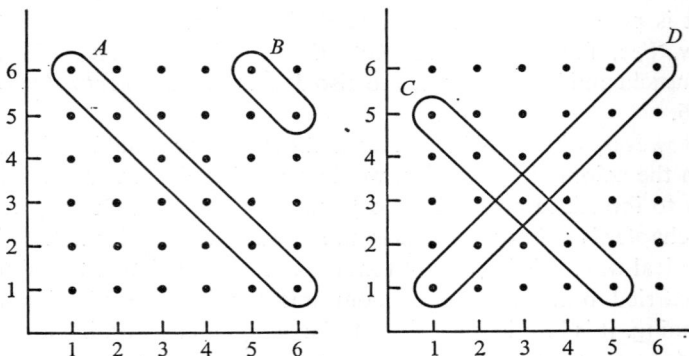

Fig. A

Exercise A (p. 2)

By dividing the class into groups, all of the experiments can be covered, although each pupil will not take part in every one.

1. No. The experiment would have to be performed many times before a conclusion like this could be drawn.

2. (*a*) This would be expected, since $240 \div 6$ is 40.
   (*b*) 1000 times.

3. One would not expect *exactly* two threes in 12 throws. If the die were thrown a large number of times, one would expect a three to occur on approximately one-sixth of the throws.

4. As the number of tosses gets larger, the proportion of 2 heads tends to $\frac{1}{4}$, of 1 head to $\frac{1}{2}$, and of 0 heads to $\frac{1}{4}$. 250 times.

5. One would expect 3 heads on $\frac{1}{8}$ of the trials. (See Exercise C, Question 11.)

6. $\frac{2}{5}$.

8. 2, 3, 4, 5, 6, 7, 8, 9, 10, 11, 12.

   2 can be scored in 1 way; 8 in 5 ways.

   The chance of scoring 8 is greater than that of scoring 2.

   The results of this question can be checked later (Exercise C, Question 3.)

4

2. EXPERIMENTAL PROBABILITY

The experimental probability of throwing:

$\quad$ (a) 2 is $\frac{39}{240}$; $\qquad$ (b) 3 is $\frac{44}{240}$; $\qquad$ (c) 1 is $\frac{40}{240}$.

The experimental probability of either a 1 or a 4 is $\frac{78}{240}$, and of not obtaining a 6 is $\frac{198}{240}$.

If the probability of drawing a heart from a hand of playing cards is 1, then all the cards in the hand are hearts. The probability that a die will turn up 7 is 0. The experimental probability that the coin will land head uppermost if tossed again is 1. The coin has two heads.

Exercise B (p. 4)

2. $\quad$ (a) $\frac{125}{800}$; $\quad$ (b) $\frac{418}{800}$; $\quad$ (c) $\frac{585}{800}$.

3. $\quad$ 1.

5. $\quad$ The teacher may like to check with the expected probability $(l-d)^2/l^2$, where l is the length of the side of the squares, and d is the diameter of a 5p piece. This result is obtained by considering the area inside a square in which the centre of the 5p piece could fall without the coin crossing an edge.

6. $\quad$ This is the well-known Buffon's Needle problem. It can be shown that if the matchstick is of length l and the lines are spaced at a distance a, then the expected probability that the match crosses a line is $2l/\pi a$.

$\quad$ This experiment can be used to obtain an approximation to π.

8. $\quad$ Check later with Exercise C, Question 3.

9. $\quad$ Check later with Exercise D, Question 9.

10. The expected probabilities are: (a) $\frac{1}{6}$; (b) $\frac{1}{2}$.

12. The experimental probability should tend to $\frac{1}{6}$.

3. EXPECTED PROBABILITY

(2, 3) represents a 2 on the red die, and a 3 on the blue. There are 6 points which represent a total of 7. The probability of scoring 7 is $\frac{6}{36}$.

Exercise C (p. 8)

It may seem tedious to write out all the elements in the set of possible outcomes, but it does help avoid to mistakes.

1. $\mathscr{E} = \{1, 2, 3, 4, 5, 6\}, \quad S = \{2, 3, 5\},$

$$p(S) = \frac{n(S)}{n(\mathscr{E})} = \frac{3}{6} = \frac{1}{2}.$$

N.B. 1 is by definition not a prime, but 2 is. (See T.G. to Book 1, p. 65.)

2. $S = \{HH, HT, TH, TT\}, \quad E = \{HH\}.$

(a) $p(S) = \dfrac{n(S)}{n(\mathscr{E})} = \dfrac{1}{4};$ (b) $p(\text{not } S) = 1 - p(S) = \frac{3}{4}.$

3. It is easiest to use Figure 3.

Score	2	3	4	5	6	7	8	9	10	11	12
Probability	$\frac{1}{36}$	$\frac{2}{36}$	$\frac{3}{36}$	$\frac{4}{36}$	$\frac{5}{36}$	$\frac{6}{36}$	$\frac{5}{36}$	$\frac{4}{36}$	$\frac{3}{36}$	$\frac{2}{36}$	$\frac{1}{36}$

The sum of the probabilities is 1.

4. $\frac{3}{324}.$

5. $\mathscr{E} = \}H1, H2, H3, H4, H5, H6, T1, T2, T3, T4, T5, T6\},$
    $S = \{H5, H6\}.$

$$p(S) = \frac{n(S)}{n(\mathscr{E})} = \frac{2}{12}.$$

6. Counting picture cards as King, Queen, Jack, the probcbility is $\frac{12}{52}.$

7. $\mathscr{E} = \{1, 1), (1, 2), (1, 3), (1, 4), (2, 1), (2, 2), (2, 3), (2, 4), (3, 1),$
    $\quad\quad (3, 2), (3, 3), (3, 4), (4, 1), (4, 2), (4, 3), (4, 4)\},$
    $S = \{(3, 4), (4, 3)\}.$

$$p(S) = \frac{n(S)}{n(\mathscr{E})} = \frac{2}{16}.$$

8. *AB, AC, AD, BA, BC, BD, CA, CB, CD, DA, DB, DC.*

(a) $\frac{2}{12};$ (b) $\frac{8}{12};$ (c) $\frac{6}{12};$ (d) $\frac{6}{12}.$

9. *WW, DD, LL, WD, DW, WL, LW, LD, DL.*
    (a) $\frac{1}{9};$ (b) $\frac{4}{9}.$

10. $\frac{16}{51}$ (counting ace low); $\frac{20}{51}$ (counting ace high), if card is not replaced.

11. (*a*) {*HHH, HHT, HTH, HTT, THH, THT, TTH, TTT*};
   (*b*) (i) $\frac{1}{8}$, (ii) $\frac{3}{8}$, (iii) $\frac{3}{8}$, (iv) $\frac{1}{8}$;
   (*c*) $\frac{1}{8}$;   (*d*) 0 (!);   (*e*) No.
12. (*a*) 1:7;   (*b*) 3:5;   (*c*) 3:5;
   (*d*) 1:7;   (*e*) 7:1;   (*f*) 1:1.

4. RANDOM SELECTION

(*a*) (i) Write each of the names on a piece of paper and mix them up in a 'hat'.

(ii) Number the boys 1 to 6.

(iii) By tossing coins. See Exercise D, Question 8.

(*b*) 7 turns up most frequently.

(*c*) Since they were entering school together, it is likely that they will have travelled together by the same means and perhaps from the same district.

(*d*) The telephone directory was opened at a page of Mc's or Mac's.

Exercise D (p. 10)

1. No. You will have mainly housewives who are doing the shopping.

2. Information like this is obtained by taking a sample. The sample has to be chosen to be representative of the whole population.

3. By using only people who possess telephones the sample is biased towards a certain social class.

4. How was the sample chosen? Were they people who were buying Whoosh when they were 'interviewed'?

5.

1	2	3	4
4	1	2	3
3	4	1	2
2	3	4	1

Patterns of this type occur in the study of groups: they will be met again in Chapter 11.

In agricultural experiments fertility gradients can be eliminated by using this pattern. If each row were treated with only one fertilizer, then a north–south fertility gradient would give false results. Fertilizer on each square with a certain number would share the advantages and disadvantages of varying fertility.

6. (*a*) The tables have the same pattern

$$T \leftrightarrow 0$$
$$H \leftrightarrow 1.$$

(*b*) (i) 3, (ii) 3.

7.

Pennies				Binary numbers			
4th	3rd	2nd	1st	Eights	Fours	Twos	Units
T	*T*	*T*	*T*	0	0	0	0
T	*T*	*T*	*H*	0	0	0	1
T	*T*	*H*	*T*	0	0	1	0
T	*T*	*H*	*H*	0	0	1	1
T	*H*	*T*	*T*	0	1	0	0
T	*H*	*T*	*H*	0	1	0	1
T	*H*	*H*	*T*	0	1	1	0
T	*H*	*H*	*H*	0	1	1	1
H	*T*	*T*	*T*	1	0	0	0
H	*T*	*T*	*H*	1	0	0	1
H	*T*	*H*	*T*	1	0	1	0
H	*T*	*H*	*H*	1	0	1	1
H	*H*	*T*	*T*	1	1	0	0
H	*H*	*T*	*H*	1	1	0	1
H	*H*	*H*	*T*	1	1	1	0
H	*H*	*H*	*H*	1	1	1	1

(*a*) 6; (*b*) $\frac{5}{16}$.

8. Toss 4 coins and 'translate' the outcome into binary numbers.
(*a*) Toss 6 coins.
(*b*) Toss 9 coins.

9.

Number of pennies tossed	Number of heads showing						Total number of outcomes
	0	1	2	3	4	5	
1	1	1	0	0	0	0	2
2	1	2	1	0	0	0	4
3	1	3	3	1	0	0	8
4	1	4	6	4	1	0	16
5	1	5	10	10	5	1	32

10. (*a*) The next row is

$$1 \quad 6 \quad 15 \quad 20 \quad 15 \quad 6 \quad 1.$$

(*b*) (i) $\frac{22}{64}$, (ii) $\frac{42}{64}$.

2

ISOMETRIES

In this chapter we combine transformations. The initial work is
geometrical. Next comes the use of letters to denote transformations
and this leads to an algebra of transformations. Chapter 3 contains
the treatment of transformations by matrix methods. The two
chapters need to be taken closely together.

1. POTATO PRINTING

The use of a potato printer in motivating the work that follows is
usually very successful. The class could be instructed to read this
section and to bring to school next day the properly cut potatoes.
This will bring out very strongly the ideas of directly and oppositely
congruent figures. The technical terms should be left until the end
of the investigation.

For practical work it is more convenient, certainly less messy, to
use a transparent plastic sheet or tracing paper. For use with the
former, wax pencils are required and one sheet can be kept in the
pupil's exercise book and used many times. Greaseproof paper
raided from the larder makes an adequate substitute for the latter;
so does 'Bronco'-type toilet paper which is easy to dispense! The
large quantity needed, however, is surprising. It is important to
allow time for strong visual impressions of these transformations
to develop and the use of actual material should not be discontinued
too soon.

Once the ideas are clear, the class will draw diagrams to illustrate
each question and will make up their own questions and discuss
solutions. It is then good to introduce some 'mental' geometry. The
class is required to picture transformations and corresponding
images in their heads. This use of the imagination strengthens the
geometrical intuition and will be helpful when plans and elevations
are met in a later book.

The Union Jack has not been drawn accurately, as pupils will quickly point out. The distortion makes it possible for all the triangles to be congruent and for their diagonal sides to be in the same straight line.

2. COMBINING TRANSFORMATIONS

Half-centimetre squared paper is recommended for the initial work and care should be taken to make the transformations simple. For example, translations whose vectors have integral components, rotations about grid points, etc. It should not be necessary for centres of rotation to be *constructed at this stage*.

There is sometimes confusion between a transformation and an image. The reason seems to be that the transformation and the image of the transformation are not properly distinguished from each other. Children should be encouraged to talk precisely about these things and not to call an image 'a transformation' or vice versa.

Exercise A (p. 14)

Tracing paper, etc., will be useful in most of this exercise.

1. (a) Half-turn about O; (b) translation $\begin{pmatrix} 10 \\ -6 \end{pmatrix}$.

2. (a) Half-turn about $(5, 0)$; (b) translation $\begin{pmatrix} 0 \\ -6 \end{pmatrix}$.

3. (a) and (b) No. After a reflection it will be oppositely congruent to both triangles 7 and 8 and so a translation will not do.

4. The most obvious pair is

$$\begin{pmatrix} -10 \\ 0 \end{pmatrix} \quad \text{and} \quad \begin{pmatrix} 0 \\ 6 \end{pmatrix},$$

the order being immaterial. There are an infinity of other such pairs and this should be stressed. Start with pairs that can be tried out on the diagram such as

$$\begin{pmatrix} -6 \\ 4 \end{pmatrix} \quad \text{and} \quad \begin{pmatrix} -4 \\ 2 \end{pmatrix}.$$

They will already 'know' theoretically that all that is required is a pair $\begin{pmatrix} a \\ b \end{pmatrix} \quad \text{and} \quad \begin{pmatrix} c \\ d \end{pmatrix}$

such that $a+c = {}^-10$ and $b+d = 6$, but it will often take a little while before they have the confidence to select a and b at random and work out c and d without reference to the figure.

5. Half-turn about $(5, {}^-3)$; half-turn about $(0, 0)$; no.

6. $\begin{pmatrix} 12 \\ 0 \end{pmatrix}$; $\begin{pmatrix} 2 \\ 6 \end{pmatrix}$ followed by $\begin{pmatrix} -12 \\ 0 \end{pmatrix}$.

7. (*a*) No; rotation—reflection will produce opposite congruence, translation produces direct congruence;
(*b*) no; translation—rotation direct, reflection opposite;
(*c*) yes; reflection—reflection direct, rotation also direct.

8. (*a*) Reflection in line $y=0$;   (*b*) half-turn about $(5, 3)$;
(*c*) no single transformation in the present repertoire, since triangles 2 and 8 are oppositely congruent but not in mirror positions. It is worth pointing out that we have not yet *closed* the set of isometric transformations, i.e. it is not always possible to find a single rotation, reflection or translation to map a figure onto a congruent figure whatever its position. The remaining isometry (hinted at in the summary) is the *glide-reflection*, which will be met in a later book.

9. Reflection in the line $x+y = 0$.

10. (*a*) Impossible, since corresponding sides are not both parallel and in the same sense in any of the four triangles;
(*b*) it is easy to see the single reflections under which $\triangle 2 \to \triangle 7$ and $\triangle 1 \to \triangle 8$. For $\triangle 2 \to \triangle 1$ (and similarly for $\triangle 7 \to \triangle 8$) a pair of reflections will do: reflect $\triangle 2$ in $y = 3$ and the image in $x = 5$. For $\triangle 2 \to \triangle 8$ (and similarly for $\triangle 1 \to \triangle 7$) we require a triple of reflections: reflect $\triangle 2$ in $y = \frac{1}{2}$ and the image in $x = 5$, and that image in $y = {}^-2\frac{1}{2}$.

11. (*a*) Translation $\begin{pmatrix} -2 \\ -8 \end{pmatrix}$;
(*b*) impossible, the congruence is opposite, but the figures are not symmetrically placed about any mirror-line.

12. Onto either $\triangle 7$ or $\triangle 8$, to either of which it is now directly congruent, but without having corresponding sides parallel. The centres of rotation can be found by drawing the mediators between two pairs of corresponding points (see Book 2, Chapter 5).

11

3. THE ALGEBRA OF TRANSFORMATIONS

The use of letters to denote transformations has strong links with the use of letters to denote functions, a topic which will be dealt with later in Chapter 10. A single capital letter is used to denote a transformation and in the text we shall use bold type for this letter. With a letter following in brackets we mean the *image* under the transformation. The letter in brackets is to be read as a figure or object, e.g. $X(F)$ denotes the image of the figure labelled F under reflection in $x = 0$. Pupils should be discouraged from referring to the 'transformation $X(F)$'. (Teachers might also fight the similar temptation to refer to the 'function sin x'—an analogous argument shows that this should be the 'function sine'.)

On first acquaintance it is easier to think of a transformation acting on a particular figure or object. With particularly slow groups the objects transformed can be the children themselves. Draw two chalk lines at right-angles on the floor and label them $x = 0$ and $y = 0$ (see Figure B). A, B and C denote children. $B = X(A)$, i.e. child B is the image after reflection in $x = 0$ of child A. This can be dramatized by raising opposite arms, touching opposite ears, etc. C could be defined by the equation $C = H(A)$ where H is a half-turn about $(0, 0)$.

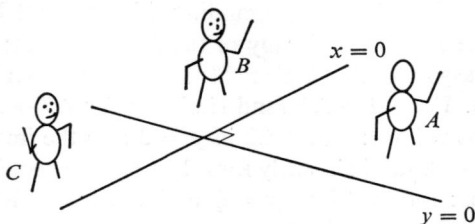

Fig. A

After some practice, particular images cease to be so important and the domain of the transformation is taken to be the whole of the plane containing $x = 0$ and $y = 0$, together with any figures drawn in it.

The order of symbols causes no difficulty if $BA(P)$ is thought of as $B(A(P))$, i.e. the image under B of $A(P)$. It is best to encourage this type of logical thought rather than rely on rote learning of rules such

12

as 'done first, written second' which so easily become mere parrot cries, and which seem to make difficulties where none actually exist.

Exercise B (p. 17)

1. (a) True;   (b) true;   (c) false;   (d) true.

2. (a) True;   (b) false;   (c) false;   (d) true.

3. (a) $\triangle 1$;   (b) $\triangle 7$;   (c) $\triangle 7$;   (d) **YA** or **BY**.

4. The translation $\binom{10}{6}$ followed by the translation $\binom{10}{6}$ again, i.e. the translation $\binom{20}{12}$. **CCC** denotes the translation $\binom{30}{18}$, coordinates are (38, 19). **C⁴** or **CCCC** denotes the translation $\binom{10}{6}$ repeated four times, i.e. the translation $\binom{40}{24}$.

N.B. The numbers governing the translation are *not* raised to the power, but multiplied by it (this is because the combination of translations corresponds to the *addition* of vectors).

5. (a) False;   (b) true;   (c) true.

6. (a), (c), (d) Yes; (b) and (e) need more care. The answer is no. The figure as a whole will *look* the same, but the opposite sides will have been interchanged as the numbers will show. Under the identity transformation every part of the figure occupies the same position as it did before. (b) and (e) are known as *symmetry* transformations of the pattern. It is possible to argue, on purely physical grounds, that a 360° rotation is not the same as the stay-put proper, atoms may have been lost, heat generated, etc. So far as the mathematical abstractions with which we deal are concerned, such an argument does not concern us. Rotations of other multiples of 360° are similarly considered to be equivalent to the identity transformation, together with double reflections, etc.

7. (a) **I**;   (b) **H**;   (c) **Y**;   (d) **I**;   (e) **I**.

8. It is simply **R**. (a) **R**; (b) **R**; (c) **R²**.

9. **E** denotes the translation $\begin{pmatrix} 1 \\ 11 \end{pmatrix}$; **F** denotes the translation $\begin{pmatrix} -7 \\ 1 \end{pmatrix}$;
G denotes the translation $\begin{pmatrix} 6 \\ -12 \end{pmatrix}$.

10. M_2 is not **I**, although it leaves $P(2, 2)$ unchanged. It would alter the position in the plane of all points not on $x = 2$. Under the identity transformation every point of the plane remains fixed.

For the points see Figure B.

No, there is no transformation M_a equivalent to M_1 for *all* points of the plane.

11. Turn left, rotating on the left heel, take one step forward.

12. $z = 3$; other values are $z = 6, 9, \dots$. Fractional values could be conceived but only positive integral powers of a transformation are defined.

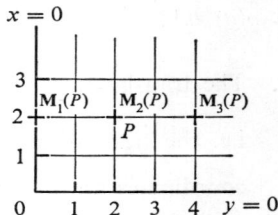

Fig. B

4. TRANSLATIONS COMBINED

In a later book we shall look systematically at the group of all isometries in a plane. It is still too early at present and, as has been pointed out already, we do not yet know all the isometries. A start is made here to draw the threads together. The tables at the end of the chapter will be amplified and completed later. It is recommended that children be helped to make up their own tables of combination before they have their attention drawn to the ones printed.

Translations were met in Chapter 7 of Book 2. There we were interested in the vectors which specified the translations and did not develop a notation for the translations themselves. It is important to be clear that an interpretation of

$$a+b = c$$

is that the translation **A**, specified by **a**, followed by the translation **B**, specified by **b**, is equivalent to a translation **C**, specified by **c**; in the algebra of transformations this would be written

$$BA = C.$$

14

$RS(P)$ is obtained by completing the parallelogram, $SR(P) = RS(P)$. RST is also a translation, since any combination of translations is a translation. Figures that can be mapped onto each other by one or more translations must be *similarly situated*, i.e. all sides parallel and in the same sense in corresponding positions. This term is not used in the pupils' text though some teachers might like to introduce it.

$$RST = RTS = SRT = STR = TRS = TSR = Q \quad \text{say.}$$

There are six possible permutations in all. The image under Q of a point P, together with its intermediate positions, is shown in Figure C. The figure reminds one of a parallelepiped or 'squashed box'. The three-dimensional effect is not accidental, since the result is equally true in three dimensions—a fact worth bringing out.

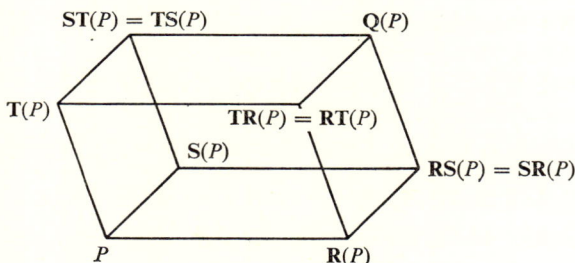

Fig. C

5. INVERSE TRANSFORMATIONS

We met the identity transformation in one of the questions in Exercise B. Now we look at the inverse of a transformation. This matches with inverse functions which have already been used in the solution of equations. It is immaterial whether A^{-1} is read 'A inverse' or 'A negative one'. $A^{-1}A = AA^{-1}$ for any transformation, even if two such transformations do not necessarily commute (e.g. two reflections do not usually commute).

The inverse of any transformation is a transformation of the same type: in particular the inverse of a translation is itself a translation, so R^{-1} is a translation and so is S^{-1}.

Exercise C (p. 20)

1. Translation across the page from left to right through:
   (*a*) 4 units; (*b*) 6 units; (*c*) 8 units;
   (*d*) ⁻2 units (i.e. from right to left); (*e*) ⁻6 units.

   T⁰ might be a useful notation for **I**, but is not often used.

2. (*a*) (1, 4); (*b*) (1, 4); (*c*) (⁻2, 2); (*d*) (⁻2, ⁻3);
   (*e*) (2, ⁻2); (*f*) (0, 5); (*g*) (⁻1, 1).

3. (*a*) (1, 3); (*b*) (4, 1); (*c*) (1, ⁻1);
   (*d*) (3, 3); (*e*) (3, 3); (*f*) (4, ⁻2);
   (*g*) (2, 5); (*h*) (⁻4, ⁻3); (*i*) (1+*b*, 1+*a*).

4. (*a*) The translation $\begin{pmatrix}-5\\-3\end{pmatrix}$.

   (*b*) Any $\begin{pmatrix}a\\b\end{pmatrix}, \begin{pmatrix}c\\d\end{pmatrix}$ such that $a+c =$ ⁻5, $b+d =$ ⁻3.

   (*c*) Any $\begin{pmatrix}a\\b\end{pmatrix}, \begin{pmatrix}c\\d\end{pmatrix}, \begin{pmatrix}e\\f\end{pmatrix}$ such that $a+c+e =$ ⁻5, $b+d+f =$ ⁻3.

   (*d*) (7, 11), (6, 7), (9, 6).

   (*e*) (2, 6) → (4, 2), (4, 1) → (6, ⁻3).

5. A(*P*) = (2, 2); **B**(*P*) = (⁻3, ⁻1); **c** = $\begin{pmatrix}0\\11\end{pmatrix}$, **C**(*P*) = (⁻1, 9).

6. $\begin{pmatrix}-8\\-9\end{pmatrix}$; (*a*) **M**; (*b*) **M**⁻¹.

7. See Figure D. The vectors may be in any position. It is confusing if they both start from (0, 0), hence the (quite arbitrary) choice of (0, 0) and (⁻2, 0) respectively for the starting points; **K²**, **K**⁻².

8. $R_1(O) = (1, 0)$; $R_2R_1(O) = (1+2, 0)$; $R_3R_2R_1(O) = (1+2+3, 0)$;
   $R_4R_3R_2R_1(O) = (1+2+3+4, 0)$.

   The points are plotted in Figure E. It is helpful to remember that

   $$1+2+3+\ldots+n = \tfrac{1}{2}n(n+1).$$

   $$R_{10}R_9 \ldots R_3R_2R_1(O) = (55, 0).$$

   $R_1R_2R_3 \ldots R_9R_{10}(O)$ is the same point; 14.

16

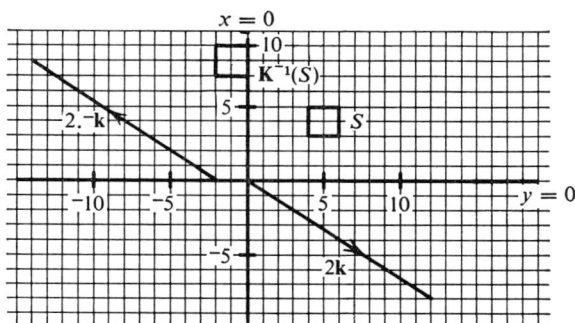

Fig. D

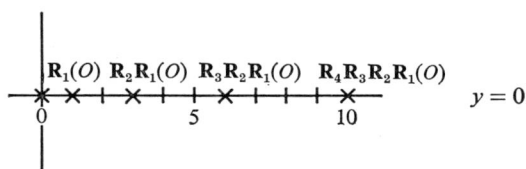

Fig. E

9. Plenty of examples should be discussed to enable pupils to see for themselves that the answer is the transformation **T**. This is not an obvious statement!

6. REFLECTIONS IN PARALLEL LINES

This work is parallel to that done with small mirrors in the Physics department. It is desirable that some connection should be shown although the thickness of the glass in actual mirrors tends to make theoretical results differ from practical ones. The class, however, should be left in no doubt that a reflection in a line is an accurately defined mathematical concept and is in no way dependent on the properties of matter! A simple shape cut from thin card makes the reproduction of a series of congruent shapes much easier.

(a) As can be seen from Figure F, the extra image is $M_1 M_2(P)$. $M_2 M_1(P)$ is directly congruent to P, the remainder are oppositely congruent.

17

(b) Reflection in m_3 maps 3 onto 4, also 4 onto 3, where m_3 is a new mirror-line, the mediator of images 3 and 4. Reflection in m_3 followed by reflection in m_3 maps the object onto itself. Reflection in m_3 is its own inverse (as is any reflection).

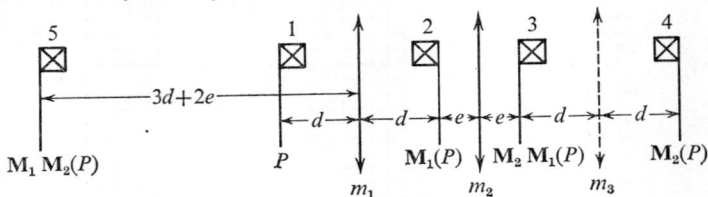

Fig. F

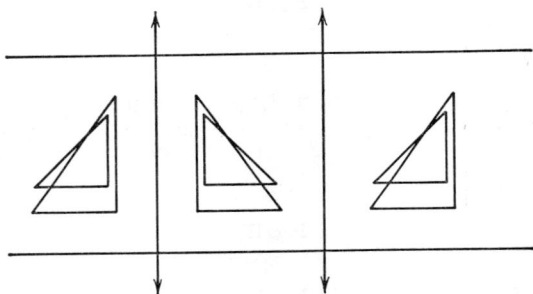

Fig. G

(c) Translation from left to right. As Figure F makes clear, the distance is $2(d+e)$, i.e. twice the distance between the original parallel lines.

(d) Again a translation, but from right to left through $2(d+e)$.

(e) ∞.

(f) With reference to Figure 15, there need be only two mirror-lines, as has been made clear in the previous work. Extra mirror-lines, themselves the reflections of mirror-lines, can be inserted and improve the symmetry, but are not needed. Each must be the mediator of an adjacent pair of motifs (see Figure G); it does not matter which two pairs are chosen. The simplest connection is that the translation should be through twice the distance between the mirror-lines. Since the frieze is infinite, however, a translation through any even multiple of the distance between the mirror-lines will do equally well. If the frieze is to be thought of as being obtained from translations alone, then it will be necessary to change the 'basic motif'.

18

Exercise D (p. 23)

1. (a) (⁻3, 1);   (b) (5, 1);   (c) (⁻5, 1);   (d) (11, 1).

   M_1M_2 is equivalent to the translation $\begin{pmatrix} -8 \\ 0 \end{pmatrix}$; M_2M_1 the transla-

   tion $\begin{pmatrix} 8 \\ 0 \end{pmatrix}$.

   They are inverse translations.

$M_1 M_2 M_1(A)$ $M_1(A)$ m_1 A m_2 $M_2 M_1(A)$ $M_2 M_1 M_2 M_1(A)$

Fig. H

2. (a) See Figure H.

   This would not make a proper frieze since the distance between one pair is not the same as the distance between every other adjacent pair, also the images face opposite ways on either side. N.B. Make sure the triangle is not symmetrical.

   (b) The answer is the same.

4. An obvious pair is $x = 0$ and $x = 3\frac{1}{2}$. Any pair of lines $3\frac{1}{2}$ units apart will do.

5. $y = {}^-2x$.

6. About 160 cm. See Figure I. (Estimating 20 cm as the width of the head.)

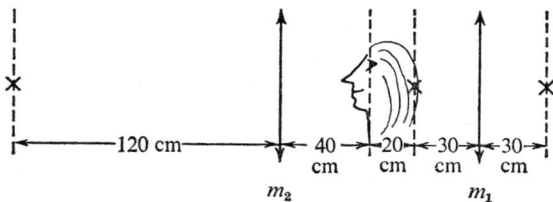

─120 cm─   40 cm 20 cm 30 cm 30 cm m_2 m_1

Fig. I

7. REFLECTIONS IN INTERSECTING LINES

It is necessary to take a good deal of care to get correct results here and with a clumsy class it might be preferable to duplicate Figure J and hand it out for the class to interpret.

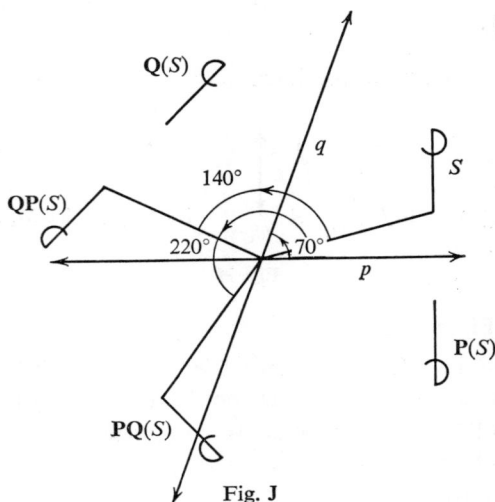

Fig. J

The single transformation that maps S onto $\mathbf{QP}(S)$ is a 140° rotation about the point of intersection of p and q. The angle is double the angle between p and q. The single transformation that maps S onto $\mathbf{PQ}(S)$ is a 220° rotation about the same point. The two angles add to 360°. $\mathbf{PQ}$ and $\mathbf{QP}$ do not map S onto the same image, that is, $\mathbf{P}$ and $\mathbf{Q}$ do not commute. It may be necessary to take a class average to get the required answer. In the exercise that follows we show the reason for all this.

Figure 9 on p. 17 concerns the special case in which the angle between the intersecting lines is 90°. The angles of the equivalent rotations are both 180° (half-turns) and so these particular reflections commute. This is no contradiction, in fact, it can provide a definition of perpendicularity in an axiomatic development of transformation geometry. For we can define two lines p and q to be perpendicular if and only if the corresponding reflections $\mathbf{P}$ and $\mathbf{Q}$ satisfy

$$\mathbf{PQ} = \mathbf{QP} \neq \mathbf{I}.$$

20

An interesting example of reflections in intersecting lines is provided by the kaleidoscope, and the class might enjoy discussing the way in which the pattern in Colour-figure 4 of Book 1 has been obtained. This leads on to the question of what angles are possible between the mirrors of a kaleidoscope.

Exercise E (p. 25)

1. P_n is (3, ⁻2) if n is even and (⁻3, ⁻2) if n is odd.

2. The images are parallel and similarly situated.

3. $M_2M_1(F)$ and $M_2'M_1'(F)$ are similarly situated. So are $M_2M_1'(F)$ and $M_2'M_1(F)$. This is a continuation of the line of thought in Question 2. The final direction of the image after two reflections depends only on the directions of the mirror-lines, not on their positions.

4. (a) 180° rotation about (0, 0);   (b) 90° rotation about (0, 0);
    (c) 270° rotation about (0, 0);
    (d) **XY** simplifies to **H** (half-turn) so that **AXY = AH**. Sketching **AH** shows that it is equivalent to reflection in $x+y = 0$.

    (N.B. the operation of combining transformations is associative, so it will not matter whether **AXY** is treated as **A(XY)** or as **(AX)Y**. The product of three reflections is a reflection (or a glide-reflection), not a rotation.)

5. Careful labelling of the known angles leads to $\angle AOD = 260°$. $\angle AOB$ was found to be 100°. The sum of these is 360°. Each is double the 'directed' angle between the two lines (see solution of Question 6). (Pupil's answer $\angle AOD = 100°$ should be accepted.)

6. The 'directed' angle between m_1 and m_2, or 'the angle between m_1 and m_2 in that order', is the anticlockwise angle through which m_1 has to be rotated in order to coincide with m_2. If the angle between m_1 and m_2 is $\theta°$, then that between m_2 and m_1 will be $180° - \theta°$. The *theorem* sums up the experience of Example 2 and Question 5. The method of proof is simply to generalize the angle summation of these questions. The two different cases are illustrated in Figure K. There is also the special case in which the angle is 90°, but this does not demand any special proof.

21

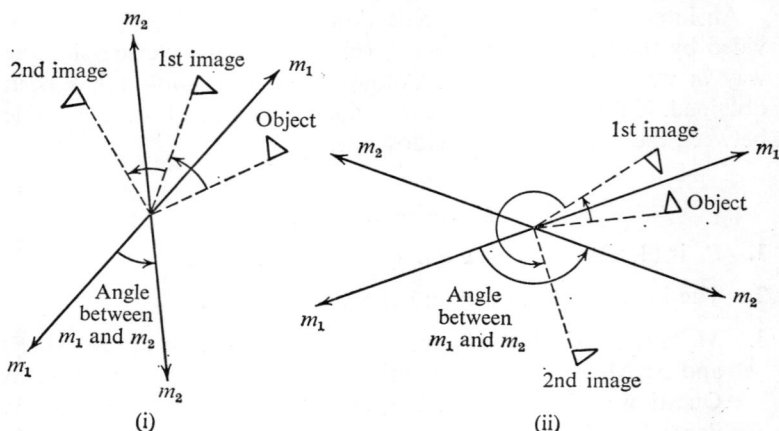

Fig. K

The systematic *proof* of theorems has not formed part of the geometrical development in this course. Nor is this policy changing. A concept of proof (i.e. logical argument resting on a set of assumptions) is being built up both in the geometry and in all the rest of the course. A brief discussion with the class might well be in order at this point.

7. We can see that $M_1M_2M_2M_1 = I$ and that $(M_1M_2)^{-1} = M_2M_1$ (remember that each of M_1 and M_2 is its own inverse). If we are told that $M_1M_2 = M_2M_1$, then each of these is H and so the lines are perpendicular.

8. (a) See Figure L. The lines v and w cannot be parallel, since this would mean that P had to be mapped onto P' by a translation, whereas the transformation is obviously a rotation. The line v is first obtained by the usual construction, the first mapping produces the dotted image. A second reflection in w, maps this onto P'. There are an infinity of pairs v, w. Any point of P, for instance, could be mapped onto the corresponding point of P'. O is the point of intersection of v and w.

(b) A general discussion of how two congruent figures are related will now follow. If the pair are directly congruent, A cannot be mapped onto B by a single reflection. A construction on the lines of (a) can always be found to map A onto B by a

22

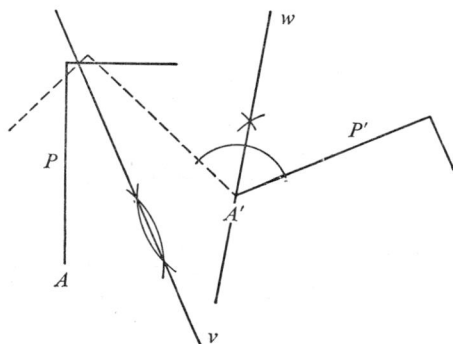

Fig. L

pair of reflections. It makes no difference if A and B are similarly situated.

(*c*) If the pair are oppositely congruent then a single reflection may be possible, but A and B must be symmetrically placed with respect to some mirror-line. They can only be similarly situated if they have a line of symmetry parallel to the mirror-line.

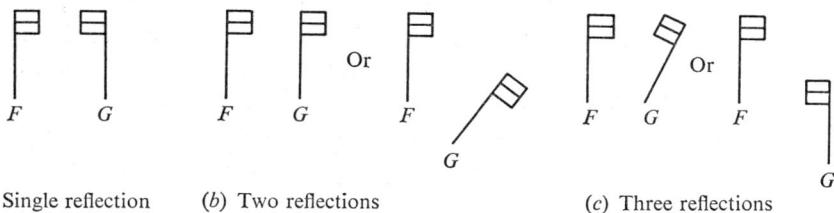

(*a*) Single reflection   (*b*) Two reflections   (*c*) Three reflections

Fig. M

9. The three possibilities are shown in Figure M. Between them they cover every possible type of positioning for F and G. Case (*c*) requires 3 reflections. Only in case (*a*) is the answer unique. In the other cases there are an infinity of pairs or triples of reflections. (The illustration for (*a*) should be repeated at (*c*).)

10. In each case, (*a*), (*b*) and (*c*), the pair H and K must be similarly situated. It is easy to place K so that H cannot be mapped onto it by a translation: merely make sure that the flags are not similarly situated.

23

3

MATRICES

Matrices form one of the most important concepts of modern Linear Algebra and as such have wide applications. Whenever a problem reduces to a set of linear equations then matrix methods are appropriate, and it is significant that a large proportion of computer time is spent in dealing with matrix operations of one sort or another.

There are many reasons why matrices are introduced into this course, but perhaps the most important is the way in which they link many apparently different branches of mathematics, thus clearly demonstrating underlying similarities of structure. In geometry they enable us to describe transformations more concisely, and in so doing much light is thrown on the properties of both the matrices and the transformations. The applications (in later chapters) to networks, relations, probability and linear equations show what a powerful aid matrices can be.

This chapter starts with the matrix as a rectangular array of numbers which stores or displays information (often called an inventory matrix) and then introduces the operations of matrix addition and multiplication before considering, briefly, some applications to geometrical transformations. It is a long chapter but the ideas are quickly mastered. If a break is thought necessary, then it could well come at the end of Section 4.

This is by no means the only way of introducing matrices, and some teachers may prefer to use:

(*a*) Matrix codes (see *Matrices* 1, *Contemporary School Mathematics*, by G. Matthews) (the definition of multiplication here appears to be completely arbitrary—for this purpose other definitions would serve as well, if not better—however, interest is provoked and work with codes certainly gives practice in matrix multiplication);

(*b*) topological networks (see Chapter 6 of this book);

(*c*) electrical networks (see *An Introduction to Matrices*, by A. E. Coulson);

(*d*) geometrical transformations (that is, starting from Section 5 of this chapter).

24

There are now many books available on matrices in addition to those already mentioned. The following selection is given in (increasing) order of difficulty:

Introduction to Finite Mathematics, by J. G. Kemeny, J. L. Snell and G. L. Thompson.

First Stages in Matrices, by G. R. Gibson and J. Mayatt.

Algebraic Structure and Matrices, by E. A. Maxwell.

Algebra, by J. W. Archbold.

A Survey of Modern Algebra, by G. Birkhoff and S. MacLane.

1. MATRICES

The name 'matrix' needs a little explanation. It is the Latin word for 'womb' and its use in a mathematical context is one of the accidents of history. By 1850 it had come to be used in mineralogy to denote the parent mass in which valuable minerals were imbedded, and out of which they have presumably been produced. In that year the mathematician Sylvester, writing a paper on the solution of simultaneous equations by means of determinants (which *determine* by their value the nature of those solutions), had occasion to say: 'We commence with an oblong arrangement of terms consisting of m lines and n columns. This will not in itself represent a determinant, but is, as it were, a Matrix out of which we may form systems of determinants...'. Since then the name, originally a figure of speech, has become a technical term for the rectangular array itself.

This section starts by recalling the use of matrices in Book 2 to present information about networks and generalizes this to any rectangular array of numerical data.

(*a*) 2 direct routes from B to C.

$$\text{From} \begin{cases} A \\ B \\ C \end{cases} \overset{\overset{\text{To}}{\overbrace{\begin{matrix} A & B & C \end{matrix}}}}{\begin{pmatrix} 1 & 1 & 1 \\ 0 & 0 & 2 \\ 1 & 1 & 0 \end{pmatrix}}.$$

(*b*) It is important to have a convention for describing the size of an array, the *order*, so that discussion of compatibility of matrices for addition and multiplication becomes possible.

(i) 2×3	(ii) 3×3	(iii) 3×2
(iv) 3×1	(v) 2×2	(vi) 1×4

25

(c) 3×3 and 2×2. *Square* is a technical term for an $n \times n$ matrix. The note about column matrices and column vectors is significant. To all intents and purposes they are the same. The word 'vector' is used usually in the geometrical context as a displacement but there is no reason why a column matrix should not be an inventory of the coordinates of a point.

Exercise A (p. 29)

1. For example:

(a) $\begin{pmatrix} 2 & 0 & 3 & 0 & 1 \\ 1 & 5 & -1 & 1 & 0 \\ -6 & 4 & 2 & 1 & 5 \end{pmatrix}$; (b) $\begin{pmatrix} 3 & 4 \\ 1 & 5 \\ 2 & 1 \\ 0 & 6 \end{pmatrix}$;

(c) $\begin{pmatrix} 0 & 3 & -1 & 8 \\ 5 & 1 & 7 & 2 \end{pmatrix}$; (d) $\begin{pmatrix} 5 \\ -3 \\ 1 \end{pmatrix}$;

(e) $(5 \quad 0 \quad -2 \quad 3)$; (f) $\begin{pmatrix} 0 & 5 \\ 2 & 6 \end{pmatrix}$.

2.

	Valves	Coils	Speakers	Resistors	Capacitors	Transistors
Beginner's Bijou	3	2	1	7	5	0
Straight Eight	8	6	2	25	24	0
Super Sistor	0	8	1	23	16	6

3.

	Velvet (m)	Binding (m)	Zip fastener (cm)	Buttons	Nylon (m)
Susan	$4\frac{1}{2}$	4	35	3	0
Bridget	$1\frac{1}{2}$	$1\frac{1}{2}$	20	0	5
Jennifer	$2\frac{1}{2}$	2	0	0	0

4.

	L.P.s	E.P.s	Singles
A	60	87	112
B	103	41	58
C	72	0	0
D	0	23	12
E	0	118	157

5.

(a)

	Butter (g)	Sugar (g)	Flour (g)	Egg (g)	Total mass (g)
Shrewsbury	125	125	200	60	510
Shortbread	300	200	500	120	1120
Lincoln	125	250	250	60	685
Bannock	500	250	1000	0	1750
Easter	125	125	250	60	560
American	100	30	500	120	750

;

(b) Good practice in using the slide rule!

Shrewsbury	250	250	390	120
Shortbread	270	180	450	110
Lincoln	180	370	370	88
Bannock	290	140	570	0
Easter	220	220	450	110
American	130	40	670	160

.

6.

$$\text{From } \begin{matrix} & \overbrace{A \quad B}^{\text{To}} \\ A \\ B \end{matrix} \begin{pmatrix} 0 & 2 \\ 1 & 1 \end{pmatrix};$$

$$\begin{matrix} & X & Y & Z & T \\ X \\ Y \\ Z \\ T \end{matrix} \begin{pmatrix} 0 & 1 & 1 & 1 \\ 0 & 2 & 0 & 1 \\ 0 & 1 & 1 & 0 \\ 1 & 1 & 0 & 0 \end{pmatrix};$$

$$\begin{matrix} & P & Q & R & S \\ P \\ Q \\ R \\ S \end{matrix} \begin{pmatrix} 1 & 1 & 0 & 0 \\ 0 & 0 & 1 & 0 \\ 0 & 0 & 0 & 1 \\ 0 & 1 & 1 & 0 \end{pmatrix}.$$

7. See Figure A. There is a unique row and a unique column corresponding to each vertex.

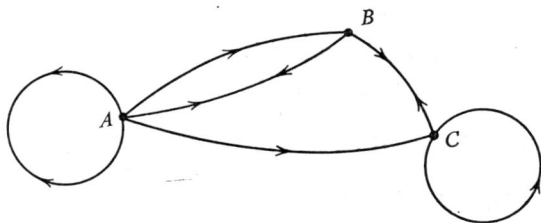

Fig. A

3-2

2. MATRIX ADDITION

(a) Addition comes naturally in an example of this kind.

$$\begin{pmatrix} 9 & 6 & 2 & 1 \\ 7 & 4 & 1 & 2 \\ 8 & 4 & 3 & 1 \end{pmatrix} + \begin{pmatrix} 6 & 4 & 2 & 0 \\ 9 & 5 & 3 & 1 \\ 6 & 3 & 1 & 2 \end{pmatrix} = \begin{pmatrix} 15 & 10 & 4 & 1 \\ 16 & 9 & 4 & 3 \\ 14 & 7 & 4 & 3 \end{pmatrix};$$

(b) This is equivalent to subtraction.

$$\mathbf{M} = \begin{pmatrix} 6 & 3 & 5 & 4 \\ 7 & 2 & 3 & -6 \end{pmatrix} - \begin{pmatrix} 3 & 2 & 5 & 0 \\ 6 & -1 & 4 & 2 \end{pmatrix} = \begin{pmatrix} 3 & 1 & 0 & 4 \\ 1 & 3 & -1 & -8 \end{pmatrix}.$$

Exercise B (p. 31)

1. (a)

	Mars	Pluto	Saturn	Venus
Boys	11	12	10	10
Girls	11	11	13	14

(b) (i) Pluto; (ii) Venus; (iii) Venus.

2.

	Overs	Maidens	Wickets	Runs
1st match	(12	4	3	25) = A
2nd match	(17	3	5	51) = B
A+B =	(29	7	8	76)

Note that if a further column were added giving the bowling *average* (i.e. runs per wicket), then addition would no longer be meaningful. The matrix sum would, however, still be defined.

3. (a) $\begin{pmatrix} 5 \\ 4 \\ 4 \end{pmatrix}$;   (b) $7\begin{pmatrix} 0 \\ 2 \\ 1 \end{pmatrix} = \begin{pmatrix} 0 \\ 14 \\ 7 \end{pmatrix}$.

4. (a) (i) $\begin{pmatrix} 5 & 6 \\ 2 & 6 \end{pmatrix}$;   (ii) $\begin{pmatrix} 4 & 0 \\ 4 & 5 \end{pmatrix}$;   (iii) $\begin{pmatrix} 3 & 4 \\ 2 & 1 \end{pmatrix}$.

(b) The following are the expected answers:

(i) $\begin{pmatrix} 4 & 10 \\ 0 & 2 \end{pmatrix}$;   (ii) $\begin{pmatrix} 3 & -3 \\ 6 & 0 \end{pmatrix}$;   (iii) $\begin{pmatrix} 7 & 11 \\ 2 & 7 \end{pmatrix}$;   (iv) $\begin{pmatrix} 2 & 2 \\ 0 & 5 \end{pmatrix}$.

5. Every time a new binary operation is defined upon a set of elements it is worth checking to see which structural laws are satisfied. This question is best discussed with the class.

(a) $\mathbf{A}+\mathbf{B} = \mathbf{B}+\mathbf{A}$ for any two matrices of the same order.

(b) $(\mathbf{A}+\mathbf{B})+\mathbf{C} = \mathbf{A}+(\mathbf{B}+\mathbf{C})$. This law was probably automatically assumed in Question 1.

6. $\mathbf{R} = \begin{pmatrix} -8 & -9 \\ 1 & -3 \\ -6 & 9 \end{pmatrix}.$

7. One way of revising simple equations:
$$a = 1, \quad b = 3, \quad c = 8, \quad d = 7, \quad e = 3, \quad f = -3.$$

3. COMBINING ROW AND COLUMN MATRICES

The point of this section is to realize that there is another common way of combining two ordered sets of numbers, other than addition. Sometimes we need to obtain $ax+by+cz$ from the ordered triples $(a\ b\ c)$ and $(x\ y\ z)$. A common example is when one set of numbers represents purchases and the other the corresponding prices. How we write the triples—whether as row or column matrices—does not matter, except that it is useful to have a specific convention. It might be argued that, to start with, pupils should be allowed to write the triples as they please and only at a later stage be taught to set out their working in a formal pattern. The individual teacher will make up his own mind on this, but his decision will probably be influenced by the group of pupils he is teaching at any particular time.

However, the pattern of matrix multiplication depends on this convention and, as will be seen in the next section, is a natural extension of it.

Readers who are familiar with vector algebra will recognize that another important example of this type of operation is the scalar (or dot) product of two vectors:

$$(a\mathbf{i}+b\mathbf{j}+c\mathbf{k}).(x\mathbf{i}+y\mathbf{j}+z\mathbf{k}) = ax+by+cz.$$

A discussion of the scalar product is left to the sixth form and those interested are encouraged to read *S.M.P. Advanced Mathematics, Book 2*.

(a) $(10\times1)+(3\times2)+(2\times4)+(6\times3) = 42$ new pence.

29

(b) $(6 \quad 4 \quad 5) \begin{pmatrix} 2 \\ 4 \\ 3 \end{pmatrix} = (43).$

(c) This question attempts to indicate why multiplication is only meaningful when the row and column matrices both have the same number of elements (the 0 in (0 6 4 5) is significant).

Exercise C (p. 34)

1. (a) (12);   (b) (4);   (c) (0);   (d) (26);   (e) (8).

Some pupils find it helpful to include the brackets but there is no reason why they should not be omitted.

2. (a) $(96 \quad 39 \quad 34 \quad 22 \quad 6 \quad 3) \begin{pmatrix} 1 \\ 2 \\ 3 \\ 4 \\ 5 \\ 6 \end{pmatrix} = (412).$

(b) 2·06 people per car. One expects comments about the inefficiency of the car when used in this way.

3. (a) $(5 \quad 1 \quad 3) \begin{pmatrix} 3 \\ 2 \\ 3 \end{pmatrix} = (26),$ $(3 \quad 2 \quad 1) \begin{pmatrix} 3 \\ 2 \\ 3 \end{pmatrix} = (16),$

$(2 \quad 0 \quad 3) \begin{pmatrix} 3 \\ 2 \\ 3 \end{pmatrix} = (15);$

(b) $(4 \quad 3 \quad 2) \begin{pmatrix} 3 \\ 2 \\ 3 \end{pmatrix} = (24),$ $(2 \quad 0 \quad 4) \begin{pmatrix} 3 \\ 2 \\ 3 \end{pmatrix} = (18),$

$(3 \quad 1 \quad 1) \begin{pmatrix} 3 \\ 2 \\ 3 \end{pmatrix} = (14).$

The First XV won the first and third matches.

4. (a) $\begin{matrix} g \\ \begin{pmatrix} 300 \\ 420 \\ 600 \end{pmatrix} \end{matrix}, \quad \begin{matrix} p \\ \begin{pmatrix} 5 \\ 6 \\ 8 \end{pmatrix} \end{matrix};$

(b) Mass: $(20 \quad 40 \quad 30) \begin{pmatrix} 300 \\ 420 \\ 600 \end{pmatrix} = (40\,800)$, 40·8 kg;

cost: $(20 \quad 40 \quad 30) \begin{pmatrix} 5 \\ 6 \\ 8 \end{pmatrix} = (580)$, £5·8;

(c)

	Small	Family	Large
Cost in new pence per gram	$\frac{5}{300}$	$\frac{6}{420}$	$\frac{8}{600}$

The large size at $\frac{1}{75}$p per gram is thus the better buy.

5. (a) $(8 \quad 3 \quad 6 \quad 7)+(4 \quad 9 \quad 6 \quad 5) = (12 \quad 12 \quad 12 \quad 12)$.
There were 12 events in the match.

(b) Each team has 2 competitors in each of 12 events, so there are $2 \times 12 = 24$ possible places.

(c) Town: $(8 \quad 3 \quad 6 \quad 7) \begin{pmatrix} 5 \\ 3 \\ 1 \\ 0 \end{pmatrix} = (55)$.

County: $(4 \quad 9 \quad 6 \quad 5) \begin{pmatrix} 5 \\ 3 \\ 1 \\ 0 \end{pmatrix} = (53)$.

Town school won.

(d) $(8 \quad 3 \quad 6 \quad 7) \begin{pmatrix} 4 \\ 3 \\ 2 \\ 1 \end{pmatrix} = (60)$, $(4 \quad 9 \quad 6 \quad 5) \begin{pmatrix} 4 \\ 3 \\ 2 \\ 1 \end{pmatrix} = (60)$.

6. (a) Cost of purchases:

$(2 \quad 3 \quad 1 \quad 4) \begin{pmatrix} 45 \\ 24 \\ 75 \\ 60 \end{pmatrix} = (477)$. 4·77 dollars.

(b) Cost of purchases in the following week:

$(1 \quad 1\frac{1}{2} \quad \frac{1}{2} \quad 2) \begin{pmatrix} 60 \\ 32 \\ 100 \\ 80 \end{pmatrix} = (318)$. 3·18 dollars.

This might be seen as $\frac{1}{2} \times \frac{4}{3} \times 477 = 318$.

Total bill decreased by 1·59 dollars.

7. This type of question often leads to surprisingly good results.

8. (a) A look at the distributive law

$$\mathbf{UW} = (3), \quad \mathbf{VW} = (^-7), \quad \mathbf{U+V} = (1 \quad 7),$$
$$\mathbf{UW+VW} = (^-4) = (\mathbf{U+V})\,\mathbf{W}.$$

(b) $3\mathbf{U}+5\mathbf{V} = (1 \quad 29), \quad 3\mathbf{UW} = (9), \quad 5\mathbf{VW} = (^-35),$
$(3\mathbf{U}+5\mathbf{V})\,\mathbf{W} = (^-26) = 3\mathbf{UW}+5\mathbf{VW}.$

9. (a) 3;   (b) 2;   (c) $^-5$;   (d) $x = {}^+4$ or $^-4$.

10. Adrian 51·0, Brian 43·6, Charles 43·1, David 47·0, Edward 54·1, Frank 45·0; order of competitors: *E, A, D, F, B, C.*

4. MATRIX MULTIPLICATION

Matrix multiplication is seen here as a natural extension of the multiplication of a row matrix.

If several row matrices are all to be combined with the same column matrix, then the row matrices are written as the successive rows of a single matrix; for example, the products on the left below are combined as a single matrix product on the right:

$$(a_1 \quad b_1)\begin{pmatrix}x\\y\end{pmatrix} = (a_1 x + b_1 y)$$
$$(a_2 \quad b_2)\begin{pmatrix}x\\y\end{pmatrix} = (a_2 x + b_2 y)$$
$$(a_3 \quad b_3)\begin{pmatrix}x\\y\end{pmatrix} = (a_3 x + b_3 y)$$

$$\begin{pmatrix}a_1 & b_1\\a_2 & b_2\\a_3 & b_3\end{pmatrix}\begin{pmatrix}x\\y\end{pmatrix} = \begin{pmatrix}a_1 x + b_1 y\\a_2 x + b_2 y\\a_3 x + b_3 y\end{pmatrix}.$$

If, further, we are now interested in the product of each of these row matrices with another column matrix $\begin{pmatrix}z\\t\end{pmatrix}$, then

$$\begin{pmatrix}a_1 & b_1\\a_2 & b_2\\a_3 & b_3\end{pmatrix}\begin{pmatrix}x\\y\end{pmatrix} = \begin{pmatrix}a_1 x + b_1 y\\a_2 x + b_2 y\\a_3 x + b_3 y\end{pmatrix}$$

and

$$\begin{pmatrix}a_1 & b_1\\a_2 & b_2\\a_3 & b_3\end{pmatrix}\begin{pmatrix}z\\t\end{pmatrix} = \begin{pmatrix}a_1 z + b_1 t\\a_2 z + b_2 t\\a_3 z + b_3 t\end{pmatrix}$$

can be combined to give

$$\begin{pmatrix} a_1 & b_1 \\ a_2 & b_2 \\ a_3 & b_3 \end{pmatrix} \begin{pmatrix} x & z \\ y & t \end{pmatrix} = \begin{pmatrix} a_1x+b_1y & a_1z+b_1t \\ a_2x+b_2y & a_2z+b_2t \\ a_3x+b_3y & a_3z+b_3t \end{pmatrix}.$$

From this follows the condition for two matrices to be compatible for multiplication: the number of columns in the left-hand matrix must be equal to the number of rows in the right-hand matrix.

This chapter is mainly concerned with developing matrix multiplication and at this stage we are not concerned with, say, identity and inverse matrices. These will arise naturally when we later seek to solve equations or combine transformations. These proper names should be used, however, if the occasion arises.

$$(a) \quad \begin{pmatrix} 10 & 3 & 2 & 6 \\ 0 & 6 & 4 & 5 \\ 5 & 5 & 0 & 8 \end{pmatrix} \begin{pmatrix} \frac{1}{2} \\ 1 \\ 3 \\ 2 \end{pmatrix} = \begin{pmatrix} 26 \\ 28 \\ 23\frac{1}{2} \end{pmatrix}.$$

(b) and (c) These questions are intended to make the pupils see what conditions must be satisfied if multiplication of two matrices is to be possible. **B** must have only 2 columns, since the rows of **B** have to combine with the columns of **A** which have only 2 elements. **C** must have 3 rows before it can be multiplied on the left by **A**.

(d) **PQ** is not possible.

$$\mathbf{QP} = \begin{pmatrix} 3 & 1 \\ 2 & 4 \\ 0 & 5 \end{pmatrix} \begin{pmatrix} 2 & 5 \\ 0 & 1 \end{pmatrix} = \begin{pmatrix} 6 & 16 \\ 4 & 14 \\ 0 & 5 \end{pmatrix}.$$

(e) It is very useful for the pupils, not only to see when multiplication is possible, but also what the order of the matrix product will be.

In this case **RS** is a 5×2 matrix.

In general
$$\mathbf{A} \ . \ \mathbf{B} \ = \ \mathbf{C}$$
$$m \times (n \ . \ n) \times p \qquad m \times p$$

Exercise D (p. 39)

1. (a) $\begin{pmatrix} 21 \\ 1 \end{pmatrix}$; (b) $(15 \ -6 \ 5)$; (c) $(6 \ 22)$;

33

(d) $\begin{pmatrix} 17 \\ 32 \\ -1 \end{pmatrix}$;   (e) $\begin{pmatrix} 16 \\ 6 \end{pmatrix}$;   (f) (45).

2. (a) £46·50.

(b) $(160 \quad 200 \quad 180) \begin{pmatrix} 150 & 0 & 0 & 200 & 500 \\ 50 & 0 & 50 & 100 & 0 \\ 0 & 250 & 200 & 500 & 0 \end{pmatrix}$

$$= (340 \quad 540 \quad 460 \quad 1420 \quad 800).$$

(c) After the first 5 deliveries the fuel left on the lorry is represented by

$$\begin{pmatrix} 150 \\ 200 \\ 300 \end{pmatrix}$$

so that the two orders that can be completed without reloading are

$$\begin{pmatrix} 100 \\ 50 \\ 100 \end{pmatrix} \quad \text{and} \quad \begin{pmatrix} 50 \\ 150 \\ 150 \end{pmatrix}.$$

3. (a) $\begin{pmatrix} 4 & 2 & 3 & 2 & 6 \\ 2 & 5 & 4 & 4 & 3 \\ 4 & 3 & 3 & 4 & 1 \end{pmatrix} \begin{pmatrix} 6 \\ 4 \\ 3 \\ 2 \\ 1 \end{pmatrix} = \begin{pmatrix} 51 \\ 55 \\ 54 \end{pmatrix} \begin{matrix} A \\ B \\ C \end{matrix}$

(b) $\begin{pmatrix} 4 & 2 & 3 & 2 & 6 \\ 2 & 5 & 4 & 4 & 3 \\ 4 & 3 & 3 & 4 & 1 \end{pmatrix} \begin{pmatrix} 8 \\ 5 \\ 3 \\ 2 \\ 1 \end{pmatrix} = \begin{pmatrix} 61 \\ 64 \\ 65 \end{pmatrix} \begin{matrix} A \\ B \\ C \end{matrix}$

C wins instead of B.

4. $(1\frac{1}{2} \quad 1 \quad 3) \begin{pmatrix} 46 & 32 \\ 30 & 22 \\ 20 & 15 \end{pmatrix} = (159 \quad 115).$

Saving = (cost at local store) − (cost in town) − (bus fare)

$\qquad$ = $159 - 115 - 25$ new pence

$\qquad$ = 19p.

34

5.

	Audio 1	Audio 2	Audio 3
Transistors	1	2	3
Resistors	10	18	24
Capacitors	5	7	10

$$\begin{pmatrix} 1 & 2 & 3 \\ 10 & 18 & 24 \\ 5 & 7 & 10 \end{pmatrix} \begin{pmatrix} 100 \\ 250 \\ 80 \end{pmatrix} = \begin{pmatrix} 840 \\ 7420 \\ 3050 \end{pmatrix} \begin{matrix} T \\ R \\ C. \end{matrix}$$

6. $(20 \quad 25 \quad 10 \quad 6)$

$$\begin{matrix} & F & P & B & R & C \\ & 1 & 4 & 8 & 14 & 2 \\ & 2 & 10 & 12 & 30 & 4 \\ & 4 & 24 & 30 & 60 & 10 \\ & 10 & 40 & 72 & 100 & 24 \end{matrix}$$

$$\begin{matrix} F & P & B & R & C \\ = (170 & 810 & 1192 & 2230 & 384). \end{matrix}$$

7. (*a*)

$$\begin{matrix} & F & P & B & R & C & \text{Cost (new pence)} \\ \text{Set 1} & 1 & 4 & 8 & 14 & 2 \\ \text{Set 2} & 2 & 10 & 12 & 30 & 4 \\ \text{Set 3} & 4 & 24 & 30 & 60 & 10 \\ \text{Set 4} & 10 & 40 & 72 & 100 & 24 \end{matrix} \begin{pmatrix} 6 \\ 4 \\ 1 \\ 2 \\ 3 \end{pmatrix} = \begin{pmatrix} 64 \\ 136 \\ 300 \\ 564 \end{pmatrix}.$$

Cost of sets:

set 1, 64p; set 2, £1·36; set 3, £3·00; set 4, £5·64.

(*b*) $(20 \quad 25 \quad 10 \quad 6) \begin{pmatrix} 1 & 4 & 8 & 14 & 2 \\ 2 & 10 & 12 & 30 & 4 \\ 4 & 24 & 30 & 60 & 10 \\ 10 & 40 & 72 & 100 & 24 \end{pmatrix} \begin{pmatrix} 6 \\ 4 \\ 1 \\ 2 \\ 3 \end{pmatrix}$ new pence.

Total cost £110·64.

The arithmetic involved in this question is considerable and it might be advisable to ask for the matrix multiplication to be *set* out rather than *carried* out. A use for a computer!

8. (*a*) $\mathbf{AX} = \begin{pmatrix} 4 \\ 6 \\ 2 \end{pmatrix}$, $\mathbf{BX} = \begin{pmatrix} 6 \\ 2 \\ 4 \end{pmatrix}$, $\mathbf{CX} = \begin{pmatrix} 2 \\ 4 \\ 6 \end{pmatrix}$,

$\mathbf{YA} = (5 \quad 1 \quad 3)$, $\mathbf{YB} = (3 \quad 5 \quad 1)$, $\mathbf{YC} = (1 \quad 3 \quad 5)$.

The components are the same numbers just moved around—that is a permutation. Matrices such as **A**, **B** and **C** are called permutation matrices (i.e. matrices representing functions that map a finite set *onto* itself).

(b) $\mathbf{D} = \begin{pmatrix} 1 & 0 & 0 \\ 0 & 0 & 1 \\ 0 & 1 & 0 \end{pmatrix}$.

There are many other 3×3 matrices which will map

$$\begin{pmatrix} 2 \\ 4 \\ 6 \end{pmatrix} \quad \text{onto} \quad \begin{pmatrix} 2 \\ 6 \\ 4 \end{pmatrix}$$

but they are not permutation matrices.

$$\mathbf{YD} = (1 \quad 5 \quad 3).$$

9. $(2x \quad 3x+y) = (6 \quad 10) \Leftrightarrow x = 3, \quad y = 1.$

10. (a) $\begin{pmatrix} 12 & -5 \\ 7 & -2 \end{pmatrix}$; (b) $\begin{pmatrix} 4 & 17 & 12 \\ 0 & -3 & -4 \end{pmatrix}$; (c) $\begin{pmatrix} 38 & 19 & 2 \\ 1 & 10 & 3 \end{pmatrix}$;

(d) $\begin{pmatrix} 4 & 7 \\ -4 & 3 \\ 8 & 2 \end{pmatrix}$; (e) $\begin{pmatrix} 5 & 6 & -8 \\ 2 & 4 & 1 \\ 0 & 3 & 9 \end{pmatrix}$; (f) $(66 \quad 30)$.

11. (a) 3×5; (b) 4×3; (c) 3×7.

12. $\mathbf{BC} = \begin{pmatrix} 6 & 8 \\ 2 & 2 \end{pmatrix} \neq \mathbf{CB}, \quad \mathbf{AB} = \begin{pmatrix} 0 & 6 \\ -3 & 3 \end{pmatrix} = \mathbf{BA},$

$\mathbf{A(BC)} = \begin{pmatrix} 18 & 24 \\ 6 & 6 \end{pmatrix} = \mathbf{(AB)\,C}.$

13. This might be done by looking at special cases or, better, by taking a general case.

(a) $\begin{pmatrix} a & 0 \\ 0 & b \end{pmatrix} \begin{pmatrix} c & 0 \\ 0 & d \end{pmatrix} = \begin{pmatrix} ac & 0 \\ 0 & bd \end{pmatrix}$. The P matrices are closed with respect to multiplication, that is, the product of two P matrices is again a P matrix.

(b) $\begin{pmatrix} a & 0 \\ 0 & b \end{pmatrix} \begin{pmatrix} 0 & c \\ d & 0 \end{pmatrix} = \begin{pmatrix} 0 & ac \\ bd & 0 \end{pmatrix}$,

$\begin{pmatrix} 0 & c \\ d & 0 \end{pmatrix} \begin{pmatrix} a & 0 \\ 0 & b \end{pmatrix} = \begin{pmatrix} 0 & bc \\ ad & 0 \end{pmatrix}$.

A P matrix multiplied by a Q matrix yields a Q matrix. In general the order does matter. What condition must be fulfilled if a P and a Q matrix are to commute?

(c) $\begin{pmatrix} 0 & a \\ b & 0 \end{pmatrix} \begin{pmatrix} 0 & c \\ d & 0 \end{pmatrix} = \begin{pmatrix} ad & 0 \\ 0 & bc \end{pmatrix}.$

A Q matrix multiplied by a Q matrix yields a P matrix. Notice the similarity between the combination of P and Q matrices and the multiplication of directed numbers:

×	P	Q		×	Pos	Neg
P	P	Q		Pos	Pos	Neg
Q	Q	P		Neg	Neg	Pos

5. MATRICES AND TRANSFORMATIONS

This is the first serious attempt to describe algebraically the transformations that have already been studied geometrically. The emphasis in this section is on describing a transformation as a mapping of the coordinates (x, y) of a general point and the reason for writing the coordinates as the elements of a column matrix is to lead into the matrix notation. However, when written in this way they can be interpreted as displacements from the origin as mentioned in the text; then they are known as *position vectors*. The idea of a position vector is invaluable at a later stage in geometry and mechanics, but its introduction at this level is not always appreciated and pupils inevitably interpret the elements of the column matrix as coordinates rather than displacements.

The transformations that interest us in this course are the general affine transformations (those which map lines into lines) and these are described algebraically by the mapping

$$\begin{pmatrix} x \\ y \end{pmatrix} \rightarrow \begin{pmatrix} ax+by+p \\ cx+dy+q \end{pmatrix}$$

which is modified later to

$$\begin{pmatrix} x \\ y \end{pmatrix} \rightarrow \begin{pmatrix} a & b \\ c & d \end{pmatrix} \begin{pmatrix} x \\ y \end{pmatrix} + \begin{pmatrix} p \\ q \end{pmatrix}.$$

Alternatively, we can use an equation form and write

$$\begin{pmatrix} x' \\ y' \end{pmatrix} = \begin{pmatrix} ax+by+p \\ cx+dy+q \end{pmatrix},$$

where (x', y') are the coordinates of the image point corresponding to (x, y). Many books use this method but since in this course we

37

have already used the mapping notation extensively it was thought more appropriate to retain it for the description of transformations.

When $p = q = 0$, the transformation will leave the origin fixed, since

$$\begin{pmatrix} 0 \\ 0 \end{pmatrix} \rightarrow \begin{pmatrix} a.0 + b.0 \\ c.0 + d.0 \end{pmatrix}.$$

The general transformation can be thought of as

$$\begin{pmatrix} x \\ y \end{pmatrix} \rightarrow \begin{pmatrix} ax + by \\ cx + dy \end{pmatrix},$$

a transformation under which the origin is fixed, followed by

$$\begin{pmatrix} x \\ y \end{pmatrix} \rightarrow \begin{pmatrix} x + p \\ y + q \end{pmatrix},$$

a translation.

(a) $A'(1, 2)$, $B'(3, 6)$, $C'(7, 3)$.

(b) $P'(p + 5, q + 3)$.

(c) The line $y = x - 3$.

Exercise E (p. 43)

1. See Figure B.

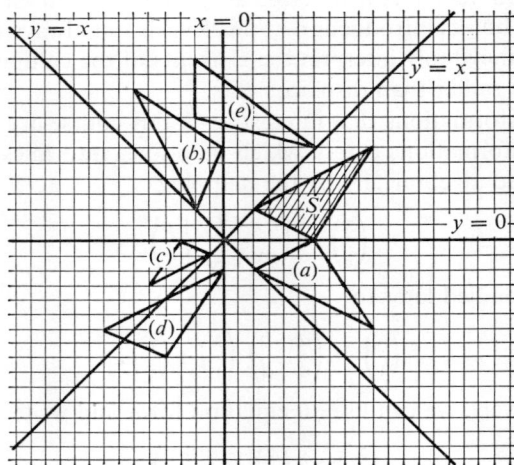

Fig. B

(a) Reflection in $y = 0$.

(b) Rotation about the origin through 90°.

(c) Enlargement, centre the origin, scale factor $-\frac{1}{2}$.

(d) Translation $\begin{pmatrix} -5 \\ -4 \end{pmatrix}$.

(e) A shear with $y = 0$ as the invariant line followed by the translation $\begin{pmatrix} 0 \\ 3 \end{pmatrix}$. (Impossible for pupils to describe: shearing comes later.)

2. (i) Reflection in $x+y = 0$.

$$\begin{pmatrix} x \\ y \end{pmatrix} \rightarrow \begin{pmatrix} -y \\ -x \end{pmatrix}.$$

(ii) Rotation about the origin through $-90°$.

$$\begin{pmatrix} x \\ y \end{pmatrix} \rightarrow \begin{pmatrix} y \\ -x \end{pmatrix}.$$

(iii) Enlargement, centre the origin, scale factor 2.

$$\begin{pmatrix} x \\ y \end{pmatrix} \rightarrow \begin{pmatrix} 2x \\ 2y \end{pmatrix}.$$

(iv) Half-turn about the origin.

$$\begin{pmatrix} x \\ y \end{pmatrix} \rightarrow \begin{pmatrix} -x \\ -y \end{pmatrix}.$$

This exercise will have served as a reminder of the transformations already met. In the remainder of the chapter we show how the matrix notation can be used to separate the numbers determining the transformation from the variables representing the coordinates of a point. The resulting 2×2 matrix is now thought of as an operator that defines the transformation.

(a) $\begin{pmatrix} 2 & -3 \\ 5 & 1 \end{pmatrix}$.

(b) $\begin{pmatrix} 7 \\ 2 \end{pmatrix}$, $\begin{pmatrix} 17 \\ -11 \end{pmatrix}$, $\begin{pmatrix} 6 \\ 7 \end{pmatrix}$.

Exercise F (p. 47)

1. (a) See Figure C.

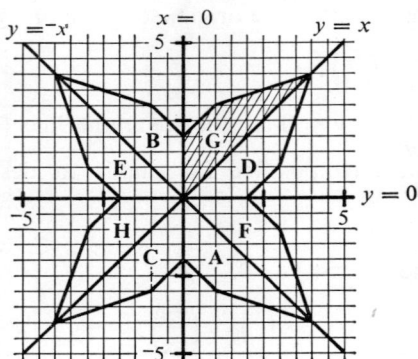

Fig. C

(*b*) **A**: reflection in $y = 0$.

    B: reflection in $x = 0$.

    C: half-turn about the origin.

    D: reflection in $y = x$.

    E: rotation about the origin through $90°$.

    F: rotation about the origin through $270°$ (or $^-90°$).

    G: identity.

    H: reflection in $y = {}^-x$.

(*c*) The figure has 4 lines of symmetry.

The matrices considered here form the group of symmetries of the square (and of course any other figure with the same symmetry).

2. (*a*) See Figure D;   (*b*) 4.

3. (*a*), (*b*) See Figure E.

(*c*) The effect of **S** is equivalent to a $45°$ rotation about the origin followed by an enlargement with scale factor $\sqrt{2}$.

(*d*) $A^†B^†C^†D^†$ on Figure E.

(*e*) The transformation defined by **T** is the inverse of the transformation defined by **S**.

T maps $A'B'C'D'$ back onto $ABCD$.

40

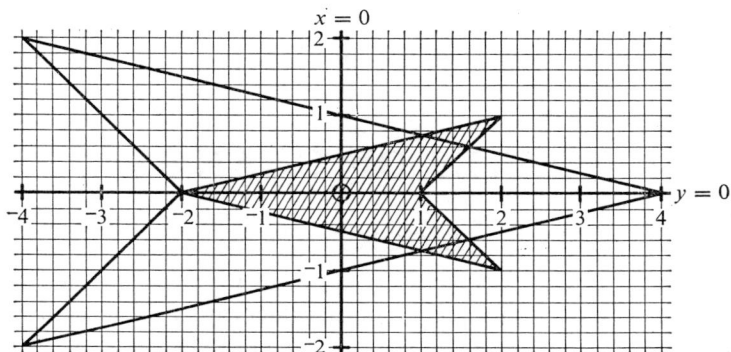

Fig. D

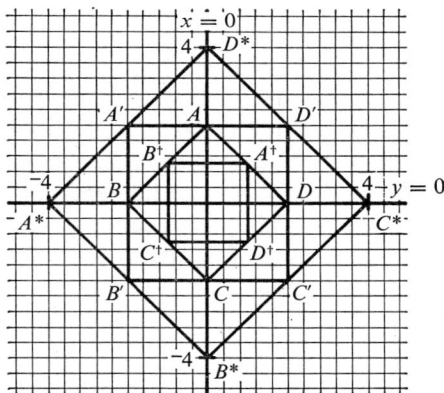

Fig. E

4. $A = \begin{pmatrix} 1 & 0 \\ 0 & 1 \end{pmatrix}$.

5. **E** defines an enlargement, centre the origin, scale factor 3.

$F = \begin{pmatrix} \frac{1}{3} & 0 \\ 0 & \frac{1}{3} \end{pmatrix}$.

6. This matrix defines a shear, see Chapter 12.
The question has been included to encourage discovery.

4   **41**

4

RATES OF CHANGE

1. CONTOURS

This is a traditional treatment, although the investigation of the gradient at a point of a curve is taken rather earlier than usual. There is plenty of scope for practical work and it is useful to cooperate with the geography department.

The contours in Figure 1 indicate a small hill. The section by the line AH is shown in Figure A. It is conveniently done by tracing the contour map and taking the horizontal distances direct, thus obviating the necessity for measurement.

The coordinates are, approximately, A (0, 150); B (3000, 250); C (6200, 350); D (7000, 450); E (9800, 450); F(10400, 350); G (10900, 250); H (11,600, 150). It is better *not* to take the same scale on both $x = 0$ and $y = 0$ since the $x = 0$ scale differences are small compared with the $y = 0$ ones. It is plainly not necessary to use the same scale on both. From our knowledge of the nature of most hills it seems best to join the points with a smooth curve. Of course the ground may be very irregular between the contours but it is reasonable to assume that this is not the case. The highest point of the road is between D and E (or at these points) and the sweep of the curve suggests that it may be midway between them.

The steepest part of the road is *likely* to be between G and F; where the contours are closest together. However, we cannot be certain of this: it could, in fact, be anywhere along the road.

2. GRADIENT OF A ROAD

It is convenient to use the *tangent* gradient throughout this chapter, i.e. we compare change in height with *horizontal* distance traversed. This will always be the most convenient gradient to use when working from maps, although it will present practical difficulties when working on the ground. The continental usage offers a useful opportunity for a gentle revision of percentage.

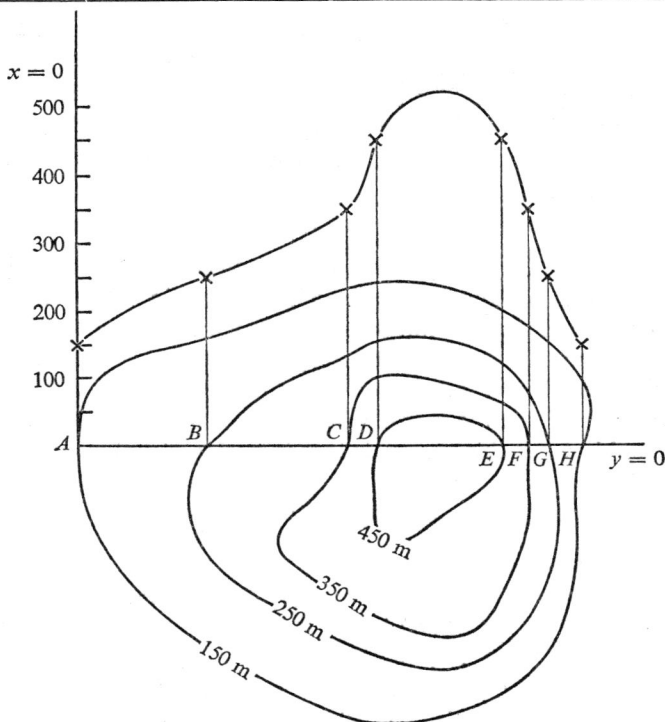

Fig. A

A gradient is dimensionless: 1 m in 8 m, 1 mm in 8 mm, 1 cm in 8 cm are all equivalent. A gradient is, in fact, a ratio (see Book 2, Chapter 11), we work with the associated fraction.

Exercise A (p. 51)

1. (a) (i) 100 m in 3200 m, or 1 in 32;
    (ii) 3%;   (iii) $\frac{1}{32}$ or 0·03.

    (b) (i) $\frac{1}{30}$; (ii) $\frac{1}{5}$; (iii) $\frac{1}{23}$. From A to D we are gaining height, from E to H losing it. This is the place to implant the idea of a *negative* gradient to distinguish the latter from the former. No great stress need be laid on this at present.

    (c) The average gradient is 0. The road has been part uphill and part downhill, again the idea that uphill is positive and downhill negative suggests the meaning behind the mathematical statement.

4-2

2. (a) 0·2;   (b) 0·25;   (c) 0·01;   (d) 0·001;   (e) no.

The symbol ∞ is sometimes seen on gradient posts by the side of railway tracks. The statement '1 in ∞' does not mean that one would have to travel a very long way in order to change height by one unit but that there is no distance, *however large*, that has this property.

3. (a) 1 in 20;   (b) 1 in 4;   (c) 1 in 12½.

4. There must be a steep hill notice somewhere between the 100 m and 150 m contours, since there is a change in height of 50 m in less than 500 m. It is not possible to say precisely where the steep part occurs. There could be steep stretches elsewhere, of course. If the road is replanned, so that there is a distance of at least 500 m between the points where it crosses the contours, then it should be possible to avoid steep hills. An S bend would achieve this.

5. 25 in 500, the mathematical gradient is $\frac{25}{500} = 0\cdot05$.

6. For an example see Figure B.

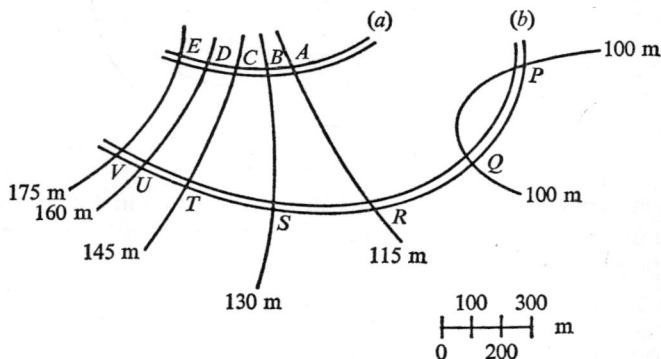

Fig. B

Road (a) has a steady gradient of about 15%. N.B.

$$AB = BC = CD = DE = 100 \text{ m}.$$

Road (b) varies from almost 0% between P and Q to about 15% between U and V.

Note that if the gradient is not zero *everywhere* between P and Q, then it must be negative somewhere. Similarly, if the gradient is

44

not 15 % everywhere between U and V, it must be greater than 15 % somewhere.

7. The hill is 1 in 10. A car would climb it easily. The diagram gives a false impression because the height scale differs from the distance scale (1 unit to 50, 1 unit to 500).

8. 'Twice as steep' is ambiguous, of course, and is intended to provoke discussion. If twice the angle is meant, then discussion should be postponed until Book 4 has been read. If it is taken to mean that the change in height is twice as great for the same change in horizontal distance, then the appropriate figures are $1:5$; 25 % respectively. It is impossible to be objective on the subject of effectiveness, it depends what you are used to. One wonders, however, about the difficulties of translation for the non-mathematically-minded tourist.

9. 'Vertical interval' means difference in height. 'Horizontal equivalent' means distance between points horizontally. This is the mathematical gradient once the units have been cancelled. Maps only give horizontal distances directly. The disadvantage comes when trying to find the gradient of a road by pacing, for it is impossible to pace the horizontal distance.

3. RATES OF CHANGE

This is the first time that a rate has been introduced specifically. A rate compares quantities that are measured in different types of units, e.g. N/cm^2, km/h, £/g. In this chapter we shall limit ourselves almost without exception to examples in which the second element is time. The more general case will be dealt with in Book 4.

The boy was moving fastest in the interval BC between 1 min and $1\frac{1}{2}$ min after leaving. He was moving slowest in the interval CD between $1\frac{1}{2}$ min and 2 min after leaving, for then he was at rest. It is important to make the point that 0 is a speed and not accept the suggestion that the interval DE is the answer.

A possible story is 'walks, runs, sees it go, waits to get his breath back, walks on very slowly' but other variations are possible.

We now draw the essential distinction between ratio and rate. A rate has to have units: 150 m per $\frac{1}{2}$ min, 150 cm per $\frac{1}{2}$ second,

150 km per $\frac{1}{2}$ hour are all different. 150 m per $\frac{1}{2}$ minute is equivalent to 5 m/s. His other speeds are 100 m/min, 0 m/min and 25 m/min in the intervals *AB*, *CD* and *DE* respectively. Since the quantities are read from the scales and actual distances do not enter into it, the scales used have no effect on the interpretation of the graph. With some children it might be wise to re-plot the data on a scale of (say) 20 s = 1 cm across the page and 100 m = 2 cm up the page, and demonstrate this.

Exercise B (p. 53)

1. See Figure C. $87\frac{1}{2}$ m; $237\frac{1}{2}$ m.

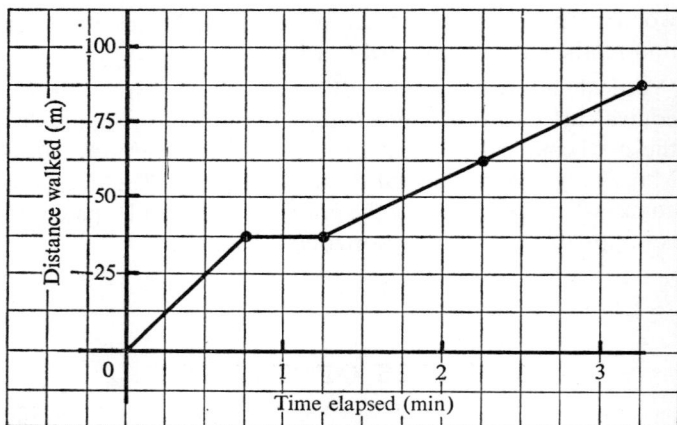

Fig. C

2. Filled at 25 l/min for 2 min; filled at 100 l/min for another 2 min (taps full on perhaps); level stationary for 1 min (cooling?); flowed out at 50 l/min for $\frac{2}{5}$ min (perhaps the plug was not properly in, the rate per min is less than that at the end when the bath was being emptied; or perhaps it was emptying through the overflow!); level stationary for $3\frac{3}{5}$ min (bathing); emptied at 230 l/min.

3. 0 degC/h; $\frac{1}{4}$ degC/h; 1 degC/h; $2\frac{1}{2}$ degC/h. Summer probably. There is no need to emphasize the physics of the situation, but it is worth noting that the morning chart is just as likely to be

46

concave upwards as to be concave downwards, as the afternoon chart is. In fact the graph indicates that there was some clouding or change of wind at about 12.00, for on a sunny day the temperature would continue to rise after noon. Another opportunity for discussing positive and negative gradients.

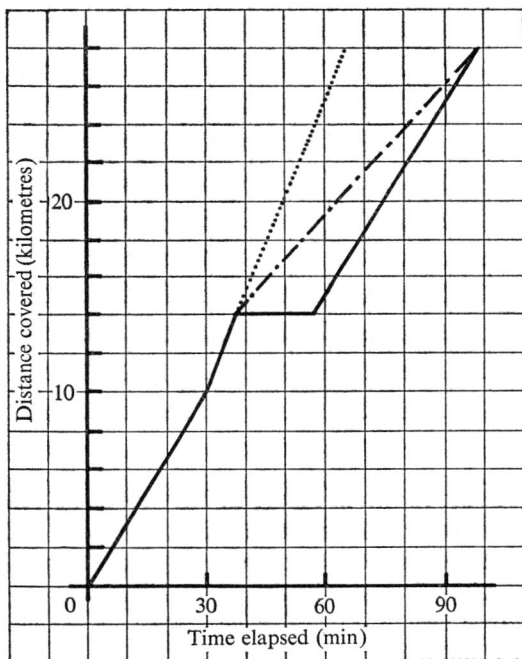

Fig. D

4. It is easy to plot the line representing $\frac{1}{2}$ h at 10 km/h. The next part is more difficult. Rather than calculating the time taken, it is better to lay off a line representing 30 km/h, by noting that this is equivalent to 15 km in $\frac{1}{2}$ h. This is shown as a broken line in Figure D. The 4 km portion can then be cut off. His average speed for the whole ride was 28 km in 98 min, about 17·2 km/h. Note that the graph continues upwards throughout, since the 'up page' scale represents distance travelled (ignoring direction). The dot-and-dashed line represents his 'straight

47

round' return speed, 14 km/h. If the scale up the page represented distance from home, then the final section would be reflected in the line 'distance = 14 km', and would cut the scale across the page at 98 min.

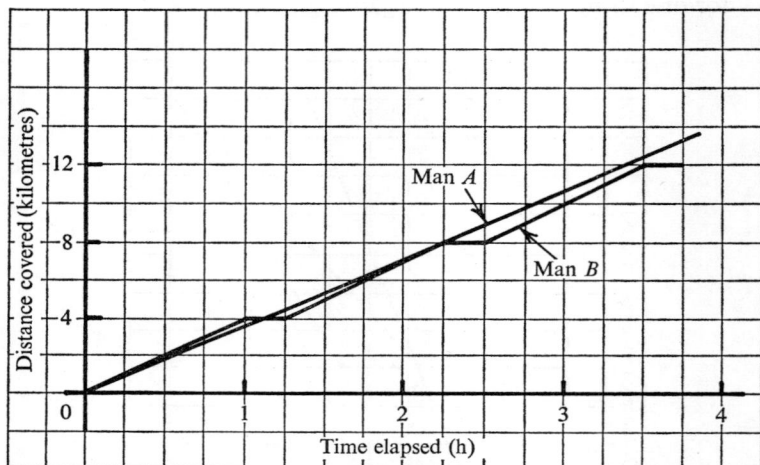

Fig. E

5. The graphs are shown in Figure E. They require careful drawing. Man B arrives first at the fourth kilometre-post and just beats man A to the eighth kilometre-post (A takes $2\frac{2}{7}$ h, B takes $2\frac{1}{4}$ h). Man A arrives first at all subsequent kilometre-posts and wins any distance events. Man B wins races of less than 4 km and between 7 and 8 km.

6. First half of 1960, $-\frac{5}{6} \times £100$ million per month; second half, $+\frac{7}{6} \times £100$ million per month. The use of the negative sign distinguishes the loss from the gain. Second half of 1959. Owing perhaps to holiday effects, perhaps to seasonal changes in earnings, etc., there is clearly a regular sawtooth pattern, though this is made to look greater than it really is by the false origin of the graph. Plotting the average figure for each year would be one way of 'smoothing' the curve. More delicate methods involve the calculation of seasonal variation and can be found in books on statistics, e.g. Chapter 8 of *Statistics, a First Course,* by R. Loveday.

48

7. See Figure F. £2·85. The savings should really be represented by a step graph, since she will add money weekly or monthly, in discrete amounts. A line graph gives the average rate.

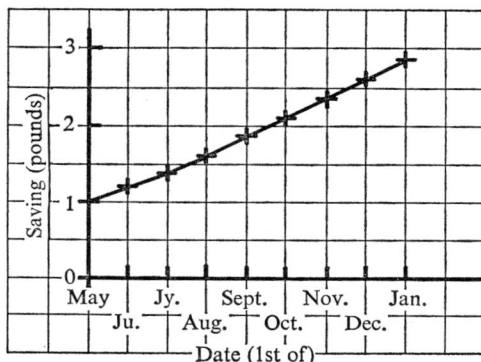

Fig. F

8. The straight line graph has been drawn so that its end-points do not coincide with grid points. The pupils will be confronted with the necessity for deciding between which points to consider the changes in speed and time. It has to be made clear that the choice makes no difference to the answer, but that it should be governed by two considerations:

(*a*) taking points well apart averages out small errors in reading;

(*b*) taking points on vertical grid lines makes the division much easier.

About 4 km/h per second, i.e. 14000 km/h per hour or $1\frac{1}{9}$ m/s per second. The magnitude of the first form of the answer often surprises pupils until they think of its implications, which lead them to see that it is rather a useless measure. Acceleration.

9. See the note on Question 8. $\frac{1}{4}$ degree Celsius per hour. An increase of $^{-}\frac{1}{4}$ degC/h. Probably not.

10. See Figure G. This is not the way that bacteria increase except in examples in textbooks! For a better model see Chapter 9, Book 2. $x + 2x = 9 \Leftrightarrow x = 3$, 3 million and 6 million bacteria per 10 h, i.e. 0·3 and 0·6 million respectively per hour.

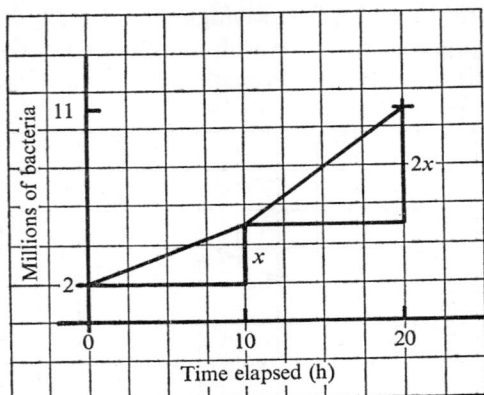

Fig. G

4. RATE OF CHANGE AT AN INSTANT

The first necessity is to get pupils to realize that there is an instantaneous rate of change. In Figure H the 'red' part is broken and the 'blue' part dotted. Where these parts meet, the rate of gain in mass was equal to the average over the 18-month period.

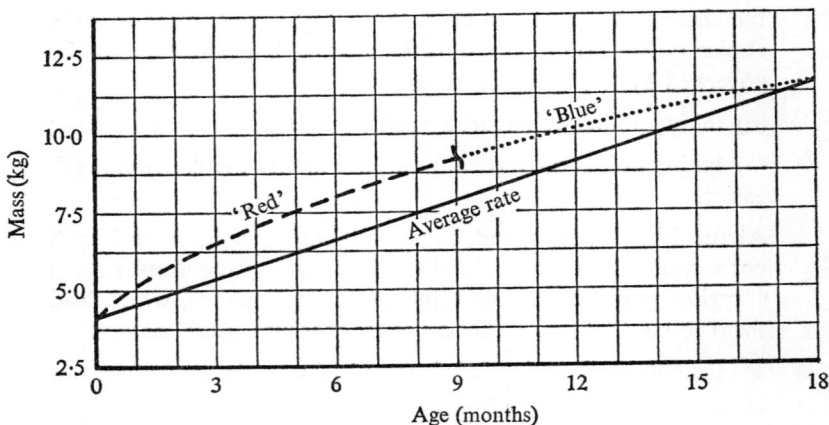

Fig. H

When the curve is turning slowly it is hard to draw tangents by eye and classes must be expected to disagree somewhat widely. An amusing way of improving the accuracy is to draw the *normal* (the line through the point of contact at right-angles to the tangent) using a small mirror (see Figure I). This is adjusted until the reflection appears to be a continuation of the curve, the normal is then ruled

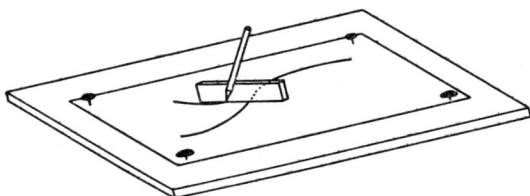

Fig. I

in and the tangent drawn at right-angles to it. It is important to make sure that the glass of the mirror is thin, a metal mirror is better still. In Example 1, A and B are points where the tangent that has been drawn cuts 'up page' grid lines differing by 10, an easy number by which to divide. Any other two points on the tangent would have done instead. See notes on Question 8 in Exercise B.

Exercise C (p. 58)

1. At the very start of his training. Just under $\frac{1}{2}$ kg per day.

2. 12 km/h per second; nearly zero. Acceleration increases in each gear, then slackens and becomes zero as the gear is changed; a three-speed gearbox perhaps. Quite an average rate of acceleration. Pupils should be encouraged to slide their rules along the curve to estimate slope. Most rapid acceleration at about 4 s, about 13 km/h per second.

3. About $\frac{2}{3}$ kg per month; about $\frac{3}{8}$ kg per month. The question that matters is 'what sort of curve is it?'. The curve is flattening, but the tangent becomes horizontal if the child stops growing, which plainly does not happen for some years. The curve tends to approach a straight line with positive gradient (or to take an upward turn).

4. Greatest at about $2\frac{1}{2}$ min;

   (*a*) 5 degC/min;   (*b*) 3 degC/min;   (*c*) $1\frac{1}{2}$ degC/min.
   See Figure J.

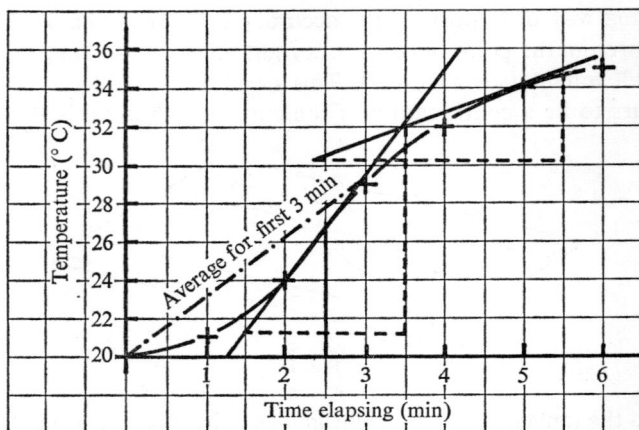

Fig. J

5. The zigzag indicates that the scale has been compressed. It could also be used to indicate the false origin in Figure 17 or, with more reason, in Figure 9.

    0·3 cm per day; 0·9 cm per day. Assuming that the rate of growth continues at the same constant rate, after 30 days the height would be 4·6 + 12 × 0·9, i.e. about 15 cm.

6. A time-based graph cannot 'curl back' on itself for this would indicate that there were two heights for the same period of growth. Height is a function of time, in the strict sense (see Chapter 10 and, Book 2, Chapter 8).

7. See Figure K. The gradients are not the gradients of a smooth curve drawn through the points. The dotted curve shows that it is still possible to fit a curve to the data, but this would hardly fit the physics of the question. We always assume that curves are 'well-behaved'.

8. The simplest method would be to use a ciné-camera and use a stop-frame every 2 s. In this question we are investigating independent and dependent variables. The function involved maps 'independent variable → dependent variable'. Usually the independent variable is 'across page'. Time is usually taken as the

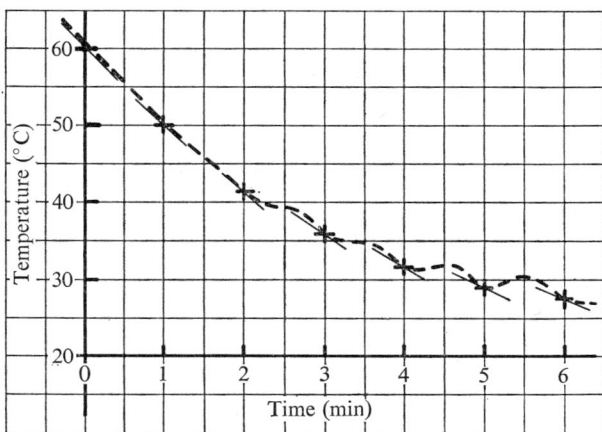

Fig. K

independent variable for reason of convenience of reference. The two graphs are shown in Figures L(i) and (ii). In Figure L(i), 'time → radius', the rate of increase was greatest at the start. When the radius is small a given volume of air will cause a large change in radius compared with the change when the radius is large. The rate is just over 2 cm/s. Figure L(ii) shows the function 'radius → time'. The rate was least when the time was least. The rate is just under $\frac{1}{2}$ s/cm. It measures the number of seconds required to give 1 cm change in radius. It is the reciprocal of the last one ($2 = 1/\frac{1}{2}$). The two curves are reflections of each other in '$y = x$'. The data could also have been collected from a ciné camera, the shots showing 2 cm, 4 cm, ... radius would then have been chosen, and the time at which they were taken worked out by counting the frames between them.

9. See Figure M. The greatest rate of increase of volume occurs at 5 seconds after the start; about 750 cm³/s. Volume is not related linearly with radius. The volume entering per second is small at first owing to the problem of 'starting' the balloon, and at the end when the rubber is reaching the end of its natural stretch.

53

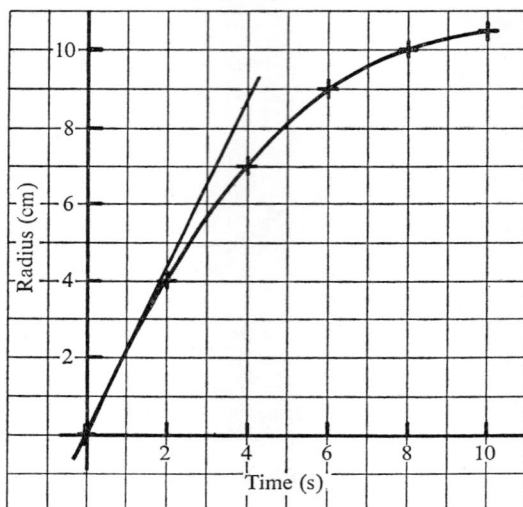

(i)

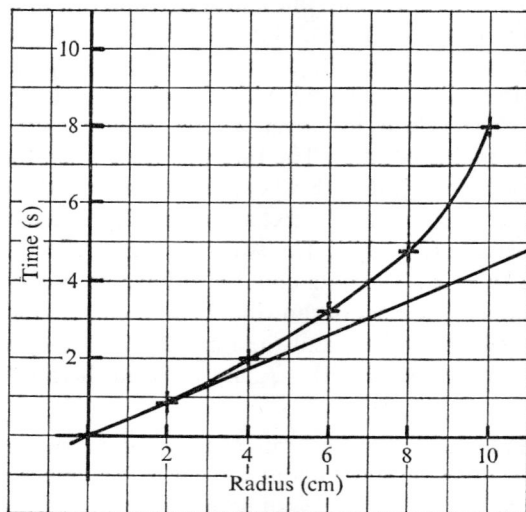

(ii)

Fig. L

54

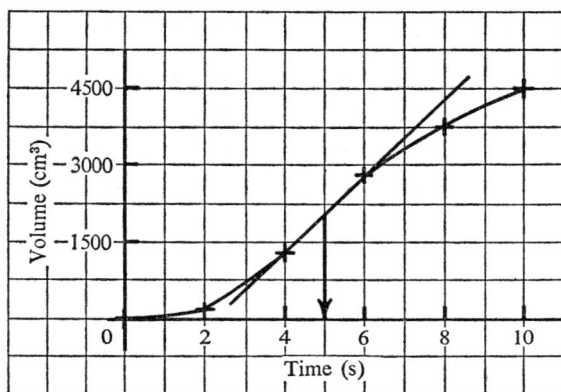

Fig. M

10. For a sphere $V = \frac{4}{3}\pi r^3$, and, therefore, the graph in Figure N is a cubic graph. No experiment is needed since the formula is known. This graph is not time-based. The shape is not under the control of the experimenter, as the other two were, for it is independent of the amount of 'puff'.

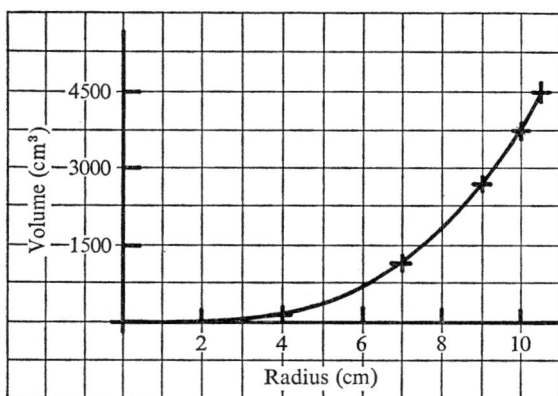

Fig. N

11. (a) Approximately 0·5 cm/h, 0·3 cm/h. The former is an increase, the latter a decrease in pressure. Indicate the former as $^+$0·5, the latter $^{-}0\cdot3$; 0, 0 cm/h, the rate of change altered from an increase $(+)$ to a decrease $(-)$.

(b) A first approximation is $75\cdot2+1\frac{1}{2}\times0\cdot6$ cm $= 76\cdot1$ cm. Since the drop from the tangent the previous day was of the order of $0\cdot2$ cm, $75\cdot9$ cm might be a better estimate. These data are quite useless for estimating the afternoon pressures.

REVISION EXERCISES

SLIDE RULE SESSION NO. 1 (p. 62)

Answers are given first to 4 s.f., then to the degree of accuracy which might be expected from a '5-inch' rule, with a reasonable allowance for error depending on the number of operations involved and on the difficulty of setting and reading-off. On an average single-operation computation an error of about $\frac{1}{3}\%$ is tolerable. On a '10-inch' rule better results would, of course, be expected. Pupils using old rules may find that they are obtaining inaccurate results through shrinkage of the slide.

1. 36270; 36300 ± 100.
2. 26650; 26600 or 26700.
3. 39·37; $39\cdot4 \pm 0\cdot1$.
4. 29·45; 29·4 or 29·5.
5. 0·022 10; $0\cdot0221 \pm 0\cdot0001$.
6. 0·1178; $0\cdot118 \pm 0\cdot0005$.
7. 0·0003108; $(3\cdot11 \pm 0\cdot02) \times 10^{-4}$.
8. 7·563; $7\cdot56 \pm 0\cdot02$.
9. 15·60; $15\cdot6 \pm 0\cdot05$.
10. 2·062; $2\cdot06 \pm 0\cdot01$.

SLIDE RULE SESSION NO. 2 (p. 62)

1. 0·000 240 2(5); $2\cdot40 \times 10^{-4}$ or $2\cdot41 \times 10^{-4}$.
2. 441·0; 441 ± 1.
3. 2·193; 2·19 or 2·20.
4. 20·66; 20·6 or 20·7.
5. 64·51; $64\cdot5 \pm 0\cdot2$.
6. 0·004388; $(4\cdot39 \pm 0\cdot01) \times 10^{-3}$.
7. 1278; 1280 ± 5.
8. 135·1; 135 ± 1.
9. 1892; 1890 ± 5.
10. 6·595; $6\cdot60 \pm 0\cdot02$.

A (p. 62)

1. $\frac{1}{4}$.
2. $(3, {}^{-}2)$.
3. $\begin{pmatrix} 16 & 19 \\ -12 & -15 \end{pmatrix}$.
4. $^{-}2$.
5. $14 \, \text{cm}^2$.
6. 14.
7. 84p.
8. $(2, 4)$.
9. 13 cm.
10. 10010_2.

B (p. 62)

1. False.
2. 28° each.
3. $x \to \frac{1}{3}x$.
4. $\frac{17}{60}$.
5. 9.
6. $(^{-}3, 6)$.
7. 0·001.
8. A cube.
9. $(5, 5)$.
10. 0.

C (p. 63)

1. $\dfrac{3\cdot62}{5\cdot11} = 0\cdot71$ to 2 S.F.   2. $\frac{6}{25} = 0\cdot24$.

3. (a) See Figure A.

   (b) (i) The translation $\begin{pmatrix} 2 \\ 2 \end{pmatrix}$;   (ii) half-turn about (2, 2).

   (c) No, as the triangles are directly congruent to one another, and a triangle and its reflected image are oppositely congruent.

4. P is the point (2, 2) (see Figure B).

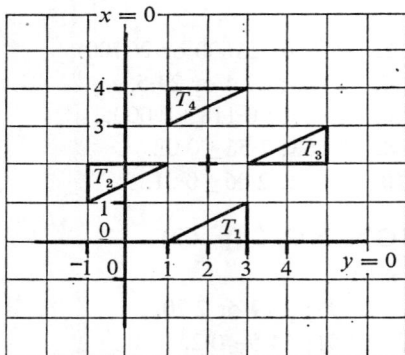

Fig. A

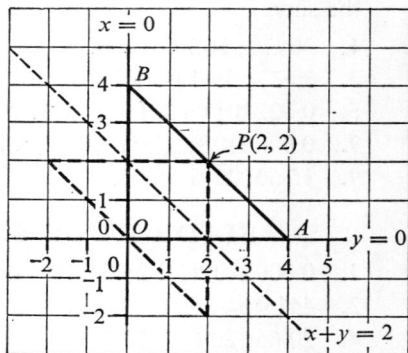

Fig. B

5. (a) $(^-3)$;   (b) $(^-3, 11)$;   (c) matrices incompatible;

   (d) $\begin{pmatrix} ^-2 \\ ^-2 \end{pmatrix}$;   (e) $\begin{pmatrix} 0 & 0 \\ 0 & 0 \end{pmatrix}$;   (f) matrices incompatible.

6. (a)

	Mass (g)		Cost (new pence)
Giant	900	Giant	12
Large	720	Large	10 ;
Standard	480	Standard	8

   (b) $(20 \quad 30 \quad 10) \begin{pmatrix} 900 \\ 720 \\ 480 \end{pmatrix} = (44\,400)$.

   Total mass is $44\,400$ g $= 44\cdot4$ kg.

58

(c) $(20 \quad 30 \quad 10) \begin{pmatrix} 12 \\ 10 \\ 8 \end{pmatrix} = (680).$

Total cost is 680p = £6·80.

7. (a) 1; (b) ⁻1; (c) 1; (d) 1; (e) 0.

8. About 6 metres per second per second.

D (p. 64)

1. $\frac{17}{44}$; $\frac{16}{41}$.

2. (a) The probability of both children being sons is in fact $\frac{1}{4}$. (The set of possible outcomes is

{(son, son), (son, daughter), (daughter, son), (daughter, daughter)},

so that there are *four* distinct possibilities. Order must be taken into account.)

(b) $\frac{7}{8}$.

3. See Figure C. There are six lines of symmetry and there is rotational symmetry of order 6.

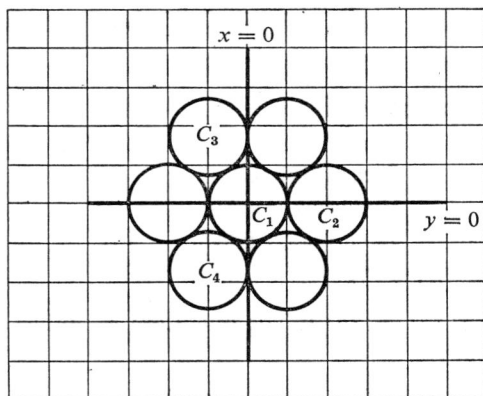

Fig. C

4. (a) $\mathbf{R}^2$ denotes a rotation of 160° about (0, 0),
$\mathbf{R}^{-1}$ denotes a rotation of ⁻80° (280°) about (0, 0),
$\mathbf{R}^4$ denotes a rotation of 320° about (0, 0).

(b) For example, $x = 5$ or ⁻4.

5. (ii) The product **ACB** can be worked out; the answer will be a 3×5 matrix.

6. New vertices are P' (5, 0), Q' (1, 8), R' ($^-$7, 4), S' ($^-$3, $^-$4).

The transformation is a combined enlargement ($\times \sqrt{5}$) and rotation (through about 26·6°) about the origin.

7. (a) 57 km/h;   (b) after 3·85;
(c) about 24 km/h per second.

E (p. 65)

1. See Figure D. Distances and directions are not faithfully reproduced.

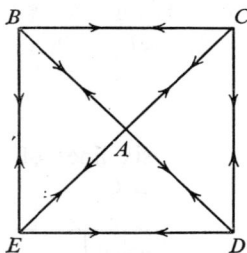

Fig. D

2. Angles of sectors are as follows:

Sunday Mail	57°
Scandalmonger	96°
Highbrow Weekly	60°
Sunday Supplement	147°

3. (2, $^-$3), (2, 3), ($^-$2, 3).

4. (a) 1; (b) 8; (c) $\frac{1}{16}$; (d) 1. The operation is neither commutative nor associative.

5. (a) $\mathbf{BD} = \mathbf{b}+\mathbf{a} = 2\mathbf{a}-\mathbf{c} \Rightarrow \mathbf{c} = \mathbf{a}-\mathbf{b}$.
(b) It is a parallelogram.

6. (a) $2\cdot2 \times 10$;   (b) $2\cdot90 \times 10^3$;   (c) $6\cdot79 \times 10^5$;
(d) 6×10^{-1};   (e) $4\cdot57 \times 10^{-4}$.

7. $33\frac{1}{3}\%$.

8. $40 \sin 36° = 23\cdot5$ cm.   (a) 2;   (b) 4.

F (p. 66)

1. (a) $119@_{12}$;   (b) $308*_{12}$;   (c) $43{,}919_{12}$;   (d) 23_{12}.

2. 3 play cricket only and 5 play tennis only. There are 26 in the form.

3. (a) $\frac{13}{24}$;   (b) $1\frac{1}{3}$;   (c) $\frac{2}{3}$;   (d) $\frac{11}{48}$.

4. $F = 8$. The solid is the regular octahedron.

5. See Figure E. $AC = x+y$.

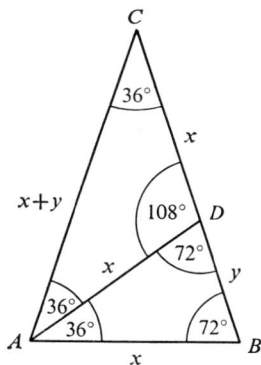

Fig. E

6. (a) $x = 5$;   (b) $x = 5$;   (c) $x = 1\frac{3}{5}$;   (d) $x = 2\cdot56$;
(e) nothing can be said: the expression is an identity relation.

7. In three ways:
(a) (0, 0) and (4, 4);   (b) (8, 4) and (4, 8);
(c) ($^-$4, 0), (0, $^-$4).

8. $\frac{1}{1500}$; $33\frac{1}{3}$ cm².

61

5

THE CIRCLE

1. WHAT IS A CIRCLE?

All pupils will have had considerable experience of the circle. It is worth asking them to write down what they understand by one. This makes a good starting point for the discussion suggested in the text as it will then be clear that a precise definition is essential.

2. THE SYMMETRY OF THE CIRCLE

A circle has an infinite number of lines of symmetry. It also possesses rotational symmetry of an infinite order. It is 'the most symmetrical plane figure there is'. It has point symmetry about its centre.

Exercise A (p. 69)

1. There are a large number of familiar objects from which the selection can be made.

2. A straight line, since the centre of a circle (the axle) is at a fixed distance from the straight line along which it rolls. A connected series of arcs of circles.

3. No.   4. No.

5. No, it is a cycloid. Testing with the eye is sufficient, but pupils should be encouraged to test with their compasses also.

6. The mediator passes through the centre, the disc folds into two semi-circles which fold on top of each other.

7. By walking along the mediators of two pairs of points estimate the position of the centre. Then test the stones for constant distance from this point using a rope. There are many more sophisticated methods, of course.

8. They are collinear. This is inevitable from the symmetry of the two circles and their point of contact.

9. All except the circle with radius 2 cm. (*a*) Yes, with radius $2\frac{1}{2}$ cm, (*b*) no largest one. The centres are collinear, they lie on the mediator of *AB*.

10. $BC = 4$ cm approx. ($r > \frac{1}{2}BC$). The line, or the line produced, bisects $\angle BAC$.

11. *O* is equidistant from *A*, *B* and *C*. The circle passes through *B* and *C*.

13. The lines 'envelop' a circle.

14. The circles 'envelop' a pair of straight lines. The idea of a moving line enveloping a curve or straight line is considered in Chapter 15; it is analogous to the idea of the locus of a point, though rather more difficult. This bears on Question 2 concerning a rolling circle.

15. It is not circular; in general it is a curve of the eighth degree. It makes no difference if the triangle is specialized.

3. THE CIRCUMFERENCE OF A CIRCLE

The object of this section is to induce pupils to discover for themselves that the circumference is a little more than six times the radius. Many will 'know' already that $C = 2\pi r$. Care will have to be taken not to allow them to use this knowledge to avoid the experience. A 13-year-old, at the end of a measuring session, was overheard by the author to say, in a very surprised voice, 'It really *is* six times'!

The easiest ways of measuring are as follows: (*a*) and (*b*) by rolling the object in question, (*c*) and (*e*) by wrapping round a thin string, and (*d*) by pacing out. When measuring the circumference of a small object the advantage of wrapping the string round a number of times should be stressed and this may be linked with the idea of averages.

The graph should be approximately straight. Difficulties may arise in finding a scale to cope with all the objects measured. The validity of using the same scale to measure both metres and centimetres could be discussed and agreed to.

Exercise B (p. 71)

1. (a) 66 cm;   (b) 48 m;   (c) 6 m;   (d) 4·20 m.

2. Men's collar sizes in 'inches' approximate to the circumference. Children will average about 30 cm, radius 5 cm.

3. 65 cm appears to be the outside diameter of the unstretched tyre. The rim is 60 cm, in diameter, the pumped-up tyre is usually a little more than 65 cm. In one revolution the bicycle moves forwards nearly 2·1 m.

4. (a) Just over 20 cm;   (b) 83 cm;   (c) 670 m.

5. Diameter of the equivalent circle. For shapes like a head, which are only roughly circular, the use of an equivalent circle is worth noting.

6. Here we are relating *diameter* and circumference, $C = 3d$ in this exercise. (a) $1\frac{2}{3}$ cm; (b) 5 cm; a clothes line is usually between $2\frac{1}{2}$ and $3\frac{3}{4}$ cm.

7. About 100 m.

8. For the hexagon,

$$6 < \text{circumference} < 6\cdot9.$$
For the 12-gon,
$$6\cdot21 < \text{circumference} < 6\cdot44$$

obviously a better estimate. The more points taken the nearer we get to the true value which is 'sandwiched' between the estimates.

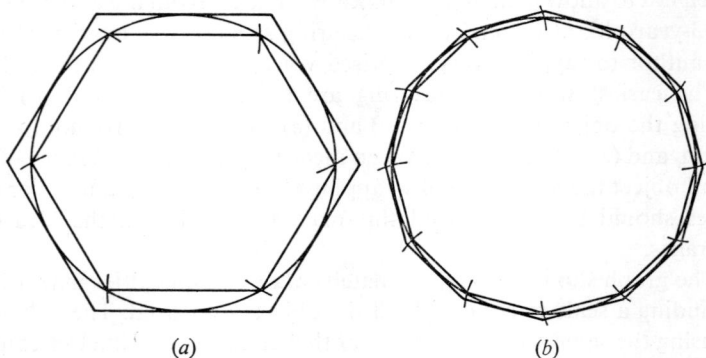

(a)   (b)

Fig. A

9. The last question should have made it clear that our estimate of 6 is on the low side, and that a suitable answer is 'rather more than 38000 km'—it is, in fact, approximately 40000 km.

10. The centres of the individual rails are coincident, the rails do not have the same radius (if they did they would have to have different centres and would no longer be parallel). The length of track is the average of the lengths of the two actual rails and the radius quoted seems to be the average radius. With radius 30 cm, six rails make a complete circle and may be called '30 cm lengths'. This provides a good example for $C \approx 6r$. The total length is therefore about 4·8 m. The 30 cm radius layout is about 3 m, that is 1·8 m shorter.

11. Using the formula $C \approx 6r$, three circles of radius 60 cm require 10·8 m, two circles of radius 45 cm require 5·4 m, total 16·2 m. Since the multiplier is actually more than 6, this would not be enough wire to make the sphere the size required: about 17 m would be needed, excluding an overlap for joining.

12. We can ignore the straights. They have run circular distances of 6×50 m; 6×51 m; 6×52 m. The outer runners have a little more than 6 and 12 m extra respectively. In practice the lanes are 'staggered'; this means that the starting lines are set back by the same distances so that they all have the same finishing line.

4. THE NUMBER CALLED π

The commonest of all errors in this type of work is the mistaking of radius for diameter and vice versa. In this exercise the radius is the length normally quoted, where diameter is used it is italicized. Pupils could well be encouraged *always* to work with radius.

Exercise C (p. 73)

1. (*a*) 38·3 cm; (*b*) 185 cm; (*c*) 113 m; (*d*) 0·283 cm.

2. (*a*) 88 m; (*b*) 22000 m; (*c*) 13·2 km;
   (*d*) 4·4 mm approximately.

   The lengths are all divisible by 7. It needs to be stressed that $\pi = \frac{22}{7}$ (to slide rule accuracy); this is an *alternative* to $\pi = 3\cdot14$.

3. False, the radius is about 80 m. 40 m is not even a rough approximation. $\pi = 3$ will be sufficiently accurate.

4. (a) 14·0 m;   (b) 0·716 cm;   (c) 812 m;   (d) 4·09 cm.

   The importance of the 'point nought' in the answer to (a) may need to be stressed.

   The slide rule setting for reading answers (b), (c) and (d) is shown in Figure B.

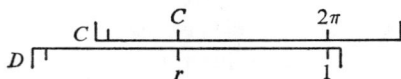

Fig. B

5. $2 \times 1·032 \times 3·142 = 6·485088$ cm. Both the figures used have been corrected to three decimal places; the answer can only be given confidently to two decimal places. The circumference measures between 6·48 and 6·49 cm approximately.

6. Take π to be 3·14 or $3\frac{1}{7}$; distance 21 m to nearest metre. The arithmetic is easier with $\pi = 3·14$ since division by 7 is then avoided: $\pi = 3$ would give an error of 1 m.

7. Take π to be 3 and assume all the turns have a radius of 1 cm (in fact most will have greater radius). Then the total length is *not less than* $1000 \times 6 \times 1$ cm $= 6000$ cm $= 60$ m. There is more than 54 m on the reel.

8. Take π to be $3\frac{1}{7}$, circumference is 132 cm; 105·6 m; 105·6 m/min $= 1·76$ m/s.

9. Take π to be 3; 8 times.

10. Take π to be 3·14; (we are going to multiply by 450 and flywheels are accurately made). Circumference measures 3·14 m. Frank travels 1413 m/min $= 23·6$ m/s (nearly 85 km/h). Moving through the air at this speed would blow him off, irrespective of the need to stick tight to provide centripetal force.

11. Taking π to be 3·14, the circumference of the earth is approximately 40000 km, a convenient figure. 1700 km/h approx. No, he is travelling along a circle of smaller radius.

5. THE AREA BOUNDED BY A CIRCLE

It is useful for pupils to make large scale models of Figures 6 and 7 and, if possible, of the further dissection into 16 ($+1$) parts. A box of processed cheese can be a useful visual aid!

Figure 6(b) is only roughly rectangular, the ends are parallel; p is a bit less than half the circumference, about $\frac{3}{2}\pi$ cm, q is a bit more than the radius $\frac{3}{2}$ cm; the areas of Figures 6(a) and (b) are plainly the same, so $\frac{9}{4}\pi$ cm² is not a bad estimate of the area.

Figure 7(b) is much more nearly rectangular, and gives a more convincing answer; again p' is about $\frac{3}{2}\pi$ cm, q' about $\frac{3}{2}$ cm, area of figure (b) and hence of circle (a) is about $\frac{9}{4}\pi$ cm².

In the case of division into 16 parts, the re-assembled figure is very nearly rectangular. Note that it is easier to obtain these figures by cutting circles from adhesive paper and sticking them onto a backing piece than it is to draw them using geometrical constructions.

The re-assembled figure will very nearly measure πr units by r units, its area is πr^2 sq. units.

The multiplier 2 disappears because the circumference is split between the top and bottom edges of the re-assembled figure.

Exercise D (p. 75)

1. (*a*) 48 cm²;   (*b*) 30000 m²;   (*c*) 1200 m².

2. 25 cm²; 5 cm.

3. (*a*) 10 km;   (*b*) 2 m;   (*c*) 7 cm.

4. 4 cm; 48 cm².

5. Presumably we do not want him to waste gold; on the other hand $\pi > 3$ and it would not do to under-order. Take $\pi = 3\frac{1}{7}$ giving an area of 710 cm².

6. It will do to take π to be 3. This gives a radius of between 6 and 7 m. The need for finding square roots is seen here.

7. 616 cm².   **8.** 1250 cm².

9. 5100 m² (taking π to be 3).

6. SQUARING WITH THE SLIDE RULE

It is better to find the approximate answer *before* turning to the slide rule. Some suitable layout, similar to the one in the worked example, should be insisted on.

Exercise E (p. 76)

1. 1156. **2.** 361. **3.** 29·2.

4. 34600. **5.** 740000. **6.** 702.

7. 26·5. **8.** 1513000. **9.** 0·270.

10. 0·828. **11.** 0·0484. **12.** 0·00706.

13. 0·00000961. **14.** 0·00001024. **15.** 11000.

16. 0·0110. **17.** 65400000. **18.** 0·362.

19. 0·384. **20.** 0·000000593.

21. (a) 11·9 cm²; (b) 378000 m²; (c) 7480 cm².

22. 7·07 cm². The setting is shown in Figure C.

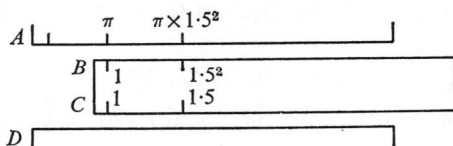

Fig. C

23. (a) 18·86 cm²; (b) 8·24 cm²; (c) 31·0 cm².

24. This is the same setting as in Figure C, but with the 10 or 100 point of the B scale set to π on the A scale.

(a) 132 cm²; (b) 269 cm²; (c) 203 cm².

25. (a) 1930 cm²; (b) 72600 m²; (c) 0·636 cm².

7. SQUARE ROOTS

It is important to build up a feeling for the number of digits in the squares and square roots of numbers of various magnitudes *before* the very simple pairing method is introduced. This section is devoted entirely to estimation.

The function 'square', i.e. $x \to x^2$, is the inverse of the function 'take the positive square root of', i.e. $x \to \sqrt{x}$.

(a) 1 or 2 digits; (b) 3 or 4 digits; (c) 5 or 6 digits; (d) $(2n-1)$ or $2n$ digits

$$x \approx 3\cdot2; \quad y \approx 32; \quad z \approx 320.$$

(a) 1 digit, it will be a number less than $3\cdot2$; (b) 1 digit, it will be a number more than $3\cdot2$; (c) 2 digits, less than 32; (d) 2 digits, more than 32; (e) n digits, first three digits are 3, 2, 0 or more. (f) $(n+1)$ digits, first three digits are 3, 2, 0 or less.

Pupils may find some difficulty in answering (e) and (f) without assistance.

N.B. 320 is only the 'dividing line' to slide rule accuracy. To 6 figures, $\sqrt{10} = 3\cdot16228$.

The final 'pairs' may be of the form 05.

Exercise F (p. 78)

1. 6.	**2.** 2.	**3.** 0·2
4. 200.	**5.** 9.	**6.** 30.
7. 0·3.	**8.** 0·9.	**9.** 80.
10. 0·8.	**11.** 800.	**12.** 0·08.
13. 20.	**14.** 0·3.	**15.** 5.
16. 0·01.	**17.** 3.	**18.** 2.
19. 20.	**20.** 0·02.	

21. $40x$; $40x = 180 \Rightarrow x = 4$ (nearest integer below).

$\sqrt{580} = 24$ (approximately).

22. $74x = 1400 - 37^2 = 31 \Rightarrow x = 0\cdot4$ (nearest below).

$\sqrt{1400} = 37\cdot4$ (approximately). A closer estimate could be obtained by using $37\cdot4$ as the first estimate:

$74\cdot8x = 1400 - (37\cdot4)^2 = 1\cdot24 \Rightarrow x = 0\cdot02$ (approximately), etc.

23. Taking 44 as an estimate gives $44\cdot7$ as a better one. From this we get $44\cdot72$ as better still, so that $\sqrt{2000} = 44\cdot7$ (3 S.F.).

8. SQUARE ROOTS USING THE SLIDE RULE

The flow diagram for square roots is shown in Figure D.

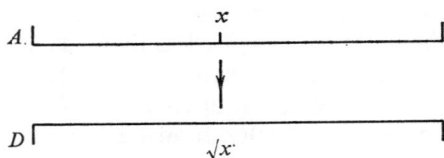

Fig. D

The rough estimate of $\sqrt{34{,}500}$ is 200. We shall therefore look below 3·45 on the A scale, not below 34·5.

Exercise G (p. 79)

1. 16·6. **2.** 5·24. **3.** 0·166. **4.** 0·00524.

5. 63·6. **6.** 2·01. **7.** 2990.

8. 299. **9.** 0·0827. **10.** 32·9.

11. 0·195. **12.** 0·0456. **13.** 237.

14. 5·21. **15.** 17·3. **16.** 23·4.

17. 0·389. **18.** 3·05. **19.** $1·865 \times 10^6$.

20. (a) 35·9 cm; (b) 61·8 m; (c) 0·953 m.

21. (a) 18·57 m; (b) 20·96 m. **22.** 8·26 cm.

23. Radius 4·2 m, circumference about 26·3 m, requiring 14 hurdles.

24. No, he divided $\sqrt{4000}$ by π, instead of finding $\sqrt{(4000 \div \pi)}$ or dividing $\sqrt{4000}$ by $\sqrt{\pi}$.

25. Shortest length needed is $2\sqrt{\pi}$, about 3·54 m.

26. $1·95^2 = 3·8025$; $2·60^2 = 6·7600$; $3·25^2 = 10·5625$.

Exact answers are required. The semi-circles have areas

$$\tfrac{1}{8}\pi \times 1·95^2; \quad \tfrac{1}{8}\pi \times 2·60^2; \quad \tfrac{1}{8}\pi \times 3·25^2.$$

The sum of the first two is equal to the third. There is no need to work them out.

27. The area of each quadrant is twice that of the corresponding semi-circle. The sum of the areas of the quadrants on the shorter sides is equal to the area of the quadrant on the larger side. Questions 26 and 27 extend the work on Pythagoras's Theorem to similar figures of any shape drawn on the sides of a right-angled triangle (see p. 268 of Book 2). With some classes these questions can be treated as exercises in computation.

28. Neither.

9. SECTORS AND SEGMENTS

Sectors are of more practical importance than segments and this section is concerned mainly with the former.

Exercise H (p. 82)

1. Segments (*a*), (*d*), (*e*); sectors (*b*), (*c*).

2. Yes, a semi-circle.   **3.** 23·9 cm.

4.

Angle between radii	Length of arc (cm)	Area of sector (cm²)
15°	3	18
30°	6	36
45°	9	54
60°	12	72

Some students should complete this table by inspection, some others may need to perform the calculations. Both length of arc and area of sector are linear functions of the angle. We use this proportionality in working out the angles in pie charts so that the areas represent the quantities involved.

5. (*a*) 45·7 cm²;   (*b*) 182·8 cm² (four times the area); (*c*) 348·2 cm² (take (*b*) from the total area).

6. 104·7 cm²; 209·4 cm³.   **7.** 90°.

8. 57·3° (i.e. 1 radian).

9. Yes; a sector; the true height is the length of the perpendicular from O to the plane of the base circle. No mention has been made in the question of the possibility of the cone being other than a right circular cone. This is a complication that can be left for the present.

10. Increasing the angle increases the base radius and decreases the height. Circumference of the base is $2\pi \times 3$ cm. If this is the curved length of a sector of a circle of radius 5 cm, then, if the angle is $\theta°$, $\dfrac{\theta}{360} \times 2\pi \times 5 = 2\pi \times 3$, giving $\theta = 216$.

The base radius cannot exceed 5 cm.

11. $2\pi r$ cm; $(360r/l)$ degrees; πrl cm².

12. $36\cdot9°$; $73\cdot8°$; $(64\cdot4 - 48\cdot0)$ cm² $= 16\cdot4$ cm².

13. (a) $9\cdot32$ m; (b) $112\cdot8°$; (c) $94\cdot2$ m²; (d) $18\,800$ m³.

10. THE CYLINDER

If the examples in Exercise H on the cone have been attempted, then the introduction of nets of cylinders should be straightforward.

The end circles have a radius of about 2·5 cm.

The net of the second cylinder will be rectangular and measure about 24 cm × 10 cm.

Exercise I (p. 84).

1. (a) 72 m²; (b) 72 m²; the area formula is symmetrical in r and h.

2. (a) 144 m³; (b) 108 m³; the volume formula is not symmetrical in r and h.

3. $8\cdot46$ cm²; $2\cdot33$ cm³.

4. 5 cm; 2·26 cm.

5. $rh = 3$, possible sets are $r = 3, h = 1$; $r = 2, h = 1\frac{1}{2}$, etc. There are infinitely many sets.

6. Approximately 28 cm.

7. Circumference = 9π cm. The area of the pipe works out as about 1·2 m². There is enough paint to paint it and about two-thirds of the next one.

8. About 1200 and 600 mm³ respectively. Ratio 1:2. The mass ratio is the same, so is the ratio of their values. Banks often 'count' silver by weighing in lots worth £5. It is possible to detect an error of 5p, even if the coins are worn, in a substantial proportion of the weighings.

9. It is to be expected that the most irregular figure has the largest surface area, i.e. the half cylinder. If the students know that the sphere is the solid of least surface area for a given volume, they may (correctly) guess that the smallest surface of these three is possessed by the cylinder.

The cube has a side of 1 cm, and a surface area of 6 cm². The half cylinder has a base radius of 0·798 cm and surface 6·1 cm². The cylinder has a base radius of 0·564 cm and surface 5·55 cm².

10. A line through the mid-point of AD and perpendicular to it in the plane of the generating circle. The locus is a circle whose centre is on the axis of rotation. If the radius of the generating circle is r units and the radius of the locus of its centre is R units, the volume V in cubic units is given by

$$V = \pi r^2 \times 2\pi R = 2\pi^2 r^2 R; \quad r = 3\tfrac{1}{2}, \quad R = 8\tfrac{1}{2}; \quad V = 2060.$$

Volume of inner tube = 2060 cm³.

11. An annulus like a napkin ring; $(3\tfrac{1}{2}, 0)$; 440 cu. units.

Exercise J (p. 85)

It is, of course, impossible to say for certain which is the most appropriate value to take for π unless the background to the problem is known. Questions 1–3 are inserted to put emphasis on the important idea that all values for π are approximate. Different pupils will choose different values and, barring arithmetical errors, will have different 'correct' answers.

1. (a) $\pi = 3$, 24 m; (b) $\pi = \tfrac{22}{7}$, 44 cm; (c) $\pi = 3\cdot14$ (slide rule), 33 cm.

2. (a) $\pi = 3\cdot14$, $2\cdot16$ cm²;   (b) $\pi = \frac{22}{7}$, 1390 m²;
   (c) $\pi = 3$, 3 km².

3. (a) $\pi = \frac{22}{7}$, $73\frac{1}{2}$ m;   (b) $\pi = 3\cdot14$, 215 m.

4. (a) $3\cdot57$ cm;   (b) $16\cdot4$ m.

5. (a) $36\frac{2}{3}$ cm;   (b) 495 cm;   (c) $7\frac{1}{3}$ m.

6. (a) $8\cdot67$ cm²;   (b) $8\cdot63$ cm².

7. (a) $93\cdot5°$;   (b) $335°$.

8. $\frac{22}{7} = 3\cdot1429$, $\pi = 3\cdot1416$; correct to two decimal places. Error $0\cdot14$ cm²; about $0\cdot04\%$. It is worth while to point out that $\frac{22}{7}$ is roughly as much too high as $3\cdot14$ is too low.

Use $\pi = 3\cdot1416$. Equatorial diameter $= 12758$ km. (Diameter of equivalent circle $= 12735$ km.) Distance between poles $= 12711$ km.

$$\frac{12758 - 12711}{12758} = \frac{47}{12758} \approx \tfrac{1}{3}\%.$$

10. Six times.   11. $88\cdot5$ mm.

12. (a) 4π m, 6π m;
   (b) 4π m², 9π m²; 2:3, 4:9, 5:2, 25:4.

13. 3:5. The radius.

14. $2\cdot04$ m; 235 rev/min.

15. $16\cdot5$ m²; $2\cdot44$ m.

16. Taking $\pi = 3$, 620 cm/s.   17. $37\cdot16$ cm.

18. The number of grid points is effectively proportional to the area; 1:3.

19. Blue $96°$, 8 children; mauve $12°$, 1 child.

6

NETWORKS

The standard mathematical term for what we, in this chapter, refer to as a network is 'graph'. Two of the books mentioned below use this word in their titles. However, since 'graph' is already used in the context of coordinate geometry we have preferred to use 'network', a word which also has the advantage of being associated with electrical circuits, railways and roads. Much of the increasing importance of the theory of graphs today lies in problems connected with these.

The chapter is a sequel to the opening chapter of Book 2 on Topology. There the idea of a matrix was introduced for the first time; since then matrices have been used in other contexts, such as transformations, and also they have been combined by addition and multiplication. Two different applications of the multiplication of matrices are introduced here, and, as has already been suggested in the commentary on Chapter 3, the work of this chapter could be an alternative starting point for considering the combination of matrices.

As the material presented here is probably the most unfamiliar of the new topics being introduced into school mathematics, some justification for its inclusion is necessary. We have already suggested that its applications are relevant and increasing and also that it provides further opportunities for consolidating work on matrix algebra. These reasons in themselves barely justify a chapter of this nature. A more powerful argument is that the material constitutes an exciting mathematical study in itself and has proved popular with pupils. In addition, it is by nature open-ended and opportunities for further investigations appear to be unlimited.

The chapter can be taken in several stages. Sections 1, 2, 3 should be done together and also Sections 4 and 5. Section 6 can be taken by itself but not before 1, 2 and 3.

The standard work on many of the problems developed here, and on many other related ones, is, *The Theory of Graphs*, by Berge. This is an invaluable source for further ideas on the topic, in spite of the notation in some places being rather difficult. A very much simpler and less extensive account of graph theory is contained in *Graphs and their Uses*, by Ore; this book, however, contains no work on matrices. Useful references to these can be found in:

> *Some Lessons in Mathematics*, ed. Fletcher;
> *Introduction to Finite Mathematics*, by Kemeny, Snell and Thompson.
>
> Applications of graph or network theory may be found in *Topology and Matrices in the Solution of Networks*, by Rogers; *Management and Mathematics*, by Fletcher and Clarke; *An Introduction to Critical Path Analysis*, by Lockyer.

The first of these three is concerned with electrical circuits and the other two with economic and business problems.

1. ROUTE MATRICES

This section and the two that follow it are variations on the same theme. The networks considered are all directed; the arcs are interpreted as:

> (i) routes on a map,
> (ii) results of games,
> (iii) relations.

Strictly speaking both (i) and (ii) can also be interpreted as relations, for example, 'is joined to' and 'beat' respectively.

It is important to realize that the networks are topological in nature and that the arcs have no metrical or directional significance. This is why the arcs are frequently drawn as curved lines; this is, of course, inevitable if, for instance, two routes join the same two nodes.

To every network there corresponds a matrix and provided we are not confined to two dimensions there is a network corresponding to any square matrix. If we are restricted to planar networks, that is to two dimensions, then there will only be networks corresponding to some square matrices. Two networks having the same matrix are said to be topologically equivalent; this idea will receive further consideration in Book 4.

The term 'leading diagonal' is again very useful; this will contain only zeros unless, as in Figure 3, there are loops joining a particular node to itself. The matrix is symmetrical about the leading diagonal if, in the corresponding network, for every route from, say, A to B, there is one from B to A.

(a) and (b) The 1 on the leading diagonal of S represents the 'circular' route from H to itself. This would be a 2 if there were two distinct routes from H to itself; removing the arrow on the loop, as in Figure A, would be sufficient to indicate this, as the route is now two-way.

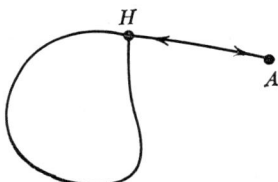

H

A

Fig. A

The text carefully outlines why forming the product of S with itself, that is S^2, produces the information about two-stage routes or journeys. It is essential for the pupil to appreciate the reasons for this and not merely to treat it as a trick.

(c)
$$S^3 = \begin{pmatrix} 1 & 2 \\ 2 & 3 \end{pmatrix}$$

and contains information on three-stage journeys from one node to itself or another node.

In this example, they are:

from A to A, $A \to H \to H \to A$ 1;

from A to H, $\left.\begin{array}{l} A \to H \to A \to H \\ A \to H \to H \to H \end{array}\right\}$ 2;

from H to A, $\left.\begin{array}{l} H \to A \to H \to A \\ H \to H \to H \to A \end{array}\right\}$ 2;

from H to H, $\left.\begin{array}{l} H \to H \to H \to H \\ H \to A \to H \to H \\ H \to H \to A \to H \end{array}\right\}$ 3.

Exercise A (p. 91)

1.

$$\begin{array}{c} A\ B\ C \\ \begin{array}{c} A \\ B \\ C \end{array} \begin{pmatrix} 0 & 0 & 1 \\ 1 & 0 & 1 \\ 0 & 1 & 0 \end{pmatrix} \end{array}.\ \text{Two-stage matrix}\ \begin{array}{c} A\ B\ C \\ \begin{array}{c} A \\ B \\ C \end{array} \begin{pmatrix} 0 & 1 & 0 \\ 0 & 1 & 1 \\ 1 & 0 & 1 \end{pmatrix} \end{array}.$$

Two-stage journeys:

$A \to C \to B,$ $C \to B \to A,$
$B \to C \to B,$ $C \to B \to C.$
$B \to A \to C,$

From now on the labels A, B, C, D, will no longer be added to the matrices.

2. $\begin{pmatrix} 0 & 1 & 0 \\ 1 & 0 & 1 \\ 0 & 1 & 1 \end{pmatrix}$. Two-stage matrix $\begin{pmatrix} 1 & 0 & 1 \\ 0 & 2 & 1 \\ 1 & 1 & 2 \end{pmatrix}$.

Two-stage journeys:

$$A \to B \to A, \qquad C \to B \to A,$$
$$A \to B \to C, \qquad C \to C \to B,$$
$$B \to A \to B, \qquad C \to B \to C,$$
$$B \to C \to B, \qquad C \to C \to C.$$
$$B \to C \to C,$$

3. $S = \begin{pmatrix} 0 & 1 & 0 & 0 \\ 0 & 0 & 1 & 0 \\ 0 & 0 & 0 & 1 \\ 0 & 1 & 0 & 0 \end{pmatrix}$, $S^2 = \begin{pmatrix} 0 & 0 & 1 & 0 \\ 0 & 0 & 0 & 1 \\ 0 & 1 & 0 & 0 \\ 0 & 0 & 1 & 0 \end{pmatrix}$.

The entries in the first columns of S and S^2 indicate the number of single-stage and two-stage journeys respectively, which end at A; since there is no route ending at A all these entries must be zeros.

4. $S = \begin{pmatrix} 0 & 1 & 1 \\ 1 & 0 & 1 \\ 1 & 1 & 0 \end{pmatrix}$, $S^2 = \begin{pmatrix} 2 & 1 & 1 \\ 1 & 2 & 1 \\ 1 & 1 & 2 \end{pmatrix}$, $S^4 = \begin{pmatrix} 6 & 5 & 5 \\ 5 & 6 & 5 \\ 5 & 5 & 6 \end{pmatrix}$.

(*a*) Six which start and end at each node; 18 altogether.

(*b*) Five between any pair of different nodes; 30 altogether.

If one attempts to enumerate these, the elusive route, between, for example, A and B, is $A \to B \to C \to A \to B$.

5. $S^3 = \begin{pmatrix} 1 & 2 \\ 2 & 3 \end{pmatrix}$, $S^4 = \begin{pmatrix} 2 & 3 \\ 3 & 5 \end{pmatrix}$, $S^5 = \begin{pmatrix} 3 & 5 \\ 5 & 8 \end{pmatrix}$,

$S^6 = \begin{pmatrix} 5 & 8 \\ 8 & 13 \end{pmatrix}$, $S^7 = \begin{pmatrix} 8 & 13 \\ 13 & 21 \end{pmatrix}$.

The numbers belong to the Fibonacci sequence. See Book 2, Chapter 6.

It is likely that some pupil will spot the series of relationships,

$$S + S^2 = S^3 \quad (\text{cf. } S \times S^2 = S^3!)$$
$$S^2 + S^3 = S^4,$$
$$S^3 + S^4 = S^5, \quad \text{etc.}$$

Teachers familiar with matrix algebra will realize that this is a particular case of the result that every square matrix satisfies its characteristic equation (the Cayley–Hamilton Theorem).

The characteristic equation is $\lambda^2 = \lambda + 1$.

6. Since there is only one route between any two points no two-stage route such as $A \to B \to A$ can exist, that is, there is no two-stage route between a point and itself. There will only be zeros on the leading diagonal of S^3 if no triangular routes (see Figure B) exist in the network.

Fig. B

2. DOMINANCE MATRICES

The networks in this section are closely related to what are known in sociology as 'sociograms'. Though, as the text states, one would hardly take the results of this section seriously in the context of games, the application of similar techniques is becoming increasingly important in the field of sociology. There, much attention is being given to the study of human (as opposed to mathematical) groups. How, for example, is a leader chosen? Berge in *The Theory of Graphs* considers this problem in considerable detail.

(*a*) The row sum gives the number of matches won by a particular contestant. The column sum gives the number of matches lost.

The following argument may be offered: *A* and *B* have both won two matches, but since *A* beat *B*, *A* can claim to be the better player.

Taking two-stage dominances into consideration confirms this verdict. However, if a similar argument is applied to *C* and *D*, it is not supported by considering two-stage dominances. *C* has a total of 3 one or two-stage dominances but *D* only 2; on the other hand *D* beat *C*.

It may be suggested that two-stage dominances against a player (the column total) should be considered as balancing out two-stage dominances in favour. This point is worth discussing if it arises. Some of the conclusions arrived at in the exercise would inevitably be invalidated if this suggestion is allowed.

Exercise B (p. 94)

1. See Figure C.

$$\mathbf{T} = \begin{pmatrix} 0 & 1 & 1 & 1 \\ 0 & 0 & 1 & 1 \\ 0 & 0 & 0 & 1 \\ 0 & 0 & 0 & 0 \end{pmatrix},$$

$$\mathbf{T}^2 = \begin{pmatrix} 0 & 0 & 1 & 2 \\ 0 & 0 & 0 & 1 \\ 0 & 0 & 0 & 0 \\ 0 & 0 & 0 & 0 \end{pmatrix}.$$

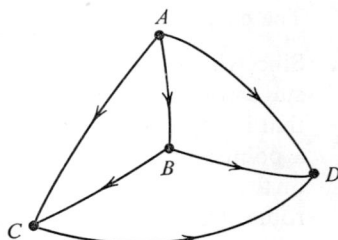

Fig. C

Totals of one and two-stage dominances:

$$A, 6; \quad B, 3; \quad C, 1; \quad D, 0.$$

2. $\mathbf{T} = \begin{pmatrix} 0 & 0 & 1 & 1 & 1 \\ 1 & 0 & 0 & 1 & 1 \\ 0 & 1 & 0 & 1 & 0 \\ 0 & 0 & 0 & 0 & 0 \\ 0 & 0 & 1 & 1 & 0 \end{pmatrix}, \quad \mathbf{T}^2 = \begin{pmatrix} 0 & 1 & 1 & 2 & 0 \\ 0 & 0 & 2 & 2 & 1 \\ 1 & 0 & 0 & 1 & 1 \\ 0 & 0 & 0 & 0 & 0 \\ 0 & 1 & 0 & 1 & 0 \end{pmatrix}.$

Totals and order of merit:

$$B, 8; \quad A, 7; \quad C, 5; \quad E, 4; \quad D, 0.$$

3. $\mathbf{T} = \begin{pmatrix} 0 & 0 & 1 & 0 & 0 & 0 \\ 1 & 0 & 1 & 0 & 0 & 1 \\ 0 & 0 & 0 & 1 & 0 & 1 \\ 1 & 0 & 0 & 0 & 1 & 0 \\ 1 & 1 & 0 & 0 & 0 & 1 \\ 0 & 0 & 0 & 1 & 0 & 0 \end{pmatrix}, \quad \mathbf{T}^2 = \begin{pmatrix} 0 & 0 & 0 & 1 & 0 & 1 \\ 0 & 0 & 1 & 2 & 0 & 1 \\ 1 & 0 & 0 & 1 & 1 & 0 \\ 1 & 1 & 1 & 0 & 0 & 1 \\ 1 & 0 & 2 & 1 & 0 & 1 \\ 1 & 0 & 0 & 0 & 1 & 0 \end{pmatrix}.$

Totals and order of merit:

Edna, 8; Betty, 7; Daphne, 6; Catherine, 5; Anne 3; Freda 3.

4. Row of zeros, no matches won. Column of zeros, no matches lost.

    If the nth row of $\mathbf{T}$ contains only zeros, then because the nth row of $\mathbf{T}^2$ is formed by combining the nth row of $\mathbf{T}$ with each column of $\mathbf{T}$ in turn, the nth row of $\mathbf{T}^2$ also will contain only zeros. A similar argument applies to columns.

Clearly if a player has won no matches he cannot exercise two-stage dominance over any other player. Also if he has lost no matches no other player can exercise two-stage dominance over him.

5. Three-stage dominances could be considered provided a situation such as that introduced in Question 6 does not arise, whereby any one of three players exercises three-stage dominance over himself via the other two. In this situation a triangular path, as shown in Figure D, occurs. This is fundamentally an inconsistency and, as far as matches between the particular three players are concerned, they are on equal terms. Consequently any numbers on the leading diagonal of $\mathbf{T}^3$ should be ignored.

Fig. D

Questions 6, 7 and 8 are optional questions for the abler pupil.

6. This extends the problem raised in Question 5.

In a tournament in which n players all play each other the maximum possible number of triangular paths of the type in Figure D is $\frac{1}{24}(n^3-n)$ if n is odd, and $\frac{1}{24}(n^3-4n)$ if n is even. In Figure 10, ACB is another such path.

(a) $n = 4$, number of paths 2 (see Figure 9);

(b) $n = 5$, number of paths 5.

Berge in *The Theory of Graphs* gives a delightful example about testing the response of a dog to six different kinds of food. The ratio of the actual numbers of triangular paths to the maximum possible numbers is called the coefficient of inconsistency of the network.

7. (a)
$$\mathbf{T} = \begin{array}{c} \\ B \\ E \\ G \\ L \\ M \\ S \end{array} \begin{array}{c} B \ \ E \ \ G \ \ L \ \ M \ \ S \\ \begin{pmatrix} 0 & 0 & 1 & 0 & 1 & 0 \\ 0 & 0 & 0 & 1 & 0 & 1 \\ 0 & 0 & 0 & 0 & 0 & 1 \\ 0 & 0 & 1 & 0 & 0 & 0 \\ 0 & 0 & 0 & 0 & 0 & 1 \\ 0 & 0 & 0 & 0 & 0 & 0 \end{pmatrix} \end{array},$$

81

$$\mathbf{T^2} = \begin{pmatrix} 0 & 0 & 0 & 0 & 0 & 2 \\ 0 & 0 & 1 & 0 & 0 & 0 \\ 0 & 0 & 0 & 0 & 0 & 0 \\ 0 & 0 & 0 & 0 & 0 & 1 \\ 0 & 0 & 0 & 0 & 0 & 0 \\ 0 & 0 & 0 & 0 & 0 & 0 \end{pmatrix}, \qquad \mathbf{T^3} = \begin{pmatrix} 0 & 0 & 0 & 0 & 0 & 0 \\ 0 & 0 & 0 & 0 & 0 & 1 \\ & & & & & \\ & & \text{rest 0's} & & & \\ & & & & & \\ & & & & & \end{pmatrix}.$$

Brazil and England have the same total (4) of one, two- and three-stage dominances. If less significance is attached to a three-stage dominance, then Brazil should be considered the favourite.

(b) The matrices are:

$$\begin{pmatrix} 0 & 0 & 1 & 0 & 1 & 0 \\ 0 & 0 & 0 & 1 & 0 & 1 \\ 0 & 0 & 0 & 0 & 0 & 1 \\ 0 & 0 & 1 & 0 & 0 & 1 \\ 0 & 0 & 0 & 0 & 0 & 1 \\ 0 & 0 & 0 & 0 & 0 & 0 \end{pmatrix}, \qquad \begin{pmatrix} 0 & 0 & 0 & 0 & 0 & 2 \\ 0 & 0 & 1 & 0 & 0 & 1 \\ 0 & 0 & 0 & 0 & 0 & 0 \\ 0 & 0 & 0 & 0 & 0 & 1 \\ 0 & 0 & 0 & 0 & 0 & 0 \\ 0 & 0 & 0 & 0 & 0 & 0 \end{pmatrix},$$

$$\begin{pmatrix} 0 & 0 & 0 & 0 & 0 & 0 \\ 0 & 0 & 0 & 0 & 0 & 1 \\ & & & & & \\ & & \text{rest 0's} & & & \\ & & & & & \\ & & & & & \end{pmatrix}.$$

England has now an equal number of two-stage dominances and is the favourite.

8. $$\mathbf{T} = \begin{pmatrix} 0 & 2 & 1 & 1 \\ 0 & 0 & 0 & 1 \\ 1 & 2 & 0 & 0 \\ 1 & 1 & 2 & 0 \end{pmatrix}, \qquad \mathbf{T^2} = \begin{pmatrix} 2 & 3 & 2 & 2 \\ 1 & 1 & 2 & 0 \\ 0 & 2 & 1 & 3 \\ 2 & 6 & 1 & 2 \end{pmatrix}.$$

David should be awarded the prize as he has more two-stage dominances than Alan.

Note that in this example a player can have two-stage dominance over himself. Alan and David have equal numbers of such dominances and so even if these are neglected the result is unaltered.

To be completely consistent the leading diagonal of **T** should contain only 1's as each player clearly should draw with himself. (The 0's imply that a player defeats himself.) However, this will not be found to affect the result of this question.

3. RELATIONS AND MATRICES

The possibility of representing a relation on a set by a matrix was mentioned on p. 134 of the *Teachers' Guide* to Book 2. For a brief introduction on relations see pp. 128–30 of that book. To the books listed on p. 130, for background reading, should be added the recent book

Modern Mathematics and the Teacher, by Lucienne Félix.

This, however, contains no work on the matrix representation of relations.

The work in this section is very similar to the idea of composition of functions used for solving simple equations in Book 2, Chapter 13.

For example, $x \to 3x+4$

was split up into $x \to 3x$ and $x \to x+4$.

Compare this to the composition of the two relations 'is the child of' and 'is the uncle or aunt of' to give the relation

'is the cousin of'.

The application of matrix notation to mappings and functions will be considered in Chapter 10. This is a suitable opportunity to introduce the transpose of a matrix, representing in this situation the inverse relation.

(*a*) The relation 'is a parent of' is not symmetric. In Figure 13, *b* is not the parent of *a* and consequently there is not a 1 opposite *b* in the first column.

$\mathbf{R}^2$ represents 'is a grandparent of'.

$\mathbf{R}^3$ represents 'is a great-grandparent of'.

Figure 13 shows only three generations of a family and thus $\mathbf{R}^3$ can only contain 0's.

(*b*) $\mathbf{R}'$ represents 'is a child of',

$$(\mathbf{R}')' = \mathbf{R}.$$

$\mathbf{R}' = \mathbf{R}$ if the matrix represents a symmetric relation, for example, 'is a cousin of'.

Exercise C (p. 96)

1. (a) All female.

(b) $\mathbf{D} = \begin{pmatrix} 0 & 0 & 0 & 0 & 0 \\ 0 & 0 & 0 & 0 & 0 \\ 0 & 1 & 0 & 0 & 0 \\ 0 & 1 & 0 & 0 & 0 \\ 1 & 0 & 0 & 0 & 0 \end{pmatrix}$, $\mathbf{S} = \begin{pmatrix} 0 & 1 & 0 & 0 & 0 \\ 1 & 0 & 0 & 0 & 0 \\ 0 & 0 & 0 & 1 & 0 \\ 0 & 0 & 1 & 0 & 0 \\ 0 & 0 & 0 & 0 & 0 \end{pmatrix}$.

(c) $\mathbf{D}'$ represents 'is the mother of';

$\mathbf{S}'$ represents 'is the sister of ';

'is the sister of' is a symmetric relation on this set but not in general.

(d) $\mathbf{DS} = \begin{pmatrix} 0 & 0 & 0 & 0 & 0 \\ 0 & 0 & 0 & 0 & 0 \\ 1 & 0 & 0 & 0 & 0 \\ 1 & 0 & 0 & 0 & 0 \\ 0 & 1 & 0 & 0 & 0 \end{pmatrix}$, 'is the niece of'.

(e) $\mathbf{SD}'$.

2. $\mathbf{R} = \begin{pmatrix} 0 & 1 & 0 \\ 0 & 0 & 1 \\ 1 & 0 & 0 \end{pmatrix}$, $\mathbf{R}^2 = \begin{pmatrix} 0 & 0 & 1 \\ 1 & 0 & 0 \\ 0 & 1 & 0 \end{pmatrix}$, 'is on the right of'.

Note that in this example $\mathbf{R}^2 = \mathbf{R}'$, and $\mathbf{R}^3$ is an identity matrix. $\mathbf{R}$ is a permutation matrix.

3. $\mathbf{Y} = \begin{pmatrix} 0 & 1 & 0 & 0 \\ 1 & 0 & 0 & 0 \\ 0 & 0 & 0 & 1 \\ 0 & 0 & 1 & 0 \end{pmatrix}$, $\mathbf{X} = \begin{pmatrix} 0 & 0 & 0 & 1 \\ 0 & 0 & 1 & 0 \\ 0 & 1 & 0 & 0 \\ 1 & 0 & 0 & 0 \end{pmatrix}$,

$\mathbf{XY} = \mathbf{YX} = \begin{pmatrix} 0 & 0 & 1 & 0 \\ 0 & 0 & 0 & 1 \\ 1 & 0 & 0 & 0 \\ 0 & 1 & 0 & 0 \end{pmatrix}$, 'is the reflection in (0, 0) of', or, 'is the image under a half-turn about (0, 0) of'.

Two reflections in perpendicular lines are equivalent to a half-turn. The order of the reflections does not matter (see Chapter 2).

4. $\mathbf{R} = \begin{pmatrix} 0 & 1 & 0 \\ 1 & 0 & 1 \\ 0 & 1 & 0 \end{pmatrix}, \quad \mathbf{R}^2 = \begin{pmatrix} 1 & 0 & 1 \\ 0 & 2 & 0 \\ 1 & 0 & 1 \end{pmatrix}.$

$\mathbf{R} = \mathbf{R}'$ because 'is perpendicular to' is symmetric.

$\mathbf{R}^2$ could be 'is parallel to' if this is taken to include 'is coincident with' and if the three lines are coplanar. The 2 in the centre of $\mathbf{R}^2$ appears because m is related symmetrically to both l and n.

5. 'Is the husband of' and 'is the sister of', or 'is the brother of' and 'is married to'.

6. $\mathbf{D} = \begin{array}{c} \\ 0 \\ 1 \\ 2 \\ 3 \end{array} \begin{array}{cccc} 0 & 1 & 2 & 3 \\ \begin{pmatrix} 1 & 0 & 1 & 0 \\ 0 & 0 & 0 & 0 \\ 0 & 1 & 0 & 1 \\ 0 & 0 & 0 & 0 \end{pmatrix} \end{array}, \quad \mathbf{T} = \begin{pmatrix} 1 & 0 & 0 & 0 \\ 0 & 0 & 0 & 1 \\ 0 & 0 & 1 & 0 \\ 0 & 1 & 0 & 0 \end{pmatrix}.$

See Figure E.

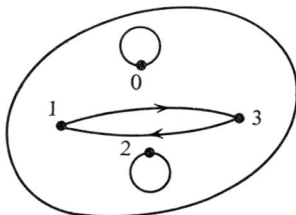

Fig. E. 'is three times'.

$$\mathbf{DT} = \mathbf{TD} = \mathbf{D}.$$

The composition of 'is twice' and 'is three times', in either order, would in ordinary arithmetic be 'is six times'. In finite arithmetic mod 4 it is therefore 'is twice'.

Notice how $\mathbf{T}$ behaves towards $\mathbf{D}$ in a similar manner to an identity matrix.

7. (a) $\mathbf{R}^2$, 'is four times'; $\mathbf{R}'$, 'is half of';
(b) $\mathbf{R}^2$, 'is a factor of'; $\mathbf{R}'$, 'is a multiple of';
(c) $\mathbf{R}^2$, 'is the fourth power of'; $\mathbf{R}'$, 'is a square root of'.

4. NETWORKS AND POLYHEDRA

Here we follow up another aspect of the study of Topology in Book 2 and link it with the construction of polyhedra in Book 1. The relevant references are:

Book 2, p. 12, Question 17; *Teachers' Guide* p. 12;
Book 1, p. 118; *Teachers' Guide*, p. 90.

$F-E+V$ can be called a topological invariant. It plays an important part in the classification of surfaces.

4.1 More precisely, a Schlegel diagram is a topological transformation of the framework of a cube, but not of its surface. In the latter case there has been cutting but no sticking together again. Good illustrations of Schlegel diagrams can be found in *Graphs and their Uses*, by Ore and in *Mathematics in the Making*, by Hogben. It is worth noting that the arcs of a Schlegel diagram need not be straight.

4.2 This is in essence a proof by induction. Proofs in texts on the theory of graphs restrict the network to one consisting of regions with no 'free' arcs, which would, for example, exclude Figure 23(*b*). Induction, however, remains the usual method of proof.

A single arc is referred to as the simplest of all networks. It would be more correct to call a single node the simplest network (see Exercise D, Question 1(*c*)). This would be a 0-node! However, we have found that the pupils do not appreciate this idea readily at first; for them, a network must contain arcs. The question of connectedness is mentioned here; it is unlikely to cause any difficulties at this stage. However, it is easily over-looked when dealing with more complicated surfaces.

Exercise D (p. 101)

1. (a) $R, 2$; $A, 2$; $N, 2$; $R-A+N, 2$.
(b) $R, 3$; $A, 4$; $N, 3$; $R-A+N, 2$.
(c) $R, 1$; $A, 0$; $N, 1$; $R-A+N, 2$.

2. Because A and N are each increased by 1.

3. See Figure F.

No. It requires the addition of arcs.

Figure G shows a possible succession.

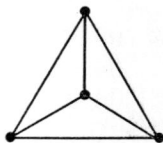
Fig. F

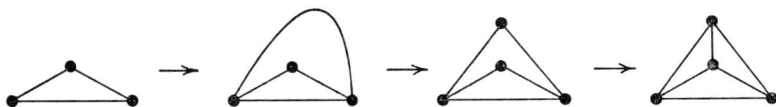

Fig. G

4. In the net several of the edges and vertices of the cube appear more than once.

Questions 5–9 form a group and should be worked together, leading to a class discussion of Question 9. They also form the first stage of a proof of the five-colour theorem. The four-colour theorem has not yet been proved though the result is not in doubt. A readable proof of the five-colour theorem is to be found in *Graphs and their Uses*, by Ore.

5. Figure F is a simple example of a 3-node network. A simpler one is that in Figure H. The Schlegel diagram for a cube is also a 3-node network.

(*a*) $A = 3(R-2)$;

(*b*) $N = 2(R-2)$.

Fig. H

6. The node-sum counts each arc twice, once at each end. Node-sum $= 2A$, for all networks.

7. aR is the total number of arcs bounding on all the regions. Every arc divides two regions and thus aR counts all the arcs twice.

Thus, node-sum $= 3N = 2A = aR$.

8. $a = 6-(12/R)$.

The proof is straightforward

$$R - A + N = 2.$$

Put
$$A = \tfrac{1}{2}aR \quad \text{and} \quad N = \tfrac{1}{3}aR,$$
$$R - \tfrac{1}{2}aR + \tfrac{1}{3}aR = 2,$$
$$\Leftrightarrow R - \tfrac{1}{6}aR = 2,$$
$$\Leftrightarrow R(6-a) = 12,$$
$$\Leftrightarrow a = 6-(12/R).$$

87

9. (a) If $a = 6 - (12/R)$ and $R > 0$, then $a < 6$.

To make the average number of arcs per region less than 6, one region, at least, must be surrounded by 5 or less arcs. In fact we can go further than this and show that in a network that has no regions surrounded by less than 5 arcs there must be at least 12 pentagonal regions.

Suppose the numbers of five-, six-, seven-, ... sided regions are R_5, R_6, R_7, ... Then

$$aR = 6R - 12$$

$$\Leftrightarrow (5R_5 + 6R_6 + 7R_7 + ...) = 6(R_5 + R_6 + R_7 + ...) - 12$$

$$\Leftrightarrow R_5 - R_7 - 2R_8 - ... = 12$$

$$\Rightarrow R_5 \geqslant 12.$$

It can further be shown that any plane network must contain at least one region surrounded by 5 or less arcs.

(b) $R \to \infty$, $a \to 6$.

This corresponds to an infinite tessellation of regular hexagons, which is a 3-node network. A network of hexagons on a sphere would contain a finite number and corresponds to a 3-node network containing a finite number of hexagons. This is shown to be impossible. It is, of course, possible to draw one hexagon but this is not a 3-node network. It is worth contrasting this with the fact that a network containing any number of hexagons can be drawn on a torus.

5. COLOURING POLYHEDRA

This is an essentially practical section and it can form the basis for a very good project. Though the exercise specifically asks for the construction of only one particular model, there is no reason why others should not be constructed in order to assist the investigation. Alternatively, polyhedra made previously can be used if they are still available.

(a) For a tetrahedron four colours are necessary. If it is not regular, then the same four colours can be permuted in 24 ways. On the other hand if it is regular, there are only two arrangements of the same four colours and these two are mirror images of each other. These are shown on Schlegel diagrams in Figure I.

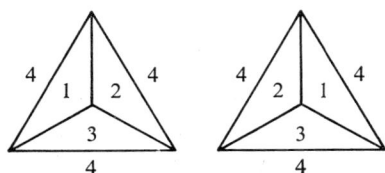

Fig. I

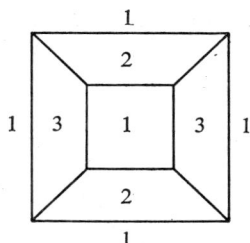

Fig. J

Exercise E (p. 103)

1. Three colours. Each pair of opposite faces have the same colour. Only one arrangement of three colours is possible (see Figure J).

2. See Figure K. Three colours.

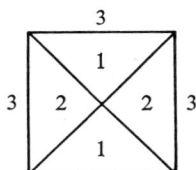

(a)

(b)

Fig. K

3. See Figure L. Either (a) or (b) will do.

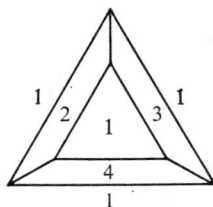

(a)

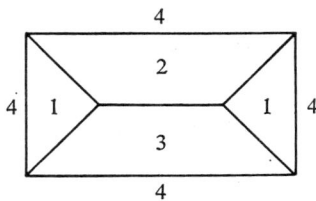

(b)

Fig. L

4. See Figure M.

5. See Figure N. There are only four ways of colouring a regular dodecahedron with the same four colours; there are two pairs of mirror images.

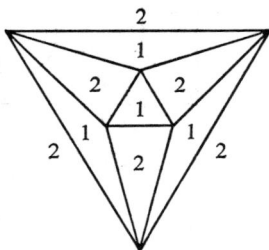

Fig. M

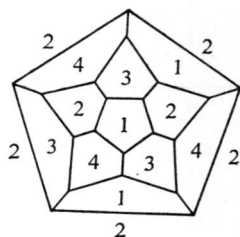

Fig. N

6. See *Mathematical Recreations and Essays,* by Rouse Ball. There are 144 ways of colouring a regular icosahedron with three colours. There are 69 pairs of mirror images and 6 which are unaltered by reflection.

7. This is similar to the four-colour problem. All arrangements in which three regions border on each other without any one of them being completely surrounded is topologically equivalent to Figure O. Notice that in this case we are not counting the infinite region on the outside. The addition of a fourth region bordering on each of these three is bound to surround one of them, thus preventing the addition of a fifth region bordering on all four others.

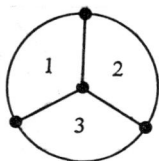

Fig. O

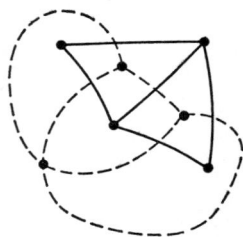

Fig. P

8. This is the 'dual' of the four-colour problem. A dual network is formed (see Figure P) by putting a node in each region and joining these nodes by arcs crossing the arcs of the original

network. The dual network is shown dotted and clearly the problem of colouring regions becomes one of colouring nodes. Duality will be considered in more detail in Book 4.

6. INCIDENCE MATRICES

These matrices are composed differently from route matrices but the connection with the latter is established in the section. It is possible to have incidence matrices for directed networks and this is usually necessary in electrical circuit theory.

For example, for the arc 1 in Figure Q, the entries in the incidence matrix connecting nodes and arcs would be as follows:

$$\text{Nodes}\begin{cases} \\ \\ A \\ B \\ C \\ . \\ . \\ . \end{cases}\overset{\displaystyle\overbrace{}^{\text{Arcs}}}{\begin{pmatrix} 1 & 2 & . & . & . \\ 1 & . & . & . & . \\ -1 & . & . & . & . \\ . & . & . & . & . \\ . & . & . & . & . \\ . & . & . & . & . \\ . & . & . & . & . \end{pmatrix}}.$$

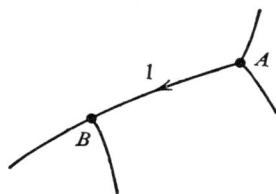

Fig. Q

The 1 indicates that arc 1 starts at A and the -1 indicates that arc 1 terminates at B. For a first look at incidence matrices it was found that this convention was unnecessarily confusing and so a simpler convention applying only to undirected networks is employed.

(a) **S** is

$$\text{Arcs}\begin{cases} 1 \\ 2 \\ 3 \\ 4 \\ 5 \end{cases}\overset{\displaystyle\overbrace{l\ \ m\ \ n}^{\text{Regions}}}{\begin{pmatrix} 1 & 1 & 0 \\ 1 & 0 & 1 \\ 1 & 0 & 1 \\ 1 & 1 & 0 \\ 0 & 1 & 1 \end{pmatrix}},$$

T is

$$\text{nodes}\begin{cases} A \\ B \\ C \\ D \end{cases}\overset{\displaystyle\overbrace{l\ \ m\ \ n}^{\text{Regions}}}{\begin{pmatrix} 1 & 1 & 0 \\ 1 & 1 & 1 \\ 1 & 0 & 1 \\ 1 & 1 & 1 \end{pmatrix}};$$

(b)

$$\mathbf{RS} = \begin{pmatrix} 2 & 2 & 0 \\ 2 & 2 & 2 \\ 2 & 0 & 2 \\ 2 & 2 & 2 \end{pmatrix} = 2\mathbf{T}.$$

7-2

R is 'nodes × arcs' and **S** 'arcs × regions'. Combining **R** with **S** has the effect of cancelling the arcs and yields a matrix of the form 'nodes × regions'.

The incidence of node A on region l is arrived at in two ways in the product **RS**. When the first row of **R** is combined with the first column of **S**, we have:

A is incident on 1 which is incident on l	$(1 \times 1) = 1$
A is not incident on 2 which is incident on l	$(0 \times 1) = 0$
A is not incident on 3 which is incident on l	$(0 \times 1) = 0$
A is incident on 4 which is incident on l	$(1 \times 1) = 1$
A is not incident on 5 which is not incident on l	$(0 \times 0) = 0$
	$\overline{2}$

and so on for the remaining arcs and regions.

(c) and (d) The transpose of a matrix is again used here to give a combination (nodes × arcs) with (arcs × nodes).

This gives a (nodes × nodes) matrix

$$\mathbf{RR'} = \begin{array}{c} \\ A \\ B \\ C \\ D \end{array}\begin{array}{cccc} A & B & C & D \\ \end{array}\begin{pmatrix} 2 & 1 & 0 & 1 \\ 1 & 3 & 1 & 1 \\ 0 & 1 & 2 & 1 \\ 1 & 1 & 1 & 3 \end{pmatrix}, \quad \mathbf{M} = \begin{array}{c} \\ A \\ B \\ C \\ D \end{array}\begin{array}{cccc} A & B & C & D \\ \end{array}\begin{pmatrix} 0 & 1 & 0 & 1 \\ 1 & 0 & 1 & 1 \\ 0 & 1 & 0 & 1 \\ 1 & 1 & 1 & 0 \end{pmatrix}.$$

The numbers on the leading diagonal of **RR'** are the order of the nodes A, B, C and D. A and C are 2-nodes, B and D are 3-nodes.

This arises because the combination of, for example, the second row of **R** with the second column of **R'** gives

$$B \text{ is on 1 which is on } B,$$
$$B \text{ is on 2 which is on } B,$$
and $$B \text{ is on 5 which is on } B.$$

The order of the node B is therefore arrived at. For the remainder of the matrix the routes are counted, A is on 1 which is on B, giving the route $A \to B$ and so on.

Thus apart from the leading diagonal, **RR'** is the same as **M**.

Exercise F (p. 107)

1. See Figure R.

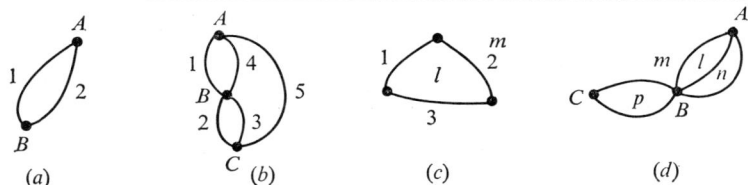

Fig. R

In (b) and (d) there are other possibilities but they will be topologically equivalent to those shown.

2. $\mathbf{R} = \begin{pmatrix} 1 & 1 & 1 & 1 & 0 \\ 1 & 1 & 1 & 0 & 1 \\ 0 & 0 & 0 & 1 & 1 \end{pmatrix}$, $\quad \mathbf{S} = \begin{pmatrix} 1 & 0 & 0 & 1 \\ 1 & 1 & 0 & 0 \\ 0 & 1 & 1 & 0 \\ 0 & 0 & 1 & 1 \\ 0 & 0 & 1 & 1 \end{pmatrix}$,

$\mathbf{T} = \begin{pmatrix} 1 & 1 & 1 & 1 \\ 1 & 1 & 1 & 1 \\ 0 & 0 & 1 & 1 \end{pmatrix}$.

3. (a) $\mathbf{R'R} = \begin{pmatrix} 2 & 1 & 0 & 1 & 1 \\ 1 & 2 & 1 & 0 & 1 \\ 0 & 1 & 2 & 1 & 1 \\ 1 & 0 & 1 & 2 & 1 \\ 1 & 1 & 1 & 1 & 2 \end{pmatrix}$. No.

(b)
$$\begin{array}{c c} & \begin{array}{c c c c c} 1 & 2 & 3 & 4 & 5 \end{array} \\ \begin{array}{c} 1 \\ 2 \\ 3 \\ 4 \\ 5 \end{array} & \begin{pmatrix} 0 & 1 & 0 & 1 & 1 \\ 1 & 0 & 1 & 0 & 1 \\ 0 & 1 & 0 & 1 & 1 \\ 1 & 0 & 1 & 0 & 1 \\ 1 & 1 & 1 & 1 & 0 \end{pmatrix} \end{array}.$$

This matrix differs from $\mathbf{R'R}$ only in the leading diagonal, where the zeros indicate that no node 'links' one arc with itself. Compare with route matrices.

4. $\mathbf{R'R} = \begin{pmatrix} 2 & 2 & 1 & 1 \\ 2 & 2 & 1 & 1 \\ 1 & 1 & 2 & 1 \\ 1 & 1 & 1 & 2 \end{pmatrix}$;
$\quad \begin{array}{c c} & \begin{array}{c c c c} 1 & 2 & 3 & 4 \end{array} \\ \begin{array}{c} 1 \\ 2 \\ 3 \\ 4 \end{array} & \begin{pmatrix} 0 & 2 & 1 & 1 \\ 2 & 0 & 1 & 1 \\ 1 & 1 & 0 & 1 \\ 1 & 1 & 1 & 0 \end{pmatrix} \end{array}.$

The 2's on the leading diagonal of any $\mathbf{R'R}$ matrix indicate that each arc is between two nodes. The other 2's, in the (arcs × arcs) matrix occur because arcs 1 and 2 are incident on each other at both nodes A and B.

93

5. (a) $\mathbf{TT'} = \begin{pmatrix} 2 & 2 & 1 & 2 \\ 2 & 3 & 2 & 3 \\ 1 & 2 & 2 & 2 \\ 2 & 3 & 2 & 3 \end{pmatrix}$; (b) $\begin{array}{c} \\ A \\ B \\ C \\ D \end{array} \begin{array}{cccc} A & B & C & D \\ \end{array} \begin{pmatrix} 0 & 2 & 1 & 2 \\ 2 & 0 & 2 & 3 \\ 1 & 2 & 0 & 2 \\ 2 & 3 & 2 & 0 \end{pmatrix}$.

(i) The matrix in (b) differs from $\mathbf{TT'}$ only in the leading diagonal.

(ii) Nothing.

Notice that the matrix in (b) relates the nodes to each other with respect to the regions. A route matrix relates the nodes to each other with respect to the arcs.

6. $\mathbf{S'S} = \begin{pmatrix} 4 & 2 & 2 \\ 2 & 3 & 1 \\ 2 & 1 & 3 \end{pmatrix}, \quad \mathbf{T'T} = \begin{pmatrix} 4 & 3 & 3 \\ 3 & 3 & 2 \\ 3 & 2 & 3 \end{pmatrix}$.

Both these matrices relate regions to regions, $\mathbf{S'S}$ with respect to arcs which surround them and $\mathbf{T'T}$ with respect to the nodes on their boundaries.

The 2 in the first row and second column of $\mathbf{S'S}$ indicates that regions l and m have *two* arcs in common; the 3 in the first row and second column of $\mathbf{T'T}$ indicates that regions l and m have *three* nodes in common (A, B, D) on their boundaries. The leading diagonal of $\mathbf{S'S}$ gives the number of arcs surrounding each region and the leading diagonal of $\mathbf{T'T}$ the number of nodes on the boundary of each region. These numbers are obviously equal.

7. (a) $\mathbf{R} = \begin{array}{c} \\ A \\ B \\ C \\ D \end{array} \begin{array}{ccc} 1 & 2 & 3 \\ \end{array} \begin{pmatrix} 1 & 0 & 0 \\ 1 & 1 & 1 \\ 0 & 1 & 0 \\ 0 & 0 & 1 \end{pmatrix}, \quad \mathbf{RR'} = \begin{pmatrix} 1 & 1 & 0 & 0 \\ 1 & 3 & 1 & 1 \\ 0 & 1 & 1 & 0 \\ 0 & 1 & 0 & 1 \end{pmatrix},$

$\mathbf{M} = \begin{pmatrix} 0 & 1 & 0 & 0 \\ 1 & 0 & 1 & 1 \\ 0 & 1 & 0 & 0 \\ 0 & 1 & 0 & 0 \end{pmatrix};$

(b) $\mathbf{S} = \begin{pmatrix} 1 \\ 1 \\ 1 \end{pmatrix}, \quad \mathbf{T} = \begin{pmatrix} 1 \\ 1 \\ 1 \\ 1 \end{pmatrix}, \quad \mathbf{RS} = \begin{pmatrix} 1 \\ 3 \\ 1 \\ 1 \end{pmatrix},$ **RS** is not equal to **2T**.

However, arc 1 could be said to bound region *l* twice and similarly for arcs 2 and 3 (see Figure S).

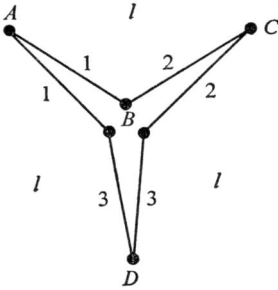

Fig. S   Fig. T

Also *B* could be said to be incident on region *l*, 3 times. Therefore we could have

$$\mathbf{S} = \begin{pmatrix} 2 \\ 2 \\ 2 \end{pmatrix}, \quad \mathbf{T} = \begin{pmatrix} 1 \\ 3 \\ 1 \\ 1 \end{pmatrix},$$

and

$$\mathbf{RS} = \begin{pmatrix} 2 \\ 6 \\ 2 \\ 2 \end{pmatrix}.$$

In this case **RS** is equal to **2T**.

Similar difficulties arise in the case of loops at nodes, as in Figure T.

Exercise G (p. 108)

Miscellaneous

1. 2.

2. This was originally proposed in the form of a round tour of the world through 20 cities at the vertices of a dodecahedron. Paths on the cube, octahedron and dodecahedron are easily found.

Simple networks on which Hamiltonian paths are not possible are shown in Figure U though the first contains a 1-node. If the requirement that the path must start and finish at the same point is dropped, then the problem is easier. Hamiltonian paths have an important application in operational research.

Fig. U

3. See *Mathematical Recreations and Essays*, by Rouse Ball, p. 126 (11th edition).

Number of				Result of cut	
Twists	Edges	Sides	Cut	Loops	Other observations
1	1	1	$\frac{1}{2}$	1	Loop twice as long, 4 twists, 2 edges.
1	1	1	$\frac{1}{3}$	2 linked	Short loop, 1 twist, similar to original; long loop, 4 twists, 2 edges.
2	2	2	$\frac{1}{2}$	2 linked	2 loops, similar to original but half as wide.
2	2	2	$\frac{1}{3}$	2 linked	2 loops similar to original, one twice as wide as the other.
3	1	1	$\frac{1}{2}$	1	8 twists, knotted, 2 edges.
3	1	1	$\frac{1}{3}$	2 linked	Short loop, 3 twists, similar to original; long loop, 8 twists knotted, 2 edges.

4. Shortest route: 15, 5, 9, 10, 7

46 kilometres.

Salesman's route: 15, 5, 9, 11, 8, 7, 10, 9, 5, 15;

or: 15, 5, 9, 10, 7, 8, 11, 9, 5, 15;

94 kilometres.

Further applications of this sort of network will be considered in connection with duality in Book 4.

5. It is a 3-node network as each utility supplies three houses and each house receives three utilities.

$$N = 6, \quad A = 9 \quad \text{and} \quad R - A + N = 2 \Rightarrow R = 5.$$

$$a = 6 - \frac{12}{R} \quad \text{and} \quad R = 5 \Rightarrow a = 3\cdot6.$$

All regions have four arcs on the boundary as no utilities are joined to each other and no houses are joined to each other directly. This implies $a = 4$. Thus the assumption that the network could be drawn is false. The problem has no solution.

7

3-DIMENSIONAL GEOMETRY

No apology is needed on behalf of three-dimensional geometry and there is little novelty in its treatment in this chapter. Perhaps there is greater emphasis than usual on really getting to understand the fundamental ideas, but no teacher will find the basic material unfamiliar.

This is not, of course, the first encounter with solids. We have met them before in Book 1 (Chapter 8, 'Polygons and Polyhedra') and again in Book 2 (Chapter 10, 'Solids'). Some thinking back to these two chapters will be called for.

Teaching aids

Supplies of card, rods, string, drinking-straws and pipe-cleaners will be useful for discussion purposes. It is essential for framework models of the cube and pyramid to be available to every pupil (see Book 2, Chapter 10, for details of construction), and it is desirable for a general collection of other models to be at hand.

1. POINTS, LINES AND PLANES

There are difficulties in making rigorous definitions here. Some teachers may like to talk about such concepts as 'straightness'; but we prefer, frankly, to dodge such discussions at this stage. This is not the place in which we wish to be drawn into an airing of Euclid's defects. For our purposes intuitive ideas are good enough.

Discussion (p. 111)

1. No; a pencil-drawn dot has countless different positions within its area. A true 'point' would be completely invisible, i.e. it would have no area.

2. Similarly, a line (having no breadth) is really invisible. (See W. W Sawyer's *Mathematician's Delight* p. 36.)

98

3. Since only one measurement is necessary to specify the position of a point on a circle relative to some fixed origin, the statement is true. It is a one-dimensional figure in two-dimensional space.

4. True. The converse is false, of course, and it might be interesting to mention the hyperbolic paraboloid here. (See Cundy & Rollett's *Mathematical Models*.)

5. Two coordinates necessary (latitude and longitude): so it is two-dimensional. It is a two-dimensional figure in three-dimensional space.

6. (a) ∞;   (b) 1;   (c) 0 or 1;   (d) ∞;   (e) ∞;
(f) 1, unless A, B, C are collinear, in which case ∞;
(g) 0 in general. Could be 1, or ∞ if A, B, C, D are collinear.
(h) ∞;   (i) 1;   (j) 1;   (k) 0.

7. It contains either the whole line or just a single point of it.

8. (a) No; in a plane two non-parallel lines do intersect.
(b) Yes; it *is* possible for two non-parallel lines in space not to intersect.

9. (a) Two non-intersecting planes must be parallel.
(b) Two intersecting planes meet in a line.

10. (a) Yes.
(b) Either a point or the line l itself.

Exercise A (p. 113)

(Point out that strictly speaking AB, for example, is a line *segment*, and that $ABCD$ is just part of a plane.)

1. *B.*

2. A triangular pyramid (a non-regular tetrahedron). Triangle EGB is equilateral.

3. A square.

4. (a), (b), (d), (g), (h), (j) determine planes; (c), (e), (f), (i) are skew.

5. (a), (b), (e), (g), (j) determine planes.

2. ANGLES

Angle between a line and a plane

Appeal to intuition is probably sufficient to put over the idea of a projection. A formal definition would inevitably be somewhat frightening.

Exercise B (p. 116)

1. (*a*) 45°; (*b*) 45°; (*c*) 45°; (*d*) 0° (parallel); (*e*) 90°.

2. 8.

3. *AB, BC, CD, DA, EF, FG, GH, HE.*

4. (*a*) *BD*; (*b*) *FC*; (*c*) *HC*; (*d*) *EG*; (*e*) *A*.

5. (*a*) ∠*FDE*; (*b*) ∠*BHA*; (*c*) ∠*FCB*; (*d*) 90°; (*e*) 0°.

6. (*a*) *EX*; (*b*) *AX*, where *X* is intersection of *FH, EG*.

7. (*a*) (i) *RO*, (ii) *OV*; (*b*) *OV*; (*c*) 90°; (*d*) ∠*VPO*.

8. (*a*) *BC*; (*b*) *BC*; (*c*) *BD*; (*d*) *MN*; (*e*) *EH*.

9. (*a*) 90°; (*b*) 45°; (*c*) 90°; (*d*) 90°; (*e*) 90°.

10. (*a*) Yes; (*b*) yes; (*c*) no; (*d*) yes; (*e*) no.

11. (*a*) ∠*CBG* or ∠*DAH*; (*b*) ∠*CGB* or ∠*DHA*;
(*c*) ∠*ADB* or ∠*EHF*; (*d*) ∠*AFE* or ∠*DGH*;
(*e*) ∠*AFB* or ∠*DGC*.

12. (*a*) ∠*CBG*; (*b*) ∠*BDF*; (*c*) ∠*BGF*;
(*d*) ∠*AGD*; (*e*) ∠*EBH*.

13. No; no; *NM*; *FB*.

14. It is the distance between the point and its projection on the plane.

15. (*a*) 4 cm; (*b*) 4 cm; (*c*) 4 cm; (*d*) 2 cm; (*e*) $2\sqrt{2}$ cm.

Exercise C (p. 118)

1. (*a*) See Figure A.

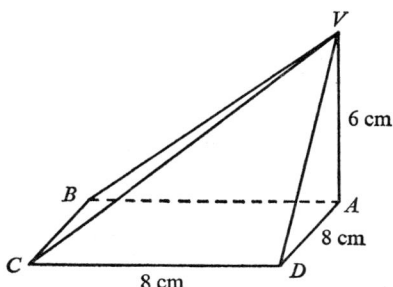

Fig. A

(*b*) (i) $BV = 10$ cm;
(ii) $CV^2 = 8^2 + 8^2 + 6^2 \Rightarrow CV = 12\cdot8$ cm;
(iii) $DV = 10$ cm.
(*d*) (i) $\angle ABV = 36\cdot9°$;
(ii) $\angle ACV = 27\cdot9°$;
(iii) $\angle BVC = 38\cdot7°$.

2. (*a*) (i) 5 cm, (ii) 5 cm, (iii) $\sqrt{(5^2+4^2)}$ cm $= \sqrt{(41)}$ cm $= 6\cdot4$ cm;
(*b*) (i) $53\cdot1°$, (ii) $38\cdot7°$, (iii) $90°$, (iv) $53\cdot1°$, (iv) $90°$;
(*c*) $143\cdot1°$.

3. Dodecahedron.

4. (*a*) All edges of tetrahedron are diagonals of equal faces of cube;
(*b*) 6 cm;
(*c*) *AE*, *BF*, *CG*, *DH* are all perpendicular to both *p* and *r*;
(*d*) 45°.

5. (*a*) Lines are skew.
(*b*) Lines intersect or are parallel.
(*c*) Lines coincide with one another.

6. Either *p* lies completely in the plane or it is perpendicular to the plane.

7. (*a*) Parallel; (*b*) perpendicular; (*c*) parallel;
(*d*) parallel or skew; (*e*) infinite.

101

8

LINEAR PROGRAMMING

The purpose of this chapter is twofold:

(1) to develop and provide practice in a number of basic algebraic skills, and

(2) to give an inkling of a type of problem with which an increasing number of mathematicians in industry and government service are concerned.

It is the experience of many teachers that linear programming provides motivation for most of the linear algebra that has been traditionally covered for 'O' level. At the same time the importance of orderings is clearly seen since in practical problems orderings occur as frequently as equations. Solution sets, also, now come into their own, for in the questions discussed there are usually many possible solutions. The questions are necessarily contrived so as to restrict the orderings to two variables. This enables the solutions to be represented graphically. However, pupils can usually see without any difficulty how a more complex problem could be represented by a set of linear orderings in several variables, although no method of solution is as yet available to them.

Perhaps the most valuable part of this chapter is in the first stage of every question where the given situation has to be translated into a set of algebraic relations. Once this stage has been reached the technique of plotting lines and shading areas is straightforward. The solution sets have been kept finite by restricting the problems to those in which the variables must be integers (for example, numbers of aeroplanes). This enables us to consider members of the solution sets one-by-one when it is desired to maximize a profit or a factory output and there is no need to resort to any complicated techniques.

There will be a further chapter on linear programming in this series of texts but to anyone wishing to extend his knowledge of the subject we would recommend *An Introduction to Linear Programming and the Theory of Games*, by S. Vajda.

1. GRAPHING SOLUTION SETS

This section draws on previous experience and tackles the problem of representing solution sets of ordered pairs as points on a graph. The number of members in each solution set is small so that they can be found by 'trial and error' and such techniques as shading regions to represent orderings are left until later sections.

Games are generally good for supplying motivation and they provide some useful examples. This is not surprising, since the development of linear programming was closely associated with the theory of games.

In teaching this chapter much use can be made of pin-boards or peg-boards. Members of a solution set can be readily shown on these and mistakes can easily be rectified. Small wooden coloured beads can be purchased at most D.I.Y. shops at a reasonable price and these can be placed on the pins as an alternative to rubber bands —the latter, however, are still necessary for marking in boundaries. The teacher will find a large peg-board treated with blackboard paint and fixed to the wall invaluable. Colours also help to clarify graphical work and their use should be encouraged.

Because so much of the work is graphical, a large supply of graph paper is essential and it will be found that $\frac{1}{2}$ cm paper is easier to use than $\frac{1}{5}$ cm paper, for the scale is then simply 1 unit to the side of a square.

(*a*) (6, 2), (6, 3), (6, 4), (6, 5), (6, 6), (5, 3), (5, 4), (5, 5), (5, 6), (4, 4), (4, 5), (4, 6), (3, 5), (3, 6), (2, 6).

(*b*) See Figure A.

(*c*) $r \leqslant 6$ and $b \leqslant 6$.

(*d*) $8 \leqslant r+b$ or $7 < r+b$.

(*e*) (6, 1), (6, 2), (5, 1), (5, 2), (5, 3), (4, 2), (4, 3), (4, 4), (3, 3), (3, 4), (3, 5), (2, 4), (2, 5), (2, 6), (1, 5), (1, 6).

(*f*) See Figure B.

(*g*) (3, 3), (4, 4).

The ordered pairs represent the possible throws for a pair of dice so that both dice show the same number and the total thrown lies between five and nine.

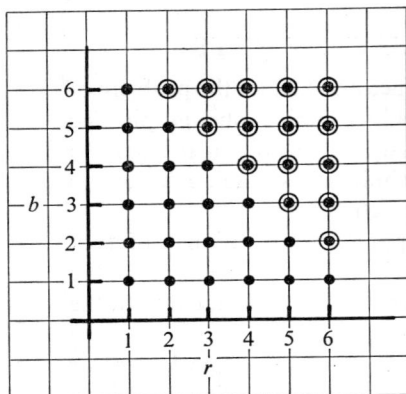

Fig. A

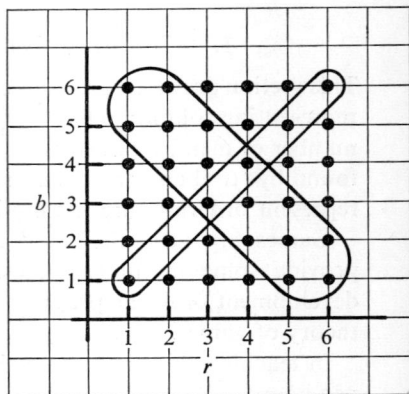

Fig. B

Exercise A (p. 123)

1. (a) and (b). See Figure C.

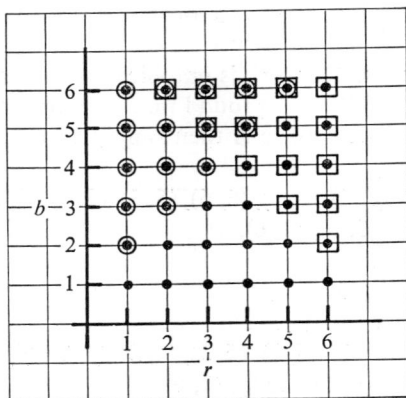

Fig. C

(c) *P* represents the possible ways in which a red die and a blue die can be thrown so that the number showing on the red die is less than that on the blue.

Q represents the possible ways in which two dice can be thrown so that the total showing is greater than 7.

$P \cap Q$ represents the possible ways in which a red die and a blue die can be thrown so that the number showing on the red die is less than that on the blue *and* so that the total thrown is greater than 7.

(d) $n(P \cap Q) = 6$.

2. This game could well be played by members of the form and analysed in some detail in the way indicated.

(a), (b) and (c). See Figure D.   (c) $\frac{2}{5}$.

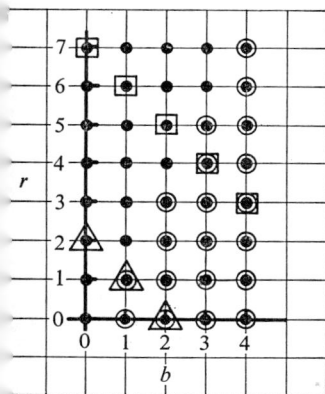

Fig. D

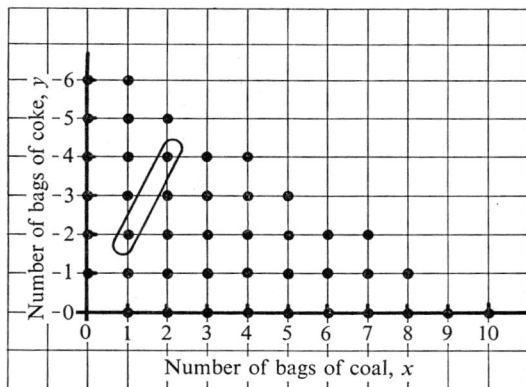

Fig. E

3. (a) (5, 6), (6, 5), (7, 4), (8, 3);

(b) (i) 6, (ii) 3;   (c) $3 \leqslant w \leqslant 6$.

4. (a) 10 bags of coal;

(b) 0, 1, 2, 3 or 4 bags of coal;

(c) See Figure E. One hopes that pupils will notice that in all these examples the region in which the dots occur is always bounded by straight lines.

(d) $2x + 3y \leqslant 20$.

(e) (i) See Figure E.

(ii) This question assumes whole bags and the solution is given by 2 coal and 4 coke for a mass of 300 kg.

5. (*a*) and (*c*) (see figure F).

(*b*) $r+b = 6$.

(*d*) Either 2 books and 4 records or 3 books and 3 records.

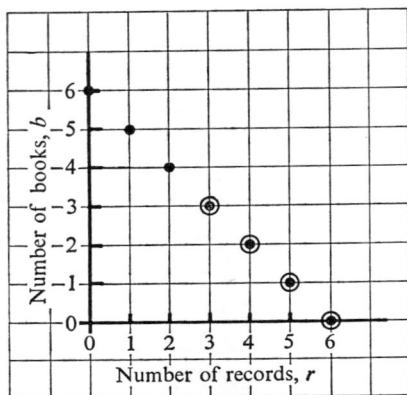

Fig. F

6. $c \geqslant 0$ and $b \geqslant 0$ because it is meaningless to carry a negative number of cars or buses. If b buses are carried, this is equivalent to three times as many cars, hence $3b$ cars. If c cars and b buses are carried, this is equivalent to carrying $c+3b$ cars which must not exceed 12.

(*a*), (*b*) (see Figure G).

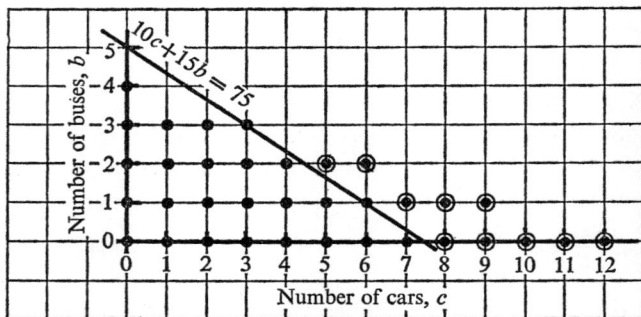

Fig. G

106

(*b*) Any point on the line $10c + 15b = 75$ represents a load where the ferry breaks even.

(*c*) (i) 12, (ii) 7;   (*d*) (i) 30p, (ii) 15p.

2. GRAPHING EQUATIONS AND ORDERINGS

The link is now made between plotting members of a solution set and the graphical representation of linear orderings which was first met in Book 1. Some practice may be needed to give confidence in plotting lines accurately and quickly and this may be tackled first, although seeing that such work has a useful application makes it more interesting.

When discussing the graphical representation of an ordering such as

$$2x + 3y \leqslant 12,$$

it is helpful to distinguish the three parts of the plane given by

$$2x + 3y < 12, \quad 2x + 3y = 12 \quad \text{and} \quad 2x + 3y > 12,$$

and to note that two of these parts are required (see Figure H).

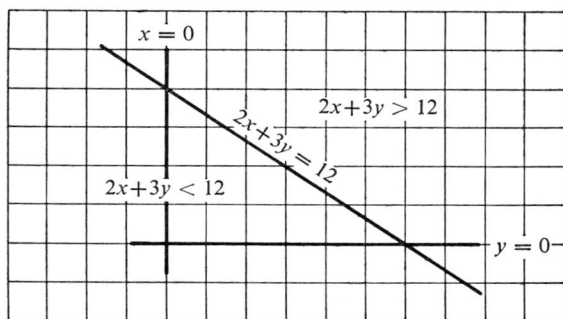

Fig. H

In linear programming problems it is the convention to shade out the region not required. The additional convention which distinguishes between the graphical representation of such orderings as $2x + 3y > 12$ and $2x + 3y \geqslant 12$ is also a useful one.

107

1. See Figure I.

Exercise B (p. 129)

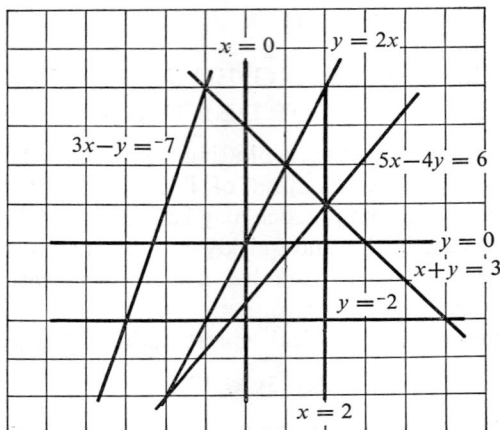

Fig. I

2. See Figure J.

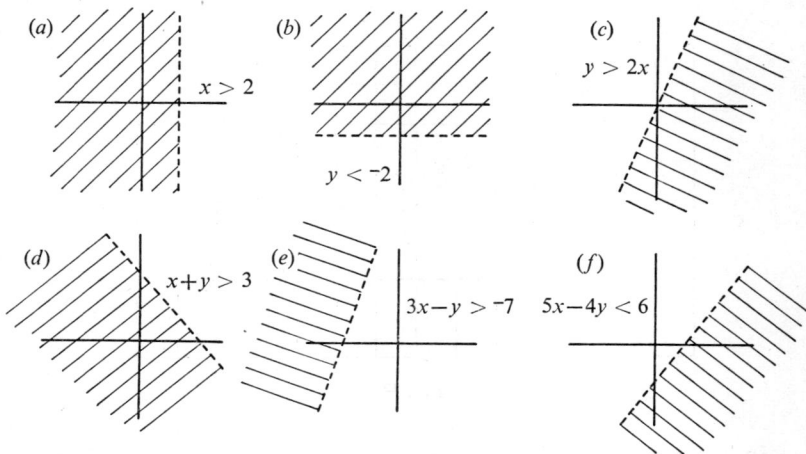

Fig. J

3. (a) (1, 2);   (b) (2, 1);   (c) (⁻1, 4);
    (d) (⁻2, ⁻4);   (e) (⁻3, ⁻2).

4. See Figure K.

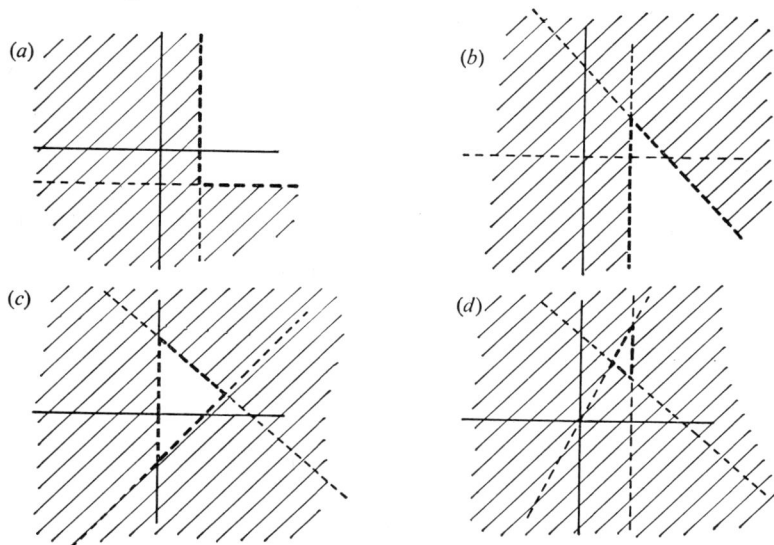

(a)

(b)

(c)

(d)

Fig. K

5. $y \geqslant {}^-2$, $3x - y \geqslant {}^-7$, $x + y \leqslant 3$.

6. See Figure L.

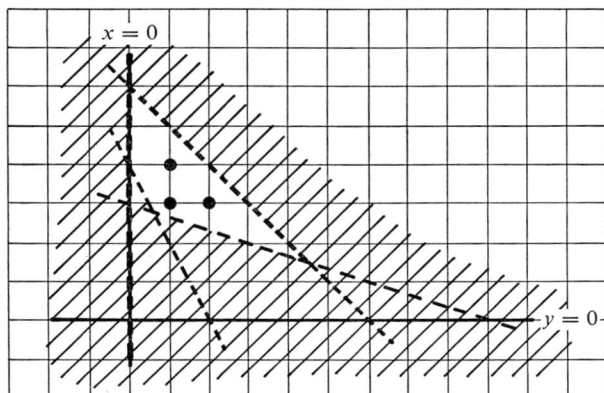

Fig. L

109

7. (*a*) *b* bangers cost $2b$ pence, *r* rockets cost $3r$ pence. Total cost has to be at most 20 new pence.

(*b*), (*c*) and (*d*) (see Figure M).

(*e*) (i) 5, (ii) 8 as (5, 3) or (4, 4). By buying as many bangers as possible, which also gives the maximum number of fireworks, John does not spend all his money. The solutions that use up all the available money are (1, 6) and (4, 4).

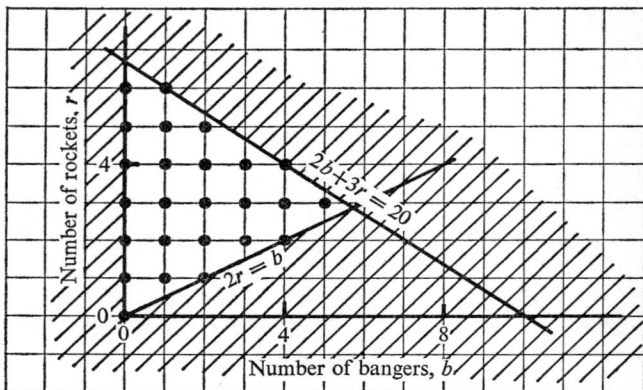

Fig. M

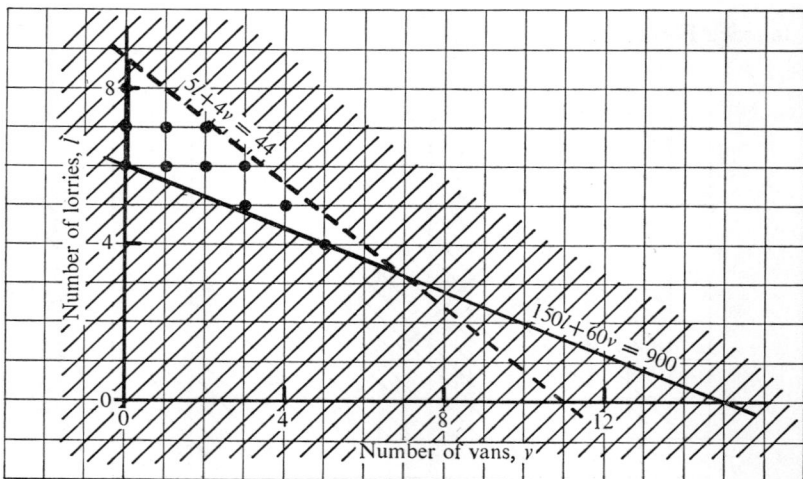

Fig. N

8. (*a*) $150l + 60v \geqslant 900$;   (*b*) $5l + 4v < 44$;   (*c*) See Figure N.
     (*d*) (i) 9,
         (ii) 6 lorries at a cost of £30,
         (iii) 7 lorries and 2 vans at a cost of £43.

3. LINEAR PROGRAMMING

In this section we apply the techniques developed in the previous section to a variety of situations. One characteristic of the problems is that they look long. An attempt has been made to break them down into small stages so that the pupil can build up his solution gradually, but the time will come when he has to start from scratch and sort out the situation on his own. The last question in the exercise cannot be solved graphically but it has been introduced to show how the linear programming technique can be extended. The authors have used this problem on several occasions to introduce linear programming to a class by first discussing it, looking at possible solutions by trial and error, and then challenging the class to arrange the output so as to maximize the profit (5p for the best production manager is always a good incentive!).

Exercise C (p. 132)

1. (*a*) (i) $x + 2y \leqslant 28$,   (ii) $3x + y \leqslant 24$.
     (*b*) See Figure O.
     (*c*) (i) 8,   (ii) 14.
     (*d*) 4 bats and 12 rackets.

Points on the line $x + 2y = 28$ represent solutions which require all the machine time. Similarly points on the line $3x + y = 24$ represent solutions which require all the craftsman's time. The only point satisfying both these conditions is where the lines intersect.

     (*e*) (i) £8,   (ii) £7,   (iii) £10.

It is worth noting that if the factory produces only bats, then only 8 machine hours out of a possible 28 are utilized and the factory could be made more efficient by reducing the number of machines or by greatly increasing the number of craftsmen, in which case the output would increase. This last suggestion is, however, governed by the availability of the men with the right skills, by the size of the factory, and by whether or not it would be possible to sell a larger output.

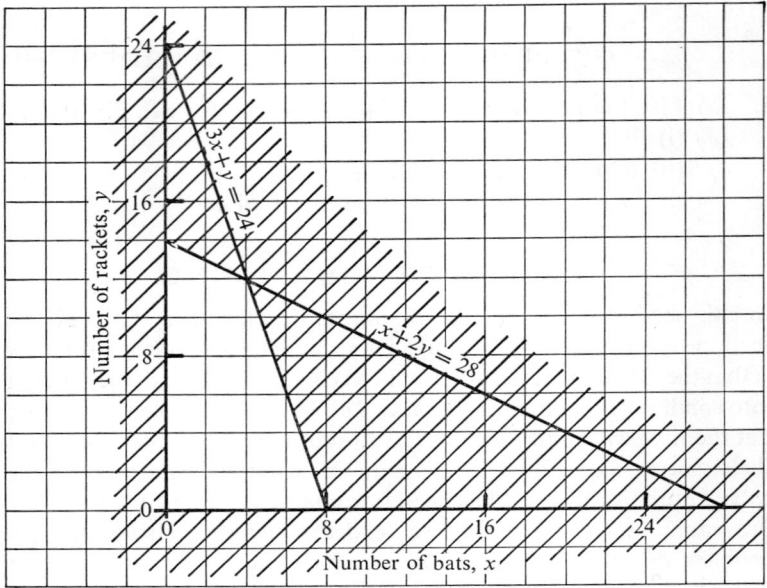

Fig. O

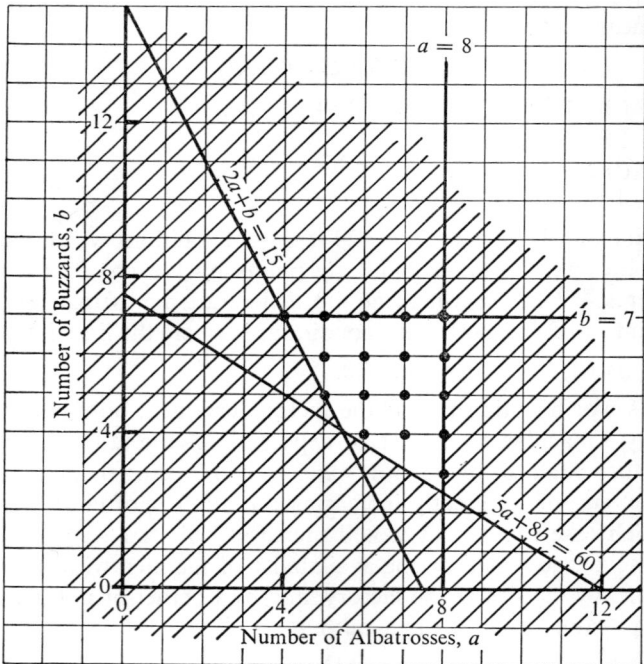

Fig. P

2. (*a*) $5a+8b \geqslant 60$ comes from $50a+80b \geqslant 600$, the limitation on passengers. $2a+b \geqslant 15$ comes from $6a+3b \geqslant 45$ the limitation on baggage.

(*b*) See Figure P.

(*c*) 10 planes as (5, 5) or as (6, 4).

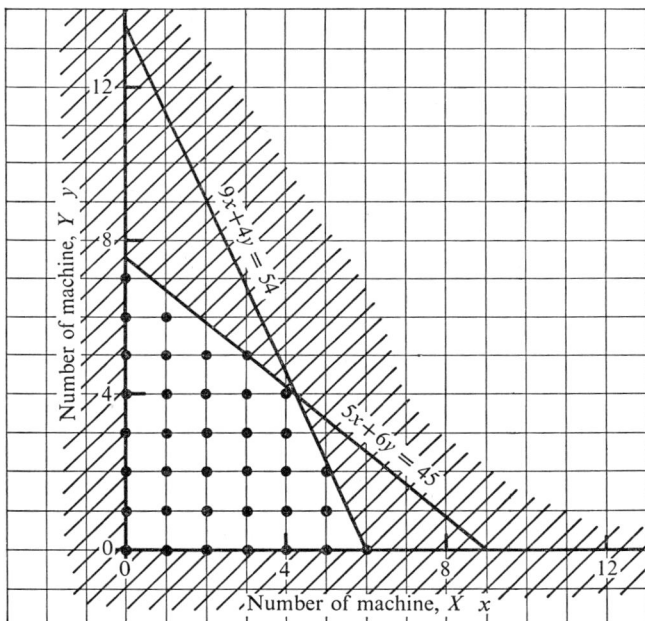

Fig. Q

3. (*a*) (i) $5000x+6000y \leqslant 45,000$ which simplifies to $5x+6y \leqslant 45$.

(ii) $9x+4y \leqslant 54$.

(*b*) See Figure Q.

(*c*) (i) It is expected that this should be done by computing the output for different solutions. 4 of *X* and 4 of *Y*, giving an output potential of 2000 units.

(ii) The only solution on the line $9x+4y = 54$ is (6, 0) which implies 6 of *X*.

113

(*d*) By providing work for all his employees his output is 1800 units which is 200 below the best. The solution that maximizes output only employs 52 men.

4. (*a*) $5l+3p \leqslant 60$, $3l+p \leqslant 30$.

(*b*) See Figure R.

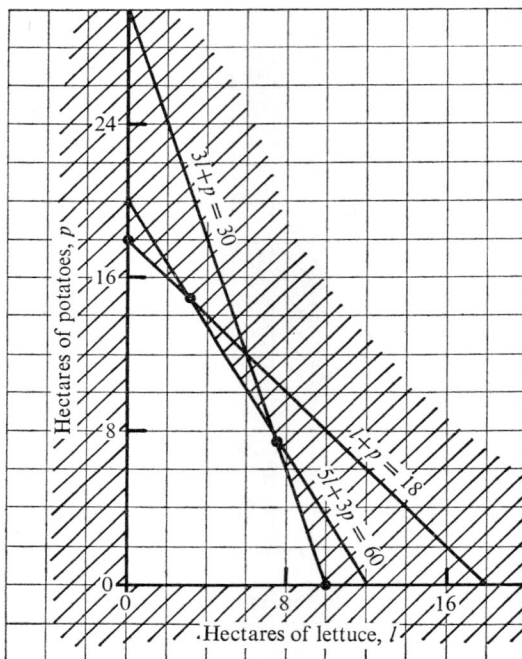

Fig. R

(*c*) When, as in this case, the variables are not restricted to taking integral values the optimal solution will be at one of the vertices of the solution polygon—more of this in the follow-up chapter.

Vertex	Profit
(10, 0)	£120
(7½, 7½)	£150
(3, 15)	£156
(0, 18)	£144

114

5. (a) (i) $x+y \leqslant 600$, (ii) $3x+5y > 1200$.

(b) Not an easy ordering to express since it imposes a restriction on y and not, as might be assumed, on x,

$$y \leqslant 400.$$

For the graph see Figure S.

(c) (i) £30.

(ii) 240 all at 25p.

(iii) £70 at (200, 400).

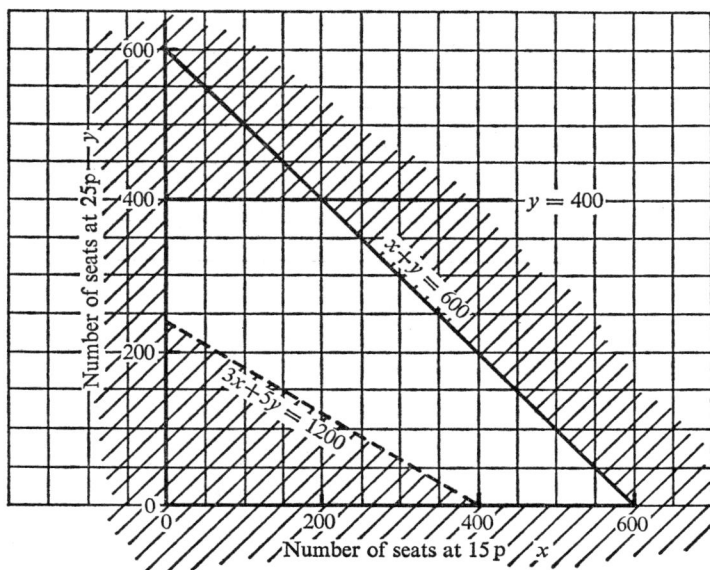

Fig. S

6. See Figure T. The relevant orderings are:

Cost: $\quad 3x+y \leqslant 600$.

Bye-law: $\quad y \leqslant 8x$.

Maximum surface area of building: about 490 m².

115

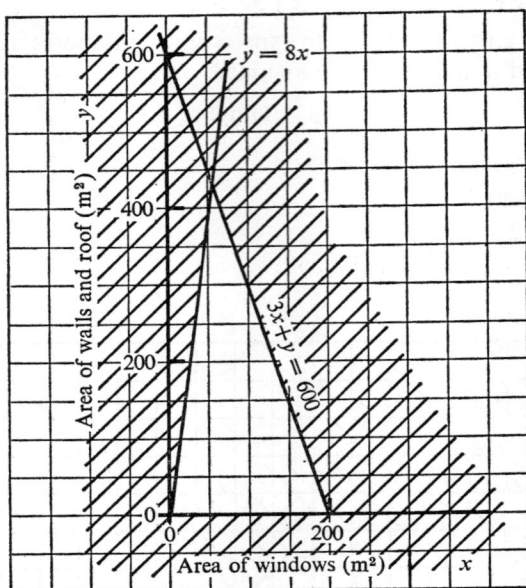

Fig. T

7. (a)

$$5a + 3b + 8c + 2d + 6e + 6f \leqslant 120,$$
$$3a + 6b + c + 2d + 5e \qquad \leqslant 70,$$
$$2a + 5b + 3c + 4d + e + 4f \leqslant 80,$$
$$6a + 2b + 4c + d + 3e + 6f \leqslant 100.$$

(b) No-one has yet exceeded a profit of £114 although this has been obtained in several ways, namely:

(0, 0, 1, 5, 4, 13),   (0, 0, 0, 6, 6, 12),   (1, 1, 0, 5, 5, 12).

These all point to the fact that the manufacturer should discontinue the production of products A, B and C.

Once pupils understand this problem it is fascinating to see the ingenuity they will display in trying to solve it.

REVISION EXERCISES

SLIDE RULE SESSION NO. 3 (p. 135)
(See note on p. 57)

1. 1559; 1559 ± 3.

2. 18·72; $18\cdot72 \pm 0\cdot03$.

3. 1·359; $1\cdot359 \pm 0\cdot003$.

4. 14·20; $14\cdot2 \pm 0\cdot03$.

5. 6·285; $6\cdot28(5) \pm 0\cdot02$.

6. 19·87; $19\cdot87 \pm 0\cdot03$.

7. 2·789; $2\cdot79 \pm 0\cdot01$.

8. 278·9; 279 ± 1.

9. 0·9107; $0\cdot911 \pm 0\cdot003$.

10. 0·1426; $0\cdot1426 \pm 0\cdot0004$.

SLIDE RULE SESSION NO. 4 (p. 135)
(See note on p. 57)

1. 703 (exact); 703 ± 1.

2. 3·465; $3\cdot46(5) \pm 0\cdot01$.

3. 0·5135; $0\cdot513(5) \pm 0\cdot001$.

4. 1711; 1711 ± 3.

5. 149·0; $149 \pm 0\cdot3$.

6. 42 (exact); $42\cdot0 \pm 0\cdot2$.

7. 0·0002190; $(2\cdot19 \pm 0\cdot01) \times 10^{-4}$.

8. 221·7; 222 ± 1.

9. 993·0; 993 ± 3.

10. 180·4; $180\cdot4 \pm 0\cdot3$.

G (p. 135)

1. $135°$.

2. Yes; $C - B - A$.

3. No.

4. Yes.

5. 1.

6. $(4, {}^-3)$.

7. $\begin{pmatrix} 2 & 1 & 2 \\ 0 & 3 & 1 \\ 1 & 0 & 1 \end{pmatrix}$.

8. Yes.

9. 52_8.

10. £2·45.

H (p. 136)

1. Yes.

2. 30.

3. 920.

4. $(4, 0)$ or $({}^-4, 5)$.

5. $({}^-5, {}^-1)$.

6. $3\cdot7 \times 10^{-4}$.

7. $1:20$.

8. $-4x^2 + 6$.

9. $x = 4$.

10. No.

I (p. 136)

1. (b) Impossible; (c) angle of sector must be greater than 320°; (d) impossible; the height would have to be at least 2·5 cm.

2. 47·8 cm³; 73·2 cm².

3.

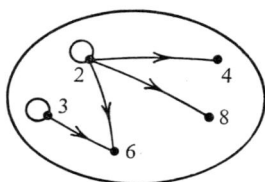

Fig. A

$$\mathbf{R} = \begin{array}{c} \\ 2 \\ 3 \\ 4 \\ 6 \\ 8 \end{array} \begin{array}{ccccc} 2 & 3 & 4 & 6 & 8 \\ \begin{pmatrix} 1 & 0 & 1 & 1 & 1 \\ 0 & 1 & 0 & 1 & 0 \\ 0 & 0 & 0 & 0 & 0 \\ 0 & 0 & 0 & 0 & 0 \\ 0 & 0 & 0 & 0 & 0 \end{pmatrix} \end{array},$$

$$\mathbf{R'} = \begin{pmatrix} 1 & 0 & 0 & 0 & 0 \\ 0 & 1 & 0 & 0 & 0 \\ 1 & 0 & 0 & 0 & 0 \\ 1 & 1 & 0 & 0 & 0 \\ 1 & 0 & 0 & 0 & 0 \end{pmatrix}.$$

$\mathbf{R} = \mathbf{R}^2$.

$\mathbf{R}^2$ represents the relation 'is a prime factor of'.

$\mathbf{R'}$ represents the relation 'is a multiple of the prime number'.

4.

$$\begin{array}{c} \\ P \\ Q \\ R \\ S \end{array} \begin{array}{cccc} P & Q & R & S \\ \begin{pmatrix} 0 & 1 & 0 & 1 \\ 0 & 0 & 0 & 1 \\ 1 & 1 & 0 & 0 \\ 0 & 0 & 1 & 0 \end{pmatrix} \end{array}, \qquad \begin{array}{c} \\ P \\ Q \\ R \\ S \end{array} \begin{array}{cccc} P & Q & R & S \\ \begin{pmatrix} 0 & 0 & 1 & 1 \\ 0 & 0 & 1 & 0 \\ 0 & 1 & 0 & 2 \\ 1 & 1 & 0 & 0 \end{pmatrix} \end{array}.$$

Taking two-stage dominances into account, a possible order would be: Rupert first, then Philip, Simon, Quentin.

5.

	1-nodes	2-nodes	3-nodes
Line	0	∞	0
Half-line	1	∞	0
Segment	2	∞	0

6. $AC = \sqrt{(200)} (= 14·1)$ cm; $AG = \sqrt{(300)} (= 17·3)$ cm.
   If $\theta = \angle GAC$, then $\cos \theta = 14·1/17·3 = 0·814$, and $\theta = 35·5°$.

7. (1, 2), (2, 1), (2, 2), (3, 1), (3, 2), (3, 3).

8. If there are a Albatrosses and k Kestrels, then
$$50a+40k \geqslant 500 \quad \text{or} \quad 5a+4k \geqslant 50$$
and
$$5a+3k \geqslant 42.$$
For the cost $7a+6k$ to be a minimum, we need
$$a = 10 \quad \text{and} \quad k = 0.$$

J (p. 137)

1. 3.74 cm^2.

2. (a) 2.5 cm.; (b) $78.5°$; (c) 3.42 cm.

3.

	N	A	R	$R+N$	$A+2$
(a)	2	2	2	4	4
(b)	3	4	3	6	6
(c)	5	6	3	8	8
Whole figure	10	12	6	16	14

For Figure 3 considered as a whole $R+N = A+4$.

4. (a)

To

$$\text{From} \begin{array}{c} A \\ B \\ C \\ D \end{array} \begin{pmatrix} 1 & 1 & 0 & 0 \\ 1 & 1 & 0 & 0 \\ 1 & 0 & 0 & 1 \\ 0 & 1 & 0 & 0 \end{pmatrix} \quad \begin{array}{c} A\ B\ C\ D \end{array}$$

A route matrix is always asymmetrical if there are one-way routes.

(b) The matrix $\mathbf{S}^2$ represents the number of two-stage routes connecting the points A, B, C, D.

$$\mathbf{S}^2 = \begin{pmatrix} 2 & 2 & 0 & 0 \\ 2 & 2 & 0 & 0 \\ 1 & 2 & 0 & 0 \\ 1 & 1 & 0 & 0 \end{pmatrix}.$$

5. $\pi \cap \pi'$ is the line containing B and C.

6. 1.19 cm.

7. $(0, 0), (0, 1), (^-1, ^-1)$.

8. If he has L hectares of lettuces, P hectares of potatoes, then $L+P \leqslant 10$, $10L+6P \leqslant 75$, $4L+2P \leqslant 30$ and $6L+4P$ is to be a maximum. Solution: $L = 3\frac{3}{4}$, $P = 6\frac{1}{4}$.

K (p. 138)

1. 20 faces. (a) $\frac{1}{20}$; (b) $\frac{1}{20}$; (c) $\frac{-3}{20}$; (d) $\frac{4}{5}$.

2. $(2, ^-3), (6, ^-6), (2, ^-8)$. The two triangles are *oppositely* congruent, so the second triangle could not be an image of the first under either a translation or a rotation. (Note the order of the vertices.)

3. The new vertices are $(^-1, 1)$, $(1, 2)$, $(^-1, 3)$ respectively.

4. 280, 780, 1750 m²/h.

5. (a) $140°$; (b) $1 \cdot 29$ cm²; (c) $4 \cdot 89$ cm²; (d) $3 \cdot 60$ cm².

6. Maximum flow is 3000 vehicles per hour.

7. (a) A half-line; (b) a line; (c) a line segment.
   $\{(x.y): x \geqslant 0\}$ is an example of a half-plane.

8. (a) $y > 2x$; (b) $xy > 48$; (c) $x^2+y^2 < 225$.
   $(4, 13), (4, 14), (5, 11), (5, 12), (5, 13), (5, 14), (6, 13)$.

L (p. 139)

1. See Figure B. The dotted lines are mediators of AB, AC.

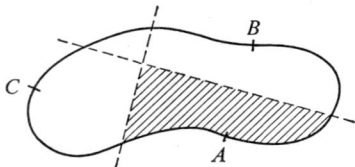

Fig. B

2. (a) e.g. isosceles triangle; (b) e.g. swastika; (c) impossible;
   (d) impossible; (e) a circle.

3. £2410; less than 20 %.

4. $9\frac{1}{2}$ square units.   **5.** $y = 2x+1$.

6. $W = 3\cdot2+0\cdot4n$ for $0 \leqslant n \leqslant 10$, where W is the mass in kilograms and n is the number of weeks after birth.

7. 450 cm²; 1890 g.

8. (a) False: π is *approximately* $\frac{22}{7}$.   (b) True.
   (c) False: it is an odd number.
   (d) False: it has 9 planes of symmetry.

TRIGONOMETRY TABLES PRACTICE (p. 140)

1. (a) 0·574;   (b) 0·997;   (c) 0·679.

2. (a) $x = 24\cdot9$;   (b) $x = 87\cdot9$;   (c) $x = 11\cdot5(\pm0\cdot1)$.

3. 1·540.   **4.** $\theta = 48\cdot6$.   **5.** 2·82.

6. (a) 0·8082;   (b) 0·1918;   sum of squares is 1.

7. (3·8, 3·2).   **8.** $AB = 1\cdot79$ cm, $AC = 4\cdot67$ cm.

9

WAVES

This is the second chapter on trigonometry in the course and in it the domains of the sine and cosine functions are extended to cover all angles. The definition of these functions as projections of a unit displacement makes this extension to non-acute angles straightforward. Once this extension has been made, the emphasis turns to the periodic character of the functions and physical examples such as tides are used for illustration. Although a fair amount of computation is required, the chapter is more concerned with ideas than manipulative techniques.

Access to tables of the sine and cosine function is not essential, but if tables are available then greater accuracy can be achieved.

1. THE SINE AND COSINE FUNCTIONS

By now the concept of a function should be appreciated and in this section we consider the nature of the cosine and sine functions for general angles.

(*a*) All one can deduce from Figure 2 is that sin 35° lies between 0·5 and 0·64 and that it is probably nearer to 0·64.

(*b*) No apparent help.

(*c*) (cos 60°, sin 60°) $\approx$ (0·50, 0·87).

(*e*) The diagrams should enable the pupils to see that all the answers depend on the values of cos 60° and sin 60°.

   (i) cos 120° = ⁻cos 60° = ⁻0·5,

        sin 120° = sin 60° = 0·87;

  (ii) cos 240° = ⁻cos 60° = ⁻0·5,

        sin 240° = ⁻sin 60° = ⁻0·87;

(iii) cos 300° = cos 60° = 0·5,

        sin 300° = ⁻sin 60° = ⁻0·87.

(*f*) Once a sketch has been made showing unit displacements at the given angles, no difficulty should be found in attaching a meaning to their sines and cosines (see Figure A).

$$\sin 420° = \sin 60° = 0·87,$$
$$\cos 480° = \cos 120° = {}^-\cos 60° = {}^-0·5,$$
$$\cos {}^-60° = \cos 60° = 0·5,$$
$$\sin {}^-300° = \sin 60° = 0·87.$$

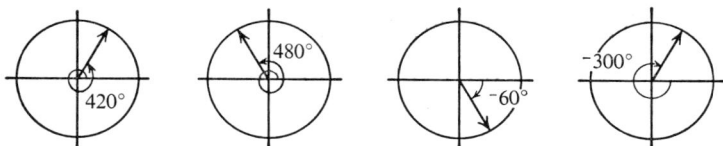

Fig. A

(*g*) By drawing unit displacements at angles of 63° and 256° and measuring the central and sideways displacements.

(*h*) From Figure 6:

    (i) $\sin 110° = 0·94,$

        $\sin 330° = {}^-0·5;$

    (ii) 30° or 150°.

(*i*) Two angles. This question could easily lead to a discussion of the angles mapped onto 0·5 by the sine function for a larger domain.

Exercise A (*p. 145*)

1.   (*a*) 0·42, ⁻0·34, ⁻0·71, 0·95;

    (*b*) 49° and 131°, 17° and 163°, 256° and 284°.

    Not much accuracy can be expected in reading the graph. For better results use tables in conjunction with the graph.

2.   (*a*) $0 < \sin θ° < 0·5$;   (*b*) $^-1 < \sin θ° < 0$.
    (*c*) $0 < θ < 90$ and $90 < θ < 180$ assuming that the domain is $0 < θ < 360$.

3.   The graph is the same shape as the sine wave but translated 90° to the left (see Figure 17).

4.   (*a*) 0·97, 0·39, ⁻0·71, 0·24;
    (*b*) 60° and 300°, 32° and 328°, 70° and 290°, 154° and 206°.

5. (*a*) 3 seats;   (*b*) (i) 70°, (ii) 160°, (iii) 250°.
1·8 m approximately.

6. (*a*) 9·5 cm;   (*b*) 60·7 cm;   (*c*) 48·8 cm.

7. (*a*) (i) 3·2 km east, (ii) 3·8 km north;
(*b*) 0·87 km.

8. 6°.

9. The first dinghy has travelled 250 m south while the second dinghy has travelled 240 m south.

10. (*a*) (i) $x = 30$, (ii) $x = 70$, (iii) $x = 50$,
(iv) $x = 10$, (v) $x = 67$;
(*b*) $x+y = 90$;
(*c*) $x = 45$ assuming that $0 < x < 90$.

11. (*a*) $A(5 \cos 53°, 5 \sin 53°) = (3{\cdot}01, 3{\cdot}99)$;
(*b*) $B(7 \cos 240°, 7 \sin 240°) = (-3{\cdot}50, -6{\cdot}06)$;
(*c*) $C(12 \cos 310°, 12 \sin 310°) = (7{\cdot}72, -9{\cdot}39)$.

2. WAVES

Now that the graphs of the sine and cosine functions have been discussed, we are able to look at examples of natural phenomena whose analysis leads to similar graphs. The idea of a mathematical model could be discussed here and, in particular, how to fit a mathematical function to given experimental data.

(*a*) When passing beneath the point of suspension.

(*b*) The speed of the child increases from zero at the highest point he reaches until it attains a maximum and then it decreases once more to zero. The child will then travel backwards, i.e. his forward speed will be negative, until he again reaches the highest point. This cycle is then repeated. It is not easy to describe this in words and most pupils will resort to using their hands to simulate the motion.

(*c*) 2 s.

(*d*) (i) 11.45 a.m.,   (ii) 5.15 p.m.

(*e*) 9 a.m. to 3.50 p.m. and 6·50 p.m. to 8 p.m.

(*f*) 10 m.

(*g*) From 9 a.m. to 11.45 a.m. and from 5.15 p.m. to 8 p.m.

(*h*) 2.30 p.m.

124

Exercise B (p. 148)

1. An analysis of almost any periodic motion occurring in nature leads to an approximately sinusoidal graph. Fourier analysis shows how periodic functions can be represented as infinite sums of sine and cosine functions.

   The motion of tree branches in the wind.

   The height of a cycle pedal above the ground when a cycle is being pedalled.

   The rolling of a ship at sea.

   The oscillation of a mass on a spring balance or of a cork float bobbing up and down on water.

2. Alternating current. The current first flows one way and then the other, the whole pattern repeating 50 times a second. If a graph were plotted of voltage against time, it would look like a sine wave which had a maximum value of 230 V. and a period of $\frac{1}{50}$ s. It could be represented mathematically by the function

$$t \to 230 \sin 18{,}000°t.$$

   The so called 'mains hum' often heard with older radio or T.V. sets corresponds to a note with a periodic time of $\frac{1}{50}$ s.

3. Very high frequency.

4. The groove on a gramophone record is a wavy line corresponding to the frequencies of the notes being produced.

   One effective demonstration to show the connection between vibrations, sounds and sine waves uses an oscilloscope. If the Y plates of an oscilloscope are connected through an amplifier to a microphone, then sounds can be represented on the screen as sinusoidal waves whose frequency and amplitude depend on the pitch and loudness of the notes being picked up by the microphone.

5. (a) (i) $261 \times 2^3 = 2088$, (ii) $261 \times 2^{-2} = 65 \cdot 25$;
   (b) See Figure B.

6. (a) See Figure C;
   (b) (i) 4·8 m, (ii) 4·44 m, (iii) 5·04 m, (iv) 4·26 m.

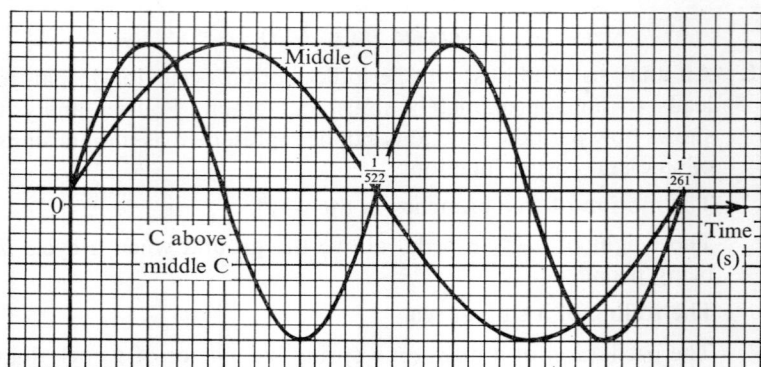

Fig. B

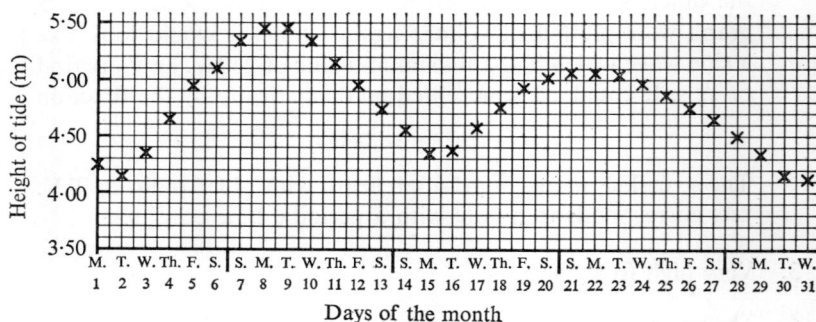

Fig. C

(c) This is not a continuous graph but a graph of discrete points. Intermediate points have no meaning although the positions of the points plotted give a good guide to the depth of the afternoon tide.

7. See Figure D. It is advisable to have a list of s.r. and s.s. time available already checked so as to avoid confusion over British Summer Time.

(a) 21 June 16 h 40 min;

(b) 22 December 7 h 50 min;

(c) (i) 14 weeks, (ii) 28 weeks, (iii) 42 weeks.

126

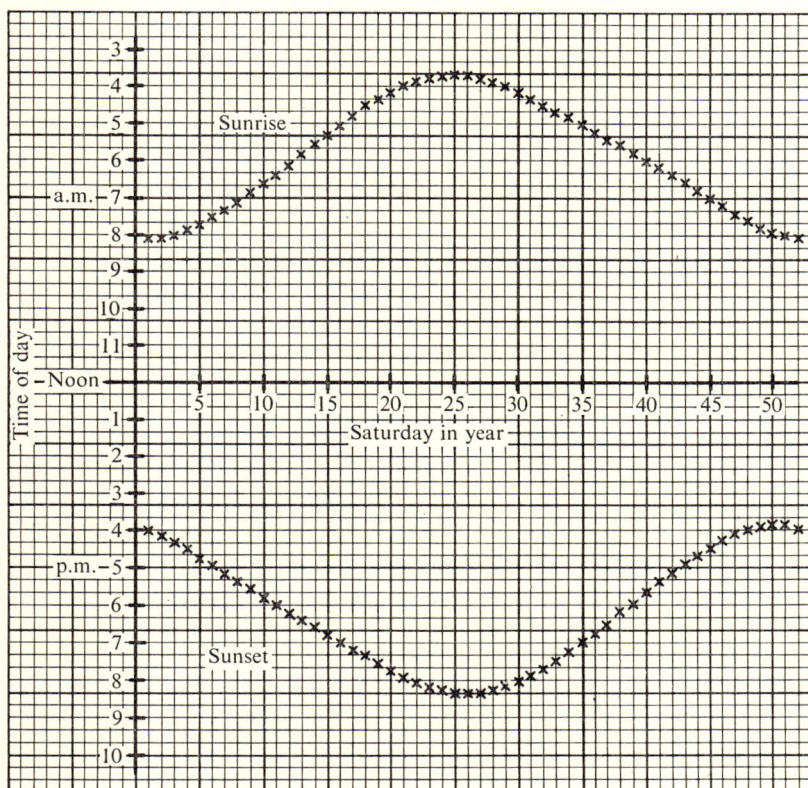

Fig. D

8. The discussion here is meant to be qualitative. The choice of suspension is subjective. What is required is evidence that the graphs have been understood. A statement such as 'I prefer the first suspension because it doesn't bounce so high or so quickly as the second' is acceptable.

9. (a) $15 + 3 \cos 210° = 15 - 3 \cos 30° = 12·4$;

(b) $15 + 3 \cos 330° = 15 + 3 \cos 30° = 17·6.$

127

Exercise C (p. 151)

Miscellaneous

The questions in this exercise are concerned more with the use of the sine and cosine in practical problems than with the sine and cosine functions as such. The exercise might best be thought of as a revision of the work in Book 2.

1. (a) (i) 7·8 m, (ii) 6·6 m, (iii) 5·4 m, (iv) 2·4 m;
   (b) (i) 7·5 m, (ii) 9 m, (iii) 9·9 m, (iv) 10·5 m;
   (c) The maximum operating radii are 8·4 m, 11·4 m, 12·9 m and 12 m respectively, so that the 18 m jib gives the largest operating radius.

2. (a) 2·3 m; (b) 20°; (c) 2·15 m.
   There are many different kinds of cranes and civil engineering equipment in use today involving jointed rods and hydraulic jacks, which are excellent sources for exercises on trigonometry and loci, at least for boys.

3. (a) 18; (b) 35° or 145°; (c) 4·6; (d) 10;
   (e) 60° or 300°; (f) 2·0.

4. This is best done on polar graph paper. See Figure E. Some discussion will probably be necessary to help the pupils plot points such as (⁻3, 120°). It can be thought of as the point reached by starting at the origin, facing the direction 120° and then walking backwards 3 paces. What happens when θ takes values between 180 and 360?

5. Again this is best done on polar graph paper (see Figure F).

6. Angle at A is approximately 25°. $BF \approx 4·56$ m. $AC \approx 21·8$ m.

7. (a) 5·19 m; (b) 6 m; (c) 163 m³ approx.
   This is a good example of short-sighted planning in which the reduction in initial outlay is soon lost because of the greatly increased heating costs.

8. $\angle AOC = 130°$
   (8 cos 130°, 8 sin 130°) $\approx$ (⁻5·14, 6·13).

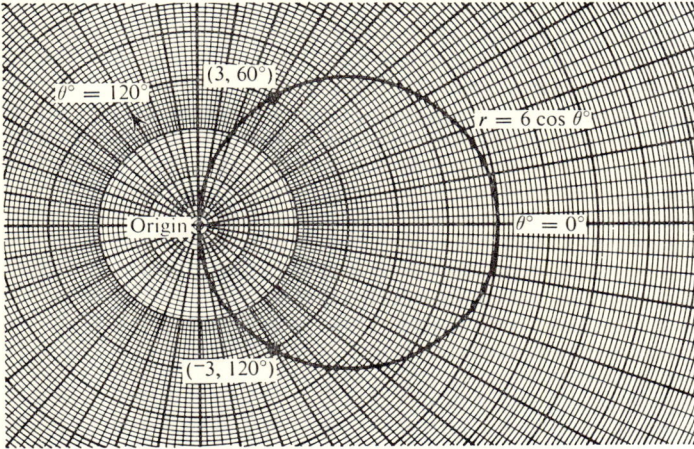

Fig. E

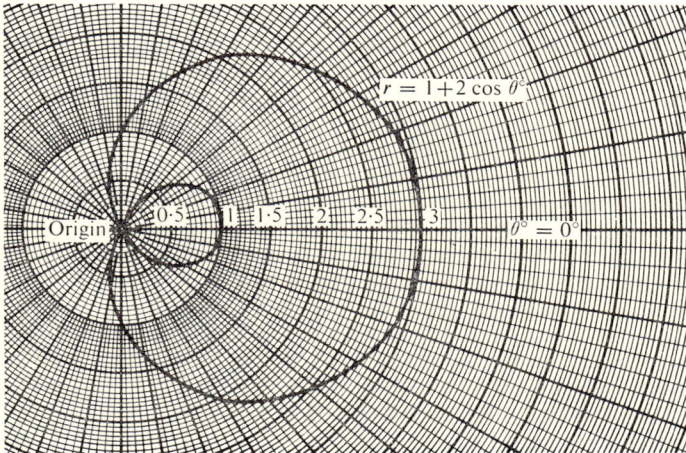

Fig. F

129

10

FUNCTIONS AND EQUATIONS

This chapter marks an important stage in the development of the S.M.P. algebra course and follows on directly from Chapters 8 and 13 in Book 2. Our fundamental approach to algebra is reflected by this extract from the preface to Book 2:

'It is necessary that pupils acquire certain manipulative techniques and it is even more necessary that they should understand what they are doing when performing these manipulations.'

In Book 1 the policy was to use algebraic notation in an intuitive manner whenever it seemed appropriate; in Book 2 the underlying ideas of structure, commutativity, associativity and distributivity of operations, and the mapping concept, were discussed and the beginnings of manipulative techniques established. In this chapter the concept of a mapping, and in particular a function, along with composite and inverse mappings, are further developed with appropriate notations; these ideas are then used to consolidate the necessary techniques involved in the manipulation of simple equations and formulae. All further manipulative methods, to be considered later, are only special cases of the methods employed here.

In the traditional course the solution of simple linear equations is invariably part of the first year's work; however, we have found that a very gradual build up to this technique is desirable but that subsequently a more rapid development is possible.

A final section is devoted to extending the use of brackets to cover the product of two binomials, or multinomials. The chapter could easily be taken in several stages, the material divides itself naturally into three possible units, Sections 1–4, 5 and 6, and 7.

1. FUNCTION NOTATION

The 'machine' analogy is again employed but the lifelike illustration of Figure 1 is immediately simplified to a box with in- and out-going arrows. The function notation is a very useful and easily understood

130

shorthand for an already familiar idea. The two ways of describing a function each have their own merit; for example, $f: x \to x - 4$ focuses attention on the mapping and the more traditional

$$f(x) = x - 4$$

on the image of the mapping. The notation is not new as it has been used in Chapter 2 in the context of transformations. The investigation of composite functions is greatly clarified by the use of this notation and the breaking down of a function into simpler functions is fundamental to any manipulative process. For example, the pupil should have a mental picture of $(3x - 1)^2$ as a succession of three machines, 'multiply by 3', 'subtract 1' and 'square'. To 'get at' x, inverse machines will have to be employed in the reverse order.

The words 'inverse' and 'reverse' call for some comment. Both involve the notion of opposite. We have inverse elements, inverse operations, inverse relations or mappings; on the other hand we associate 'reverse' with the idea of direction and talk about the effect of an operation being reversed by the corresponding inverse operation.

(a) (i) $^-7$, (ii) $^-4$;

(b) (i) 2, (ii) 0, (iii) $^-6$;

(c) (i) 11, (ii) 2, (iii) $^-1$.

1.1

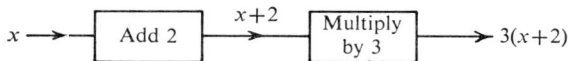

Fig. A

The composite machine in Figure A has output $fg(x)$, that is, 'g followed by f', or $x \to 3(x + 2)$.

(i) 8, (ii) 12, (iii) $^-4$, (iv) 0.

No element x is mapped onto the same image by gf and fg since the equation $3x + 2 = 3x + 6$ has no solutions.

Exercise A (p. 156)

1. (a) 'halve' or 'divide by 2';   (b) 'add 2';   (c) 'cube'.

2. (a) $x \to x - 5$;   (b) $x \to \frac{1}{7}x$;   (c) $x \to \frac{1}{3}x$;   (d) $x \to x^2 + 2$.

3. (a) 1;   (b) 0;   (c) $^-1\frac{1}{2}$.

131

4. (*a*) ⁻1; (*b*) 4; (*c*) 9.

5. (*a*) 2; (*b*) 0; (*c*) ⁻1; (*d*) $\dfrac{4x+1}{4x-1}$.
$f(x)$ is not defined for $x = 1$.

6. (*a*) 16; (*b*) 1.
'Raising to the power 0' was mentioned in Book 2, Chapter 9.

7. (*a*) 5; (*b*) 5; (*c*) 7.

8. (*a*) 2; (*b*) 0.

9. No. $x \to 2x^2$; $x \to (2x)^2$.
$x \to 3x^2$ is 'square' followed by 'multiply by 3';
$x \to (3x)^2$ is 'multiply by 3' followed by 'square'.

10. (*a*) $x \to x-3$, $x \to \tfrac{1}{2}x$;
(*b*) $x \to x+7$, $x \to x^2$;
(*c*) $x \to {}^-x$, $x \to x+5$.

11. This raises the question considered at length in the section on 'order of operations' in Book 2, Chapter 4, in a more formal manner.
$gf(x) = fg(x)$ if
either (i) f and g involve only $+$ and $-$,
or (ii) f and g involve only $\times$ and $\div$.
Another of the many possibilities is
$$f: x \to x^m \quad \text{and} \quad g: x \to x^n.$$

12. (*a*) ⁻11; (*b*) 5; (*c*) ⁻3; (*d*) 13.
$$gf: x \to 1-4x,$$
$$fg: x \to 9-4x.$$

13. (*a*) 7, 7; (*b*) ⁻5, ⁻5; (*c*) ⁻3, ⁻3.
Both gf and fg are $x \to 6x-5$.
This is an interesting extension of Question 11. More generally it can be shown that for
$$f: x \to ax+b \quad \text{and} \quad g: x \to px+q,$$
$$gf(x) = fg(x) \Leftrightarrow (a-1)q = (p-1)b.$$

Some of the more able pupils can be challenged to find a general rule, though one would not expect it to be stated in this formal manner.

14. (a) $\frac{1}{5}$ and $\frac{2}{3}$;

(b) 3 and 3.

15. (a) $2x^2+1 = 9 \Leftrightarrow x = 2$ or $^-2$;

(b) $(2x+1)^2 = 9 \Leftrightarrow x = 1$ or $^-2$.

There is no need for the use of formal methods of manipulation here.

16. A linear function and therefore defined by two ordered pairs. $f(3) = {}^-1$.

The graph is not strictly necessary; the sequence method employed in Book 1 is sufficient.

17. Double brackets are unfortunately necessary.

(a) (3, 4);   (b) (0, 6);   (c) (2, 9);   (d) (2, 9).

$$gf((x, y)) = fg((x, y)) \quad \text{for all} \quad (x, y).$$

f and g are translations.

18. $\{^-1, 0, 3, 15\}$.

$f(^-x) = f(x)$ if $x = 0$ is a line of symmetry; this is so if a curve is drawn through the marked points. Any function of the form $x \to ax^2+b$ has this property.

2. INVERSE RELATIONS

Inverse functions were introduced in Book 2. Then we were mainly concerned with establishing the idea of an inverse and discussing cases in which an inverse function could be defined for a given function. We now consider in more detail the whole problem of inverse relations or mappings.

The words 'relation' and 'mapping' can both be used to refer to the same mathematical situation. For example, the relation 'is a parent of' can be thought of as a mapping of a set of parents onto a set of children. We refer to this as the mapping, parent → child. It should be noted that some authors use the word mapping as being synonymous with function; our use of the word is more general and agrees with the definition given by Mansfield and Bruckheimer in *Background to Set and Group Theory*.

Matrix representation of relations was introduced in Chapter 6 and is employed again here in the preparatory work of Sections 2 and 3. This represents a fundamental piece of mathematics and should be covered thoroughly by the pupils. The stages of development are:

(i) any mapping of a finite set into a finite set can be described by a matrix;

(ii) the inverse mapping is described by the transpose of this matrix;

(iii) a function is described by a matrix with one non-zero element in each row;

(iv) a function having an inverse mapping which is also a function, is described by a matrix with one non-zero element in each row and column (cf. the reference to permutation matrices on pp. 35 and 84 of this guide).

Functions are in general many-to-one mappings; the type of function referred to in (iv) is a one-to-one mapping.

2.1   Figure 6 represents the relation 'is a child of'.

2.2   (*a*) Figure 5 shows a one-to-many mapping which is not a function.

(*b*) Figure 6 shows a many-to-one mapping which is a function. In general 'is a child of' will not be a function as every child has two parents. The range in Figure 6 only includes one parent in each case.

$$
\begin{array}{c}
\begin{array}{cccccc} 1 & 2 & 3 & 4 & 5 & 6 \end{array}\\
\begin{array}{c} A \\ B \\ C \\ D \\ E \\ F \end{array}
\begin{pmatrix}
0 & 1 & 0 & 0 & 0 & 0 \\
0 & 0 & 0 & 1 & 0 & 0 \\
1 & 0 & 0 & 0 & 0 & 0 \\
0 & 0 & 0 & 0 & 0 & 1 \\
0 & 0 & 0 & 0 & 1 & 0 \\
0 & 0 & 1 & 0 & 0 & 0
\end{pmatrix}
\end{array}
, \quad
\begin{array}{c}
\begin{array}{ccc} b & c & d \end{array}\\
\begin{array}{c} a \\ b \end{array}
\begin{pmatrix}
1 & 0 & 0 \\
0 & 1 & 1
\end{pmatrix}
\end{array}.
$$

The matrix on the right has two 1's in the second row. If a matrix describes a function there is only one non-zero element in each row. (ii) and (iii) are functions.

Inverse mappings described by

(i)

$$\begin{array}{c} \\ a \\ b \\ c \\ d \end{array} \begin{array}{cccc} a & b & c & d \\ \begin{pmatrix} 1 & 1 & 0 & 0 \\ 0 & 0 & 0 & 1 \\ 1 & 0 & 0 & 0 \\ 0 & 0 & 1 & 0 \end{pmatrix} \end{array},$$

(ii)

$$\begin{array}{c} \\ \alpha \\ \beta \\ \gamma \end{array} \begin{array}{cccc} a & b & c & d \\ \begin{pmatrix} 1 & 0 & 1 & 0 \\ 0 & 1 & 0 & 0 \\ 0 & 0 & 0 & 1 \end{pmatrix} \end{array},$$

(iii)

$$\begin{array}{c} \\ P \\ Q \\ R \\ S \end{array} \begin{array}{cccc} a & b & c & d \\ \begin{pmatrix} 0 & 1 & 0 & 0 \\ 0 & 0 & 1 & 0 \\ 0 & 0 & 0 & 1 \\ 1 & 0 & 0 & 0 \end{pmatrix} \end{array}.$$

Only the inverse mapping of (iii) is a function.

Note that it is possible for a mapping that is not a function to have an inverse mapping that is a function.

3. INVERSE FUNCTIONS

$$(a) \ (i) \ \mathbf{R} = \begin{array}{c} \\ 2 \\ 3 \\ 7 \end{array} \begin{array}{cccc} 6 & 8 & 9 & 21 \\ \begin{pmatrix} 1 & 1 & 0 & 0 \\ 1 & 0 & 1 & 1 \\ 0 & 0 & 0 & 1 \end{pmatrix} \end{array}, \quad (ii) \ \mathbf{R}' = \begin{array}{c} \\ 6 \\ 8 \\ 9 \\ 21 \end{array} \begin{array}{ccc} 2 & 3 & 7 \\ \begin{pmatrix} 1 & 1 & 0 \\ 1 & 0 & 0 \\ 0 & 1 & 0 \\ 0 & 1 & 1 \end{pmatrix} \end{array}.$$

$\mathbf{R}'$ describes $x \to$ factor of x.

It also describes the relation 'is a multiple of'. The fact that 'is a multiple of' and '$x \to$ multiple of x' are inverses of each other may cause some confusion but reference to matrices such as the above should clear up the difficulty.

$$(iii) \ \mathbf{RR}' = \begin{pmatrix} 2 & 1 & 0 \\ 1 & 3 & 1 \\ 0 & 1 & 1 \end{pmatrix}, \quad \mathbf{R}'\mathbf{R} = \begin{pmatrix} 2 & 1 & 1 & 1 \\ 1 & 1 & 0 & 0 \\ 1 & 0 & 1 & 1 \\ 1 & 0 & 1 & 2 \end{pmatrix}.$$

$$(b) \ (i) \ \{0, 1, 2\}; \quad (ii) \ \mathbf{F} = \begin{array}{c} \\ 0 \\ 1 \\ 2 \end{array} \begin{array}{ccc} 0 & 1 & 2 \\ \begin{pmatrix} 1 & 0 & 0 \\ 0 & 0 & 1 \\ 0 & 1 & 0 \end{pmatrix} \end{array}, \quad (iii) \ \mathbf{F}' = \begin{array}{c} \\ 0 \\ 1 \\ 2 \end{array} \begin{array}{ccc} 0 & 1 & 2 \\ \begin{pmatrix} 1 & 0 & 0 \\ 0 & 0 & 1 \\ 0 & 1 & 0 \end{pmatrix} \end{array}.$$

(iv) F' describes a function.

(v) $FF' = F'F = \begin{pmatrix} 1 & 0 & 0 \\ 0 & 1 & 0 \\ 0 & 0 & 1 \end{pmatrix}$, an identity matrix.

As F and F' both describe one-to-one mappings the result of forming a composite mapping of the two, in either order, will be to map each element of the domain back onto itself and hence we obtain the identity matrix.

(c) (i) $\{0, 1\}$, (ii) $G = \begin{array}{c} \\ 0 \\ 1 \\ 2 \end{array} \begin{array}{c} 0 \quad 1 \\ \begin{pmatrix} 1 & 0 \\ 0 & 1 \\ 0 & 1 \end{pmatrix} \end{array}$,

(iii) no, (iv) $G' = \begin{array}{c} \\ 0 \\ 1 \end{array} \begin{array}{c} 0 \quad 1 \quad 2 \\ \begin{pmatrix} 1 & 0 & 0 \\ 0 & 1 & 1 \end{pmatrix} \end{array}$,

(v) no, (vi) $GG' = \begin{pmatrix} 1 & 0 & 0 \\ 0 & 1 & 1 \\ 0 & 1 & 1 \end{pmatrix}$, $G'G = \begin{pmatrix} 1 & 0 \\ 0 & 2 \end{pmatrix}$.

(a), (b) and (c) illustrate three different cases. In (a) neither R nor R' describes a function; in (c) G describes a function but G' does not; in (b) both F and F' describe functions. Only under these circumstances will the products of the matrix with its transpose result in an identity matrix. This sort of approach is linked closely with the work on route matrices. The mappings described by R and R' are both illustrated in Figure B.

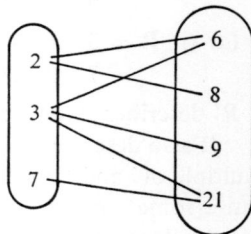

Fig. B

There are no arrows; R describes the mapping from left to right and R' that from right to left. RR' shows the numbers of two-stage routes linking 2, 3 and 7 and $R'R$ the numbers of two-stage routes linking 6, 8, 9 and 21.

It is a good idea to have a class discussion along these lines after the pupils have worked through the preparatory material in Sections 2 and 3.

1. (a) 'add 6';   (b) 'multiply by 8';
   (c) $x \to x-3$;   (d) $x \to \frac{1}{5}x$.

2. (a) No;   (b) yes;   (c) yes;   (d) yes.

3. Only (b), (c) and (d) are meaningful. (c) 7.

4. (b) and (d) in Question 2 have inverse functions.

5. Figure 8 illustrates a function having an inverse function.

   (a) 9;   (b) 4;   (c) 1;   (d) 3; 'double and add 1'.

6. (a) $f^{-1}(x) = 3x$;   (b) $f^{-1}(x) = x+4$.

7. $x \to 2x$ only has an inverse function for a finite arithmetic with a prime modulus. Hence, for {0, 1, 2, 3}, no; for {0, 1, 2, 3, 4}, yes.

8. $f^{-1}f(x) = ff^{-1}(x) = x$.

   We could say that $f^{-1}f$ and ff^{-1} both represent the *identity* function $x \to x$. The inverse of the inverse of f is f; or $(f^{-1})^{-1} = f$.

4. FINDING INVERSE FUNCTIONS

The first three sections have been concerned with exploring the idea of a function. Assuming this background knowledge, Sections 4, 5 and 6 are devoted to developing the important related techniques of solving equations and rearranging formulae. Considerable use is made of flow diagrams employing the 'function machine' approach. First of all we consider the problem of finding inverse functions, paying particular attention to functions that are self-inverse.

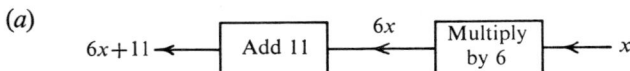

(a)

$$6x+11 \longleftarrow \boxed{\text{Add 11}} \overset{6x}{\longleftarrow} \boxed{\begin{array}{c}\text{Multiply} \\ \text{by 6}\end{array}} \longleftarrow x$$

Fig. C. $x \to 6x+11$.

(b) Note the convention that $\sqrt{}$ denotes 'the positive square root of'

$$x \to \pm \sqrt{\left(\frac{x-1}{3}\right)} \quad \text{is not a function.}$$

(i) ± 1, (ii) ± 3. $\pm a$ give the same output in Figure 10.

$x \to \sqrt{[\frac{1}{3}(x-1)]}$ is a function but cannot, in general, be said to be the inverse function of $x \to 3x^2+1$. However, if the domain of $x \to 3x^2+1$ were restricted to positive numbers, then $x \to \sqrt{[\frac{1}{3}(x-1)]}$ would be the inverse function; this sort of argument is hardly likely to be put forward by the pupils. See Exercise C, Questions 6 and 12.

4.1 (*a*) (i) $f(8) = 2$,   (ii) $f(2) = 8$

$$f(a) = b \Leftrightarrow f(b) = a.$$

(*b*) $f: x \to 12/x$, see Figure D.

(i) $f(3) = 4$, (ii) $f(4) = 3$, (iii) $f(8) = 1\frac{1}{2}$, (iv) $f(1\frac{1}{2}) = 8$,

$$xy = 12.$$

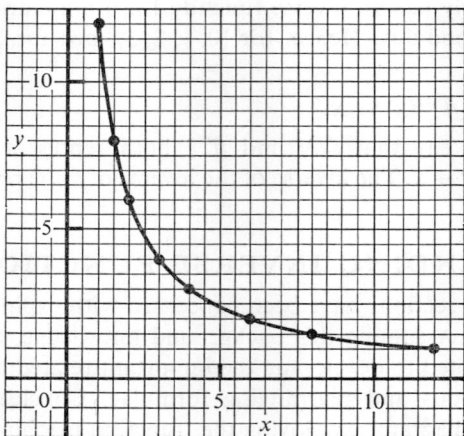

Fig. D

Figure 12, $x+y = 10$. The symmetric way in which x and y occur in these equations indicates their connection with self-inverse functions.

$y = x$ is a line of symmetry, itself representing the identity function $x \to x$ which is also self-inverse. When flow diagrams are reversed, boxes containing self-inverse functions are unaltered. This is illustrated in Example 1.

1. (*a*) See Figure E

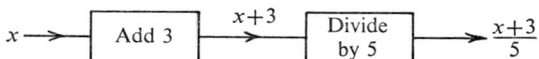

Fig. E

(*b*) See Figure F

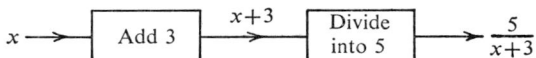

Fig. F

Note the self-inverse function in the second box. No.

Inverse of (*a*) is $x \to 5x - 3$, and of (*b*) is $x \to \dfrac{5}{x} - 3$.

2. $f(2) = 2$, $f^{-1}(2) = 2$, $f(10) = 0.4$, $f^{-1}(10) = 0.4$.

$f(x) = f^{-1}(x)$ for all x; f is self-inverse.

$$f(f(x)) = x.$$
$$g(g(x)) = x \Leftrightarrow g^{-1} = g.$$

3. The inverse functions are

(*a*) $\frac{1}{2}(x + 1)$;

(*b*) $\frac{1}{3}(x - 2)$;

(*c*) $3(5 - x)$;

(*d*) $\frac{1}{3}(2x - 7)$;

(*e*) $\frac{1}{2}(x/5 + 1)$;

(*f*) $\dfrac{4 - x}{20}$.

4. This rather difficult example emphasizes why we give the self-inverse functions, such as $x \to 3 - x$, special treatment. Treating them as composite functions is rather like using a sledge hammer to crack a nut; however, it is interesting to see that they *can* be seen as composite functions. The inverse function of 'multiply by $^-1$' is 'divide by $^-1$', which is the same; hence, $x \rightarrow {}^-x$ is self-inverse.

Figure G shows a flow diagram for $x \rightarrow 3-x$.

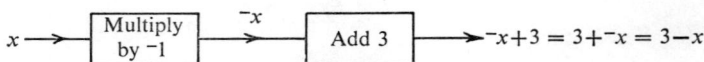

Fig. G

The reversed flow diagram is shown in Figure H.

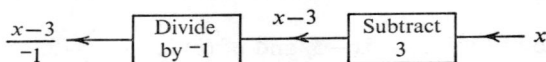

Fig. H

$$\frac{x-3}{-1} = {}^-(x-3) = {}^-x+3 = 3-x.$$

Figure H therefore illustrates the same function as Figure G, and, hence, $x \rightarrow 3-x$ is self-inverse.

5. $(fg)^{-1} = g^{-1}f^{-1}$.

This result is illustrated by reversing the flow diagram similar to Figure 3 but with f and g interchanged.

6. Inverse mappings are:

$$(a)\ x \rightarrow \pm\sqrt{\frac{3}{x}}, \qquad (b)\ x \rightarrow \pm\sqrt{4(1-x)}.$$

Neither of these is a function.

However, if the domains of the original functions were restricted to positive numbers, then the inverse mappings would be functions. See note on Section 4(b) above. One would not expect this answer from the pupils without some graphical considerations. See Questions 11 and 12 below.

140

7. See Figure I.

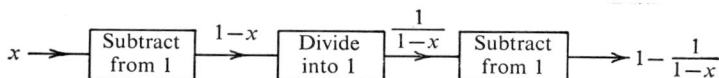

Fig. I

The reversed flow diagram is identical; the function is therefore self-inverse.

8. $f(40) = 0.643$, $f^{-1}(0.45) = 26.7$.

'Acute' ensures that the inverse mapping is a function. Range of f, $\{x: 0 \leqslant x \leqslant 1\}$.

In more general terms we say that

$$\sin^{-1} x \ (\text{'sine inverse of } x \text{' or 'inverse sine of } x \text{'})$$

is a function with domain

$$\{x: {}^-1 \leqslant x \leqslant 1\},$$

and range $\quad \{u: {}^-90° \leqslant u \leqslant 90°\}.$

This a functional way of referring to the classical 'principal value of $\sin^{-1} x$' (see Question 11).

9. Yes. No. Yes.

10. (a) $x \to a-x$; $x \to b/x$.
(b) Reflection in any line.
Half-turn about any point.
(c) $x \to$ spouse of x in a set of married people,
$x \to$ twin of x in set of people with twins.

11. $\cos^{-1}$ is only a function if the domain of $x° \to \cos x°$ is restricted to, say, $\{x: 0 \leqslant x \leqslant 180\}$. The graph of $x° \to \cos x°$ is then that part of the curve between A and B in Figure J.

141

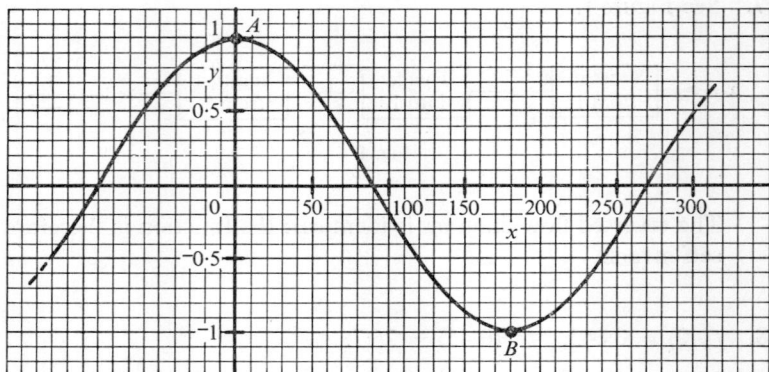

Fig. J. $x° → \cos x°$.

12. $\{x: x \geqslant 0\}$ or $\{x: x \leqslant 0\}$ (see Figure K).

$f: x → 4-x^2$ is shown in full line for the domain $\{x: x \geqslant 0\}$.

If the complete curve is drawn (that is, including the dotted part) the inverse mapping is not a function (see Question 6).

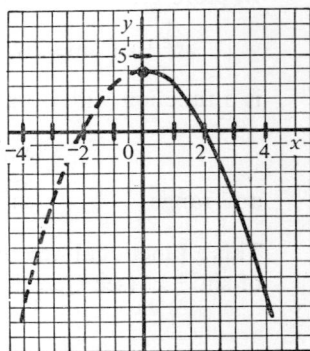

Fig. K

5. EQUATIONS

This section extends the work in Book 2, Chapter 13, to equations and orderings which involve self-inverse functions and simple graphical methods. We compare the use of the symbol ⇒, meaning 'implies' or 'only if', which was introduced in Book 2, with

(i) ⇐, meaning 'is implied by' or 'if';

(ii) ⇔, meaning 'implies and is implied by' or 'if and only if'.

In classical mathematical language:

$p ⇒ q$ means that 'p is a sufficient condition for q';

$p ⇐ q$ means that 'p is a necessary condition for q';

$p ⇔ q$ means that 'p is a necessary and sufficient condition for q'.

142

A chapter specifically devoted to logic and reasoning will be included in one of the Additional Mathematics books.

(*a*) (i) $\Rightarrow$, (ii) $\Leftarrow$, (iii) $\Leftrightarrow$.

We can say, for example, that 'I have two heads' is a sufficient condition for 'I am not a man' and 'I am not a man' is a necessary condition for 'I have two heads'.

The authors have decided that any algebraic consideration of equations in which x appears more than once should be postponed until Chapter 2 in Book 4 when the use of inverse elements is discussed at length. To forget about inverse functions and to just, for example, 'add x' to both sides would seem to be premature at this point when the ideas of inverse elements are not yet very explicit.

Exercise D (*p. 169*)

1. (*a*) $x = 2\frac{1}{3}$; (*b*) $x = {}^-1$;
   (*c*) $x = 31$; (*d*) $x = {}^-4\frac{3}{4}$.

2. (*a*) $x = 1\frac{4}{5}$; (*b*) $a = 22$;
   (*c*) $p = {}^-4$; (*d*) $h = 3\frac{1}{2}$;
   (*e*) $e = 6$; (*f*) $m = 4$;
   (*g*) $b = 0$; (*h*) $s = \frac{1}{19}$.

3. (*a*) $y = \frac{1}{2}$; (*b*) $r = 1\frac{1}{3}$;
   (*c*) $q = \frac{1}{32}$; (*d*) $d = {}^-\frac{1}{2}$;
   (*e*) $b = 0$; (*f*) $x = 1$;
   (*g*) $v = {}^-5$; (*h*) $n = \frac{1}{9}$.

4. See Figure L.
   (i) $x = 1\frac{1}{2}$, corresponding to A;
   (ii) $x = 0$, corresponding to B;
   (iii) $x = 1$, corresponding to C.

   $x = 3x - 1 \Leftrightarrow x = \frac{1}{2}$, D,
   $x = \frac{1}{3}x - 1 \Leftrightarrow x = {}^-1\frac{1}{2}$, E,
   $3 - x = \frac{1}{3}x - 1 \Leftrightarrow x = 3$, F.

5. (*a*) $x > {}^-1\frac{1}{2}$.
   This follows from Figure L,

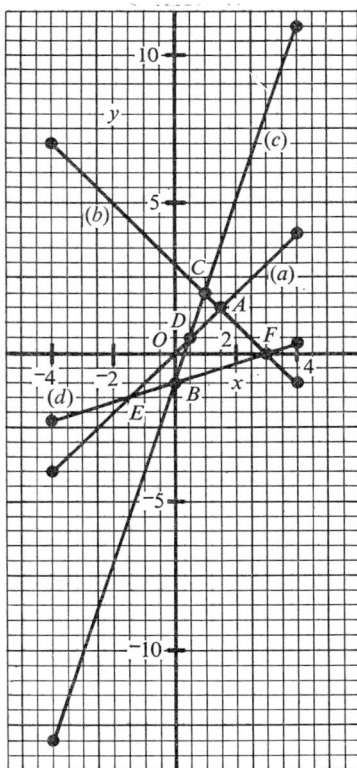

Fig. L

143

because to the right of E, that is, when $x > \frac{1}{3}x - 1$, the line representing (a) is 'above' the line representing (d).

(b) $x < 1$.　　　(c) $x \leqslant 3$.

6. (a) $x = {}^{-}2$;　　(b) $x = 2$;　　(c) $x = 3\frac{1}{2}$;　　(d) $x = {}^{-}3$.

7. See Figure M.

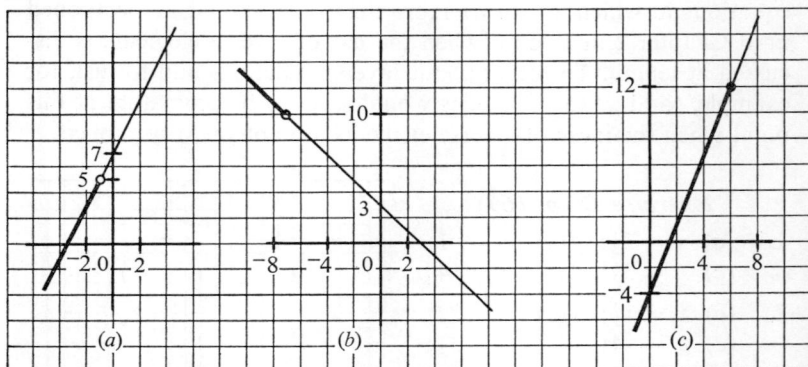

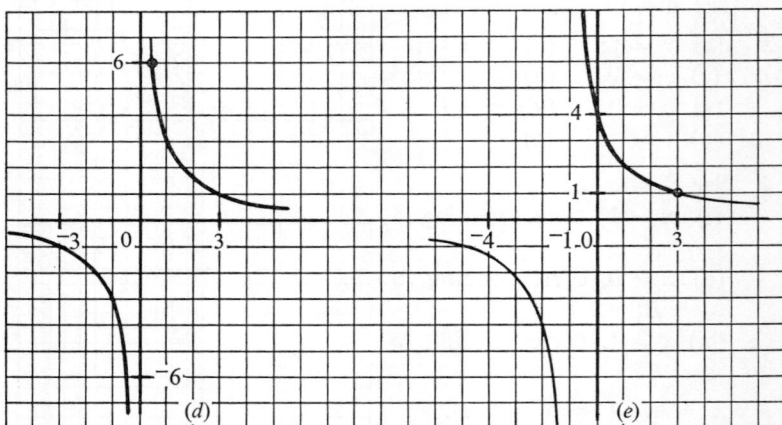

Fig. M. (a) $x < {}^{-}1$; (b) $x < {}^{-}7$; (c) $x \leqslant 6$; (d) x positive, $x \geqslant \frac{1}{2}$, x negative, $x \leqslant 0$; (e) $x + 1$ positive, $x < 3$, $x + 1$ negative, no values.

8. ' $\Leftrightarrow$ ' is not justified.　' $\Rightarrow$ ' for integral t.

6. FORMULAE

A knowledge of the technique of re-arranging formulae is particularly useful in science at this stage of the secondary course. Flow diagrams are helpful in developing this technique.

Exercise E (p. 172)

1. $c = \frac{5}{9}(f-32)$. Temperatures in Fahrenheit and Celsius.

2. $c = \sqrt{\dfrac{E}{m}}$; $c = 3 \times 10^{10}$.   **3.** $\dfrac{e}{m} = \dfrac{2V}{r^2 B^2}$.

4. (a) $P = 8a+4b$; $a = \frac{1}{8}(P-4b)$.
    (b) $S = 2a^2+4ab$; $b = (S-2a^2)/4a$.
    (c) $V = a^2 b$; $a = \sqrt{(V/b)}$.
    (d) (i) $b = 5$, (ii) $b = 4{\cdot}35$, (iii) $a = 4$.

5. $E = Pl^3/3Id$. $E = 2{\cdot}13 \times 10^6$ to 3 s.f.

6. Both are self-inverse. $n = 360/(180-\alpha)$.
    $\alpha = 90 \Leftrightarrow n = 4$.

7. $R = 12/(6-a)$. (a) $R = 12$; (b) $R = 16$.

8. (a) $d = v^2/200$;   (b) 4·5 m, 18 m;
    (c) $v = \sqrt{(200d)}$;   (d) safe speed < 95 km/h.

9. (a) 2400 volts;   (b) $I = V/R$;   (c) $W = I^2 R$, $W = V^2/R$;
    (d) (i) 31·25 ohms, (ii) 8 amp.   10 amp.

7. BRACKETS

The aim of the introductory work in this section is to establish the pattern associated with the product of two multinomials, the simplest case of two binomials receiving the most attention. This extends the work on distributivity in Chapter 13 of Book 2. Again it has not been found necessary to introduce this technical term. Tables of the type in Figure 30 are an abstraction from the 'area' diagrams of Figures 31 and 33. W. W. Sayer in *Vision in Elementary Mathematics* expounds at great length on this topic and the book is well worth consulting.

    (a) This example, drawn from Boolean algebra, gives a very clear indication of the pattern; 'and' is distributive over 'or'. In Boolean algebra 'or' is also distributive over 'and' and the dual situation is illustrated in Figure N.

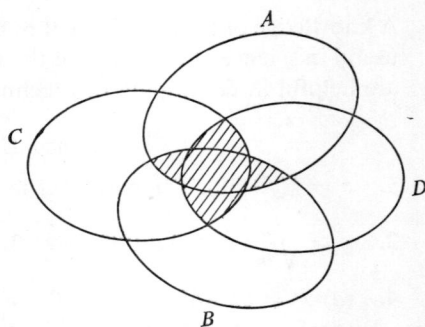

Fig. N   Fig. O

To go from L to M we have (a and x) or (b and y); this is equivalent to (a or b) and (a or y) and (x or b) and (x or y). However, this form of the logical pattern is not so succinct as that given in the text.

A similar illustration is possible using Venn diagrams and the set operations ∩ and ∪. In Figure Q the shaded region represents

$$(A \cap B) \cup (C \cap D).$$

With a little careful consideration this can also be seen to be

$$(A \cup C) \cap (A \cup D) \cap (B \cup C) \cap (B \cup D).$$

The use of colours to outline $A \cup C$, $A \cup D$, $B \cup C$ and $B \cup D$ helps to clarify the problem.

It is also important and useful to see the writing of $(a+b)(x+y)$ without brackets as a double application of the distributive property of $\times$ over $+$; first from the right and then from the left, or vice versa.

$$(a+b)(x+y) = a(x+y)+b(x+y) \quad (\times \text{ distributive from the right over } +)$$

$$= ax+ay+bx+by \quad (\times \text{ distributive from the left over } +).$$

With division, which is distributive only from the right over $+$, the process stops at the first stage:

$$(a+b) \div (x+y) = a \div (x+y) + b \div (x+y),$$

146

or
$$\frac{a+b}{x+y} = \frac{a}{x+y} + \frac{b}{x+y}.$$

The validity of the results outlined for 'and' and 'or' (and ∩ and ∪) depends on the fact that each of the connectives (as they are called in logic) is distributive both ways over the other.

(b) $(a \oplus b)(x \oplus y) = ax \oplus ay \oplus bx \oplus by.$

(c) $(10+7)(10+3) = (10 \times 10)+(10 \times 3)+(7 \times 10)+(7 \times 3).$

×	10	3
10	100	30
7	70	21

7.1 (i), (ii) and (iii) are correct.

Exercise F (p. 177)

1. (a)

×	a	$3b$
$2a$	$2a^2$	$6ab$
b	ab	$3b^2$

$2a^2 + 7ab + 3b^2$

(b)

×	c	$3d$
c	c^2	$3cd$
$3d$	$3cd$	$9d^2$

$c^2 + 6cd + 9d^2$

(c)

×	p	$-5q$
p	p^2	$-5pq$
$-4q$	$-4pq$	$20q^2$

$p^2 - 9pq + 20q^2$

2. Sausage and chips, sausage and beans, sausage and spaghetti, egg and chips, egg and beans, egg and spaghetti.

3. (a) $x^2 + 5x + 6$; (b) $x^2 + 18x + 77$;
(c) $2x^2 + 7x + 5$; (d) $15x^2 + 59x + 56$;
(e) $x^2 - x - 6$; (f) $6x^2 - x - 2$;
(g) $4x^2 - 17x + 4$; (h) $10 + a - 2a^2$.

4. See Figure P.

6 possible routes.
$(a+b)(x+y+z) =$
$\quad ax + ay + az + bx + by + bz.$

(a) $ax + bx + cx + a + b + c$;
(b) $ax - bx + cx - a + b - c$;
(c) $2x^2 - xy + 7x - 2y + 6$;
(d) $2x^2 + 3y^2 + 4z^2 + 5xy + 7yz + 6zx.$

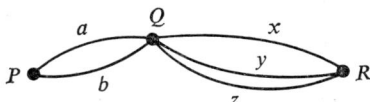

Fig. P

147

5. (a) $(p+q)^2 = p^2+2pq+q^2$;
(b) $(p-q)^2 = p^2-2pq+q^2$;
(c) $(d+e)(d-e) = d^2-e^2$;
(d) $(j+k)(j+k) = j^2+2jk+k^2$;
(e) $(x-y)(x+y) = x^2-y^2$;
(f) $(u+v)(u-v) = u^2-v^2$.

6. (a) $(x+2y)^2 = x^2+4xy+4y^2$;
(b) $(r-2s)(r-2s) = r^2-4rs+4s^2$;
(c) $(2m+3n)^2 = 4m^2+12mn+9n^2$;
(d) $(2a-5b)(2a+5b) = 4a^2-25b^2$;
(e) $(3y-4)(3y-4) = 9y^2-24y+16$;
(f) $10401^2 = 10000^2+2\times10000\times401+401^2$.

7. 950625; 999375; greater.

8. (a) 1004004; (b) 9801; (c) 1·0816;
(d) 166464; (e) 628849; (f) 0·6241.

9. (a) 97800; (b) 999516; (c) 361500;
(d) 11·91; (e) 16970; (f) 1.

10. 151·4 cm².

a^2-b^2 involves two multiplications and one subtraction.

$(a-b)(a+b)$ involves an addition, a subtraction but only one multiplication.

11. 48 m, 5808 m, 288 m/s.

The average speed from time t_1 to time t_2 is

$$\frac{12t_2^2-12t_1^2}{t_2-t_1} = 12(t_2+t_1).$$

Questions 12 and 13 link the results of this section with vectors and matrices.

12. $\begin{pmatrix} a \\ b \end{pmatrix} (x\ y) = \begin{pmatrix} ax & ay \\ bx & by \end{pmatrix}.$

The pattern is identical with Figure 30.

148

13. (a) (i) $2a+b = (a\ b)\begin{pmatrix}2\\1\end{pmatrix}$, (ii) $3a+7b = (3\ 7)\begin{pmatrix}a\\b\end{pmatrix}$.

(b) $(a\ b)\begin{pmatrix}6 & 14\\3 & 7\end{pmatrix}\begin{pmatrix}a\\b\end{pmatrix} = (6a+3b \quad 14a+7b)\begin{pmatrix}a\\b\end{pmatrix}$
$$= 6a^2+17ab+7b^2.$$

The method is hardly easier, but the structure is identical.

(c) (i) $(p+3q)(5p-q) = (p\ q)\begin{pmatrix}5 & -1\\15 & -3\end{pmatrix}\begin{pmatrix}p\\q\end{pmatrix}$,

(ii) $(a+b)^2 = (a\ b)\begin{pmatrix}1 & 1\\1 & 1\end{pmatrix}\begin{pmatrix}a\\b\end{pmatrix}$.

Expressions such as $6a^2+17ab+7b^2$ and $(a+b)^2$ are sometimes called 'quadratic forms'. When writing them as matrix products, the 2×2 matrices are not necessarily unique; for example,

$$px^2+2qxy\times ry^2 = (x\ y)\begin{pmatrix}p & q+a\\q-a & r\end{pmatrix}\begin{pmatrix}x\\y\end{pmatrix},$$

where a may be chosen at random.

In this particular question, when removing the brackets and turning the forms into matrix products, it is significant that the 2×2 matrices involved have zero determinants. This links with the standard product-sum method of factorizing quadratic expressions. There will be a further consideration of quadratic form in a later book.

11

IDENTITY AND INVERSE

1. SETS

1.1 Universal sets

In all previous work on sets a universal set has been implicit because it is impossible to answer questions without having some universe in mind. $A \cap B$ denotes children born in August who came to school on a bicycle.

The curly letter $\mathscr{E}$ for the universal set may cause confusion with the normal capital, E (Example 1) and so pupils should be taught to write it in an exaggerated style. The fact that E (even numbers) takes different forms according to the nature of $\mathscr{E}$ is the point of Example 1 and needs emphasis.

$\mathscr{E} \supset A$ means '$\mathscr{E}$ contains A as a subset'.

1.2 Complementary sets

$G \cap G' = \emptyset$.

In Figure 1 the sets are complementary, hence $A \cap B = \emptyset$ and $A \cup B = \mathscr{E}$ (note this latter relation will still have to be explained verbally). In general, sets with no members in common are called *disjoint*. With interested pupils this is a useful word which could well be introduced. The two sets A and B are necessarily disjoint since they are complementary. It is not possible to tell which is which.

Exercise A (p. 181)

1. (a) $\{^-3, 1, 2, 3\}$;   (b) $\{^-3, ^-2, ^-1, 0\}$;   (c) $\{^-3, ^-2, 0, 1, 2, 3\}$.

2. $\{2, 6\}$.   3. $\{1, 2, 3, 7, 8\}$.

4. $\{1, 2, 3, 7, 8\}$, $\{1, 2, 3, 4, 5, 6, 7, 8\}$, {integers} etc.

5. $\emptyset$. This is a special case of a subset since $A = \mathscr{E}$. N.B. The set of all subsets of A includes A itself. Some writers use a special notation for a *proper* subset, that is, a subset other than the set

150

itself. They use the symbols $\subseteq$ and $\subset$ to distinguish between subsets and proper subsets. (Compare $<$ and $\leqslant$; less than, less than or equal to.)

6. K itself.

7. *Complement*: that which completes, *compliment*: polite expression of praise.

8. (a) $5 \notin A$; $5 \in A'$;   (b) square $\in A$; square $\notin A'$;
(c) mauve $\notin A$; mauve $\in A'$;
(d) $\pi \notin A$, $\pi \notin A'$, since $\pi \notin \mathscr{E}$;   (e) $> \in A$; $> \notin A'$.

9. (a) $\{\frac{1}{2}\} \subset \{$fraction numbers$\}$;
(b) $\frac{1}{2} \notin \{$integers$\}$;
(c) $\frac{1}{2} \in \{$numbers less than 1$\}$;
(d) $\{4, 5\} \subset \{3, 4, 5\}$.

10. $A = \{$even numbers$\}$, $B = \{$integers$\}$, $C = \{$fraction numbers$\}$ is a possible set. Alternatively the members may be enumerated, for example, $A = \{a, b\}$; $B = \{a, b, c\}$; $C = \{a, b, c, d\}$. It is always true that $A \subset C$.

11. $a \in A \cap B$.

12. No. If one lets $A = \emptyset$, then there is no element b of which one can write $b \in A$.

1.3 Union of sets

The only complication here is with the overlap. $A \cup B$ includes the set $A \cap B$, i.e. members of both A and B (see Question 6). Compare the symmetric difference which was mentioned in Book 2, p. 261, and comprises members that belong to A or B but not to both.

Exercise B (p. 183)

1. (a) $\{a, c\}$;   (b) $\{a, b, c, d, e\}$.

2. (a) $\{2, 4, 8\}$;   (b) $\{2, 4, 6, 8\}$; $E \supset Y$.

3. (a) $\{C, S, H, N\}$;   (b) $\{U, I, O, S, H, N\}$;
(c) $\{C, S, H, N, U\}$;   (d) $\{U, I, O, C\}$.

4. $\{$quadrilaterals$\}$.   (a) $S \subset T$;   (b) S;   (c) T.

5. {Austin cars}, {Ford cars}, {Rover cars}; or {two wheelers}, {three wheelers}, {four wheelers}, etc. No, if the union is empty each set must be empty. There is only one empty set!

6. Always.

7. (a) and (b) $P \subset Q$. ($P = \emptyset$ would be a special case of this); yes.

8. (a) { }, {A}, {B}, {C}, {A, B}, {B, C}, {C, A}, {A, B, C}.
    (b) (i) { } and {A}, i.e. 2;
        (ii) { }, {A}, {B}, {A, B}, i.e. 4;
        (iii) see part (a) a total of 8.

    The answers appear to belong to the sequence 2, 2^2, 2^3, ... We should guess $2^4 = 16$, which is correct. The sets are { }, {A}, {B}, {C}, {D}, {A, B}, {A, C}, {A, D}, {B, C}, {B, D}, {C, D}, {B, C, D}, {C, D, A}, {D, A, B}, {A, B, C}, {A, B, C, D}.

    If the whole set has n members, then each member can either be chosen or rejected for membership of each subset, i.e. dealt with in 2 ways. The total number of ways of dealing with the members is therefore 2^n.

9. (a) A;   (b) A;   (c) $\mathscr{E}$;   (d) A;
    (e) A;   (f) $\emptyset$;   (g) $\mathscr{E}$;   (h) $\emptyset$.

10. $L = M$;   (a) L;   (b) L, or both answers could be M.

11. (a) Always true;
    (b) sometimes true, when Q is empty;
    (c) meaningless;   (d) meaningless;
    (e) sometimes true, if $P = Q$.

12. (a) All canaries are singing birds.
    (b) All singing birds are canaries, or only canaries sing.
    (c) All canaries are birds that do not sing.
    (d) A singing bird is a well-fed canary and none other.
    (e) There are no well-fed singing birds that are not canaries.
    (f) $C \cap W \neq \emptyset$.   (g) $C \cap S \cap W' \neq \emptyset$.
    (h) $C \cap S' \subset W'$ or $C \cap S' \cap W = \emptyset$.

2. IDENTITY ELEMENTS

2.1 Closed sets

The subtraction $5-8$ will not do as it requires a negative number to answer it. She can use any addition.

The set of positive integers is closed under multiplication but not under division since the answers may be fractional.

2.2 Operation tables

All the operations of this section are *binary* operations, i.e. they combine pairs of elements and so require tables with rows and columns. (*a*) In fact E and O are being used to denote *classes* of numbers, but we do not recommend that any attempt be made to introduce this term. No difficulties will arise if E is read 'any even number', etc.

Any even number added to any odd number gives an odd answer, i.e. $E+O = O$. The set $\{E, O\}$ is closed under addition. The operation table is

+	E	O
E	E	O
O	O	E.

The operation tables for $\{0, 1\}$ are

(i) for addition
(put-down digit only)

+	0	1
0	0	1
1	1	0

(ii) for multiplication

×	0	1
0	0	0
1	0	1.

The set $\{0, 1\}$ is closed under multiplication. It is only closed under addition if the 'carry' digit is ignored; in fact $1+1 = 10$, in binary.

Table (i) resembles the table for the set $\{E, O\}$ under addition; table (ii) has a different pattern.

We should expect the multiplication table for $\{E, O\}$ to have the same pattern as the multiplication table for $\{0, 1\}$. Here it is:

×	E	O
E	E	E
O	E	O

and the agreement is perfect. Pupils left to themselves may give the operation tables in a different order. They should be shown that a change of order does not matter, for instance,

×	O	E
O	O	E
E	E	E

is plainly easily turned to the previous form. On the other hand

+	O	E
O	E	O
E	O	E

is still obviously different in having a different balance of symbols.

The order of members in the labelling row and column should be the same. This is merely a convention, but a useful one.

(b) The set $\{U, V, W\}$ is closed under addition.

+	U	V	W
U	U	V	W
V	V	W	U
W	W	U	V

+	0	1	2
0	0	1	2
1	1	2	0
2	2	0	1.

That the two tables are of the same pattern is easily seen. Technically the two structures are said to be *isomorphic*, but this word is not yet necessary and need not be used in class.

The multiplication tables are

×	U	V	W
U	U	U	U
V	U	V	W
W	U	W	V

×	0	1	2
0	0	0	0
1	0	1	2
2	0	2	1.

2.3 Identity

The identity element of the set $\{K, L, M\}$ under the operation o is M. The identity element for $\{E, O\}$ under multiplication is O. The identity element for $\{U, V, W\}$ under addition is U and under multiplication is V. Our experience with numbers does not lead us to expect the same identity element for differing operations, since (i) the additive identity is 0 and (ii) the multiplicative identity is 1. The identity element when transformations are combined is the stay-put transformation, **I**.

154

Exercise C (p. 187)

Much of the value of this chapter is in getting the idea of similarity of structure (i.e. pattern of tables). This involves comparing operation tables which need to be labelled and carefully retained.

1. (a) Yes.
   (b) Yes, provided $\frac{6}{1}$, etc., are considered to be fractions; and provided division by $\frac{0}{1}$ is not permitted.
   (c) Yes.

2. (a) Strictly no, for example, $5 \sim 5 = 0$ and 0 is not a positive integer although it does belong to {integers};
   (b) yes, 0 is a rational number;
   (c) no, for example, $9 \sim 4 = 5$ and $5 \notin$ {square numbers}.

3. {Q, H, T, I} is closed under the operation 'followed by'. The operation table is:

	Q	H	T	I
Q	H	T	I	Q
H	T	I	Q	H
T	I	Q	H	T
I	Q	H	T	I

Note that rotations commute under the given operation of combination. This means that the table is symmetrical about the leading diagonal and that we are spared the embarrassment of having to opt at this stage for some convention about displaying non-symmetrical combination tables of transformations. The normal convention is illustrated in the following table:

	X	Y	Z
X		Z	
Y	Y		
Z			

These entries indicate $XY = Z$ and $YX = Y$. That is, the row is given by the element *written* first and the column by the element *written* second *regardless* of the order in which the transformations are applied; here, for example, 'first Y and then X' gives Z.

This difficulty is best avoided for the moment.

4. No; since, for example, $\{1, 2\} \cap \{2, 3\} = \{2\} \notin \{\{1, 2\}, \{2, 3\}, \{3, 1\}\}$.

5. (*a*) Addition or subtraction;   (*b*) multiplication.

6. *F* is commutative. There are many sets; an example is $\{2, 6, 10\}$. One way of generating them is to select a highest common factor (in this case 2) and then ensure that the other factors of the members are co-prime. A further example is

$$\{3, 6, 9, 15, 21, 33, \ldots\},$$

i.e. $\{3 \times 1, 3 \times 2, 3 \times 3, 3 \times 5, 3 \times 7, 3 \times 11, \ldots\}$

(the other factors are the primes).

7. **I** can be thought of as a rotation through 0°, 360°, etc. The set **I, P, Q** is closed under 'followed by'. The operation table is

	I	P	Q
I	I	P	Q
P	P	Q	I
Q	Q	I	P

The identity element is **I**.

The structure is isomorphic to $\{U, V, W\}$ under addition.

8.

⊕	Cottage	Palace	Mansion	Pigsty
Cottage	Palace	Mansion	Pigsty	Cottage
Palace	Mansion	Pigsty	Cottage	Palace
Mansion	Pigsty	Cottage	Palace	Mansion
Pigsty	Cottage	Palace	Mansion	Pigsty

The identity element is pigsty. The structure is isomorphic to that in Question 3.

9.

+	0	1	2	3
0	0	1	2	3
1	1	2	3	0
2	2	3	0	1
3	3	0	1	2

The identity element is 0.

×	0	1	2	3
0	0	0	0	0
1	0	1	2	3
2	0	2	0	2
3	0	3	2	1

The identity element is 1.

The rearrangement of the addition table puts the identity elements in the same place and is as follows:

+	1	2	3	0
1	2	3	0	1
2	3	0	1	2
3	0	1	2	3
0	1	2	3	0

This now shows that the structure is isomorphic to that in Question 8. Some care must be exercised in rearranging tables. The first temptation is merely to interchange two rows or columns, but both rows and columns have to be interchanged so that the alteration in pattern is more complex. In practice the new table has to be ruled up and each entry either re-computed or read from the old table.

10. Using **LR** to denote '**R** followed by **L**', we see that **LR** = **B**; yes.

	I	R	L	B
I	I	R	L	B
R	R	I	B	L
L	L	B	I	R
B	B	L	R	I

No. In this table only the identity element appears in the leading diagonal (all elements are self-inverse), a feature of none of the others.

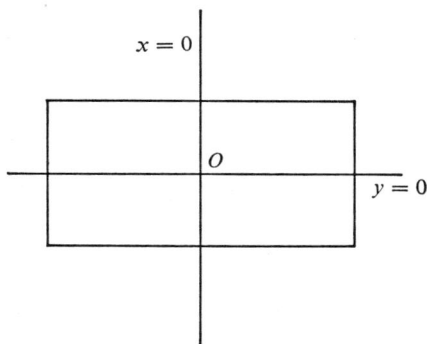

Fig. A

11. See Figure A. If **H** denotes a rotation of 180° about O, **X** denotes reflection in $x = 0$ and **Y** denotes reflection in $y = 0$, the combination table is:

157

	I	X	Y	H
I	I	X	Y	H
X	X	I	H	Y
Y	Y	H	I	X
H	H	Y	X	I

The pattern is the same as the table in Question 10, i.e. the structures are isomorphic.

12.

∩	ø	A	B	P
ø	ø	ø	ø	ø
A	ø	A	ø	A
B	ø	ø	B	B
P	ø	A	B	P

∪	ø	A	B	P
ø	ø	A	B	P
A	A	A	P	P
B	B	P	B	P
P	P	P	P	P

The identity element is *P*.   The identity element is ø.

Re-arranging

∪	P	B	A	ø
P	P	P	P	P
B	P	B	P	B
A	P	P	A	A
ø	P	B	A	ø

The tables for ∩ and ∪ are now seen to possess the same pattern and become identical if $P \to ø$ and $A \to B$, $B \to A$, $ø \to P$.

13. (*a*) The idea of a substructure is implicit in part (i) of this question. Some teachers may prefer to start by producing the entire multiplication table for the set {0, 1, 2, 3, 4, 5} mod 6.

×	0	1	2	3	4	5
0	0	0	0	0	0	0
1	0	1	2	3	4	5
2	0	2	4	0	2	4
3	0	3	0	3	0	3
4	0	4	2	0	4	2
5	0	5	4	3	2	1

(i) The structure for the subset {1, 5} can then be picked out as shown. It is

×	1	5
1	1	5
5	5	1

The identity element is 1.

(ii) Similarly we get

×	0	2	4
0	0	0	0
2	0	4	2
4	0	2	4

The identity element is 4.

(b)

(i)
×	1	2	3	4
1	1	2	3	4
2	2	4	1	3
3	3	1	4	2
4	4	3	2	1

(ii)
×	1	3	7	9
1	1	3	7	9
3	3	9	1	7
7	7	1	9	3
9	9	7	3	1

(iii)
+	0	1	2	3
0	0	1	2	3
1	1	2	3	0
2	2	3	0	1
3	3	0	1	2

In part (iii) re-arrange in the order 0, 1, 3, 2.

14. Yes. That each operation considered so far, as applied to the elements selected, is commutative. (As mentioned in the note on Question 3, transformations do not commute in all cases.)

−	0	1	2	3
0	0	3	2	1
1	1	0	3	2
2	2	1	0	3
3	3	2	1	0

The set is closed under subtraction. The operation − is non-commutative and so the line of symmetry cannot be present. There is no identity element since, although 0 acts as the identity when taken second (i.e. $3-0 = 3$, etc.), it does not serve in the same way when taken first (i.e. $0-3 \neq 3$).

3. INVERSE ELEMENTS

This is a straightforward idea and pupils should have no difficulty in picking inverse pairs from the tables they have constructed in the previous section. It should be pointed out that any element commutes with its inverse (as defined). Since all the tables we have considered have been for commutative operations, this property has not been properly displayed.

(*a*) 0 is self-inverse. The inverse of **A** (**A**⁻¹) is the transformation which combines with **A** to give the identity transformation. Reflection in a line; half-turn.

(*b*) The identity element is 1; 0 and 2 have no inverse; 1 and 3 are self-inverse.

(*c*)

×	1	2	3	4	(mod 5)
1	1	2	3	4	
2	2	4	1	3	
3	3	1	4	2	
4	4	3	2	1	

The identity element is 1; every element has an inverse; 1 and 4 are self-inverse.

(*d*) The additive inverse of 5 is ⁻5, the multiplicative inverse of 5 is $\frac{1}{5}$.

Exercise D (*p. 191*)

1.

+	U	V	W
U	U	V	W
V	V	W	U
W	W	U	V

(*a*) *U*;　(*b*) *U, W, V*;　(*c*) *U*.

2. (*a*) There is no identity element.
(*b*) By definition none of 0, 1 or 2 can have an inverse since there is no identity.

3. *A* and *B* do not form an inverse pair. Since 'inverse of' is a symmetrical relation (i.e. if *A* is the inverse of *B*, then *B* is the inverse of *A*) it follows that neither of the statements is true. It is not possible, by definition, for one to be true without the other.

4.

×	1	2	3	(mod 4)
1	1	2	3	
2	2	0	2	
3	3	2	1	

(*a*) No;　(*b*) 1;　(*c*) none of them;　(*d*) 1 and 3 are self-inverse.

160

5.

∩	∅	A	B	P
∅	∅	∅	∅	∅
A	∅	A	∅	A
B	∅	∅	B	B
P	∅	A	B	P

(a) Only P has an inverse, P;   (b) P.

Exercise E (p. 192)

Miscellaneous

1. (a)

×	1	2	(mod 3)
1	1	2	
2	2	1	

(b)

×	1	2	3	(mod 4)
1	1	2	3	
2	2	0	2	
3	3	2	1	

(c)

×	1	2	3	4	(mod 5)
1	1	2	3	4	
2	2	4	1	3	
3	3	1	4	2	
4	4	3	2	1	

(d)

×	1	2	3	4	5	(mod 6)
1	1	2	3	4	5	
2	2	4	0	2	4	
3	3	0	3	0	3	
4	4	2	0	4	2	
5	5	4	3	2	1	

(e)

×	1	2	3	4	5	6	(mod 7)
1	1	2	3	4	5	6	
2	2	4	6	1	3	5	
3	3	6	2	5	1	4	
4	4	1	5	2	6	3	
5	5	3	1	6	4	2	
6	6	5	4	3	2	1	

Some elements have no inverse in the cases mod 4 and mod 6. It is fairly easy to see, though less easy to set down in a few words, that a necessary and sufficient condition for every element to have an inverse is that the modulus should be prime.

2.

÷	Second number			
First number	1	2	3	4 (mod 5)
1	1	3	2	4
2	2	1	4	3
3	3	4	1	2
4	4	2	3	1

The demonstrates again the importance of following a fixed convention when constructing a table for a non-commutative operation: $a * b$ is always found by looking in *row a* and *column b*.

	Second number			
$\div$	1	2	3	(mod 4)
First number $\begin{cases}1\\2\\3\end{cases}$	1 2 3	. 1 or 3 .	3 2 1	

You find that $1 \div 2$ and $3 \div 2$ do not exist and $2 \div 2$ has two possible answers. The operation of division is not uniquely defined on this set.

3. See Figure B.

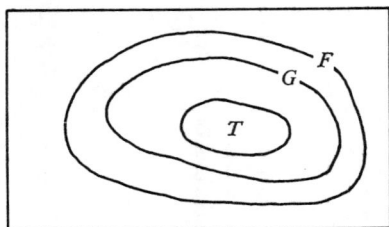 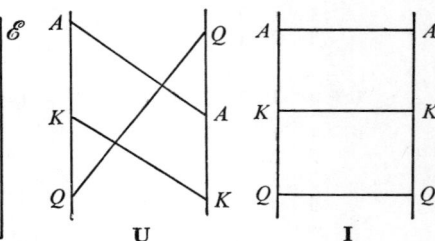 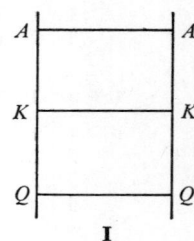

Fig. B	Fig. C	Fig. D

4. There are 6 different arrangements.

M means that the top and bottom cards are interchanged, **N** that the top two cards are interchanged.

The illustration of **U** is shown in Figure C.

The permutation **V** means that each card is moved up one, the top-most being replaced at the bottom.

There is one more permutation, this is the stay-put permutation which we shall, of course, call **I**. It is shown in Figure D.

The operation table is

	Second permutation					
	L	**M**	**N**	**U**	**V**	**I**
First permutation $\begin{cases}\mathbf{L}\\\mathbf{M}\\\mathbf{N}\\\mathbf{U}\\\mathbf{V}\\\mathbf{I}\end{cases}$	I U V M N L	V I U N L M	U V I L M N	N L M V I U	M N L I U V	L M N U V I

(a) **L, M, N, I**;
(b) **(L, M), (M, N), (N, L), (U, L), (U, M), (U, N), (V, L), (V, M) (V, N)**;
(c) **(U, V)**.

5. (i) Arithmetic mod 5.
   (a) 1, 4;   (b) no solution;   (c) 2, 3;   (d) 3.
   (ii) Arithmetic mod 6.
   (a) 1, 5;   (b) 3;   (c) 2, 4;   (d) 2.

6.

Δ	ø	A	B	P
ø	ø	A	B	P
A	A	ø	P	B
B	B	P	ø	A
P	P	B	A	ø

The identity is ø, each element is self-inverse.

7. (a) 3, $\frac{1}{3}$; only these two;   (b) 3, ⁻2; only these two;
   (c) they are self-inverse;
   (d) $\frac{3}{2}$, $\frac{2}{3}$, $\frac{1}{3}$, 3; we are back at the starting value, the sequence then continues ⁻2, ⁻$\frac{1}{2}$, $\frac{3}{2}$, $\frac{2}{3}$, $\frac{1}{3}$, 3, ⁻2, etc.;
   (e) $\frac{2}{3}$, $\frac{3}{2}$, ⁻$\frac{1}{2}$, ⁻2, 3; the same values as before, and again the sequence continues through the same values (but in reverse order);
   (f) there are just the six different answers possible, hence there can only be six different functions and a 6 × 6 table will suffice;
   (g) the table can be presented in two ways, either

Function performed second

	I	f	g	fg	gf	gfg
I	I	f	g	fg	gf	gfg
f	f	I	gf	gfg	g	fg
g	g	fg	I	f	gfg	gf
fg	fg	g	gfg	gf	I	f
gf	gf	gfg	f	I	fg	g
gfg	gfg	gf	fg	g	f	I

Function performed first

or

Function written second

	I	f	g	fg	gf	gfg
I	I	f	g	fg	gf	gfg
f	f	I	fg	g	gfg	gf
g	g	gf	I	gfg	f	fg
fg	fg	gfg	f	gf	I	g
gf	gf	g	gfg	I	fg	f
gfg	gfg	fg	gf	f	g	I

Function written first

163

Although, as previously remarked, the second of these presentations is more usual (and easier to use), it is not worth while attempting to establish a convention at this stage.

8. $\frac{1}{3}$; $x \to \frac{1}{3}x$; 2; $x \to 2x$.
   (*a*) 2;   (*b*) 3;   (*c*) 4;   (*d*) 2.

9. A binary operation on the set S can be thought of as a function from $S \times S$ to S. That is, the function maps every ordered pair (a, b) where a and b belong to S onto a third element $c \in S$. The domain of the function is, therefore $\{(a, b): a \in S, b \in S\}$ and the range is S (or a subset of S).

12

SHEARING

The purpose of the work in this chapter is twofold. First, the visual image of the shearing of a pile of books, or cards, gives the pupil a dynamic insight into certain aspects of area and volume, for example, the area of parallelograms and the volume of prisms. Secondly, using matrices to describe the shearing transformation enables us to extend the work begun in Chapter 2 on matrices and transformations; in particular, using the invariance of area under shearing as a starting point, an opportunity is afforded of introducing the determinant of the general 2×2 matrix as the area scale factor of a transformation. The word 'determinant' is avoided but will be introduced when the inverse of a matrix is discussed in Book 4.

One important point that must be stressed at this stage is that shearing as defined in this chapter also preserves straightness, that is a shear maps a straight line onto a straight line. Question 1 of Exercise C draws particular attention to this point. Area is still invariant if the sides of the pile are curves but the transformation, though akin to a shear, is not one. Similarly, volume is still preserved if the edges of the transformed cuboid in Figure 26 are curved.

Invariance is one of the keynotes of the development; in particular, a great deal of attention is focused on the invariant line of the transformation. A concise summary of shearing is given on p. 201 of the text. In addition the following properties are invariant:

(i) parallelism;

(ii) ratios of segments *along* a line.

It is important to note that the invariant line is pointwise invariant. All lines parallel to the invariant line are also in a sense invariant since the shear maps each line onto itself. In the latter case, however, individual points are not mapped onto themselves (see Question 14 of Exercise A).

Shearing has its applications in the world of art and in biology. Figure A is based on the drawings of the German artist Dürer. The same coordinates are used in both drawings. *On Growth and Form*, by D'Arcy Thompson, has many biological examples of shearing and other transformations. Very ordinary fish, for example, become strange, exciting, but none the less real, fish.

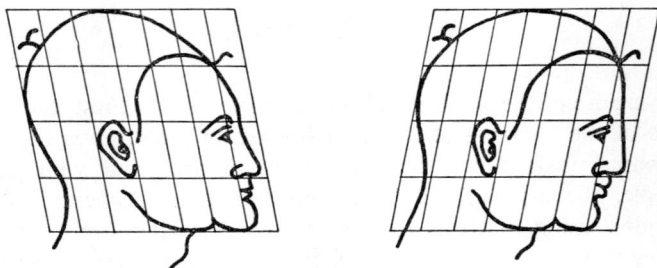

Fig. A

For those who wish to delve deeper into the nature of the shearing transformation, there is an interesting development of its properties in the *Teacher's Guide to Book T*, pp. 26–31. However, quite a number of the points covered there are mentioned in this commentary in the relevant places.

A shear can also be seen as a particular, or degenerate, case of the affine transformation known as a perspective affinity or axial stretching. For a fascinating study of these transformations see *Transformation Geometry*, by Max Jeger.

Historically, shearing belongs to the pre-calculus days of mathematics and two mathematicians who made considerable use of it are Archimedes 287–212 B.C. and Cavalieri, 1598–1647.

1. THE SHEARING TRANSFORMATION

(*a*) The transformation is first illustrated with reference to a pile of books. The transformed profile in Figure 1 (*b*) is not strictly a parallelogram because of the 'stepped' sides, but in the pack of cards in Figure 2 this difference, though still present, is no longer apparent to the eye. Note that in Figures 1 and 2 the pile in its original and sheared form have been drawn separately for clarity; in either case the bottom book, or card, has not been moved and corresponds to the invariant line.

166

It is, of course, possible to think of the two figures as the actual positions of the top part of a pile of which the lower part is not shown; the invariant line would then be lower down the page where corresponding edges of the original and sheared piles meet. (See Section 1.1(*b*) below.)

1.1 The triangular tessellation is once again found to provide a useful starting point for the investigation of a transformation.

(*a*) $RQVW \rightarrow KQVR$ with the line QV invariant,

$RQVW \rightarrow SRVW$ with the line VW invariant.

There are, of course, an unlimited number of possibilities if the tessellation is regarded as infinite.

(*b*) This is an important stage in the development. The invariant line does not necessarily have to coincide with one of the sides of the figure being transformed

$$LSRK \rightarrow JPNH \text{ with the line } BA \text{ invariant.}$$

(*c*) J is an invariant point and HK the invariant line. It may be helpful to consider triangle EFJ as part of parallelogram $EFKJ$ which is sheared into parallelogram $DEKJ$.

(*d*) This considers the problem of what happens when the invariant line passes through the figure. Points on opposite sides of the invariant line move in opposite directions.

The invariant line of the shear mapping $BFUP$ onto $LSPH$ is JQ.

(*e*) (i) $RSXW$, (ii) $BFJD$.

Exercise A (p. 197)

Questions 1 and 2 are based on the property of shearing that each point moves a distance proportional to its distance from the invariant line.

1. (*a*) 2 cm; (*b*) 4 cm. **2.** 4·5 cm.

With a generous use of colours, all the results of Questions 3–10 can be indicated on one figure. Only some of the results are shown in Figure B.

3. Two shears: $ABFE \rightarrow ABED \rightarrow AEJD$.

See Figure B, intermediate position shaded.

(*a*) three shears: $ABFE \rightarrow ABED \rightarrow ZAED \rightarrow DAEJ$,

(*b*) four shears: $ABFE \rightarrow EBFK \rightarrow JEFK \rightarrow JDEK \rightarrow JDAE$.

Other variations are possible Note that these mappings are not point-for-point equivalent. In the case of two shears A was invariant; in (*a*) $A \rightarrow D$ and in (*b*) $A \rightarrow J$.

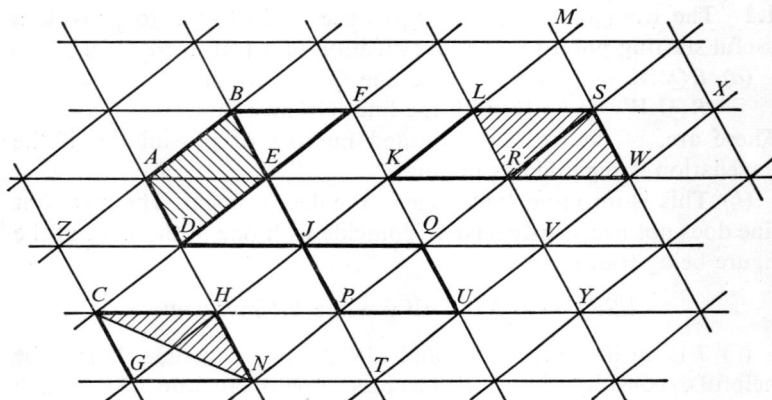

Fig. B

4. (*a*) $CHG \rightarrow CHN \rightarrow GHN$.

See Figure B, intermediate position shaded.

(*b*) $LRW \rightarrow SRW \rightarrow SRU \rightarrow RQU$.

Other possibilities in both cases.

5. $HPTN \rightarrow HQVP$ with HJ invariant.

$ \rightarrow JQUP$ with PQ invariant.

Alternatively, $HPTN \rightarrow KQTP \rightarrow JQUP$.

Any translation can be considered as equivalent to two shears with invariant lines parallel to the direction of the translation.

6. (*a*) $LSRK \rightarrow LSWR \rightarrow JQUP$.

See Figure B, intermediate position shaded.

$LSRK \rightarrow FLRK \rightarrow JQUP$.

(*b*) $LSRK \rightarrow LSWR$

$ \rightarrow UPJQ$ (half-turn about the mid-point of QR).

168

See Figure B, intermediate position shaded.

$LSRK \rightarrow FLRK$

$\quad\quad \rightarrow UPJQ$ (half-turn about the mid-point of KQ).

Note that the intermediate positions in (a) and (b) are the same but that the mappings are not point-for-point equivalent.

7. (a) QR; (b) FJ.

8. (a) $AFLE$; (b) EPY.

9. $EFKJ, KRQJ, JKQP, EKJD, RWVQ, \ldots$
All are parallelograms.

Parallelism is invariant under shearing.

10. For two shears to be equivalent to a single shear the invariant lines must be parallel or coincident.

Questions 11–13 take up again the property mentioned in connection with Questions 1 and 2.

11. $x = 0 \rightarrow y = \tfrac{1}{2}x$; $(0, 3) \rightarrow (6, 3)$.

12. $(0, 0) \rightarrow (0, 0)$, $(0, 1) \rightarrow (0, 1)$, $(1, 0) \rightarrow (1, 1)$, $(1, 1) \rightarrow (1, 2)$;
a parallelogram;

$(2, 2) \rightarrow (2, 4)$, $(3, 1) \rightarrow (3, 4)$, $(0, 4) \rightarrow (0, 4)$, $(^-1, 2) \rightarrow (^-1, 1)$, $(^-1, ^-1) \rightarrow (^-1, ^-2)$.

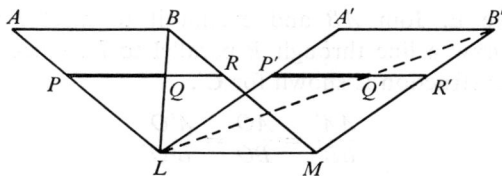

Fig. C

13. We must either assume that, under a shear, points move distances proportional to their distance from the invariant line and deduce the invariance of straight lines, or vice versa. For example, in Figure D,

$$\frac{AA'}{BB'} = \frac{OA}{OB} \text{ is an assumed}$$

property of shearing and from properties of enlargement we can deduce that $OA'B'$ is a straight line.

In Figure C we show that if P' lies on LA', then Q' must lie on LB' (where $A'B' = AB$ and $P'Q' = PQ$).

The same enlargement brings triangle LPQ to LAB and LPP' to LAA' (from shearing properties), so $\dfrac{LA'}{LP'} = \dfrac{LA}{LP} = \dfrac{AB}{PQ} = \dfrac{A'B'}{P'Q'}$. The argument of the previous page then shows that $LQ'B'$ is a straight line.

14. This has been referred to in the introductory remarks. Lines parallel to the invariant line are not point-wise invariant. Every point of the invariant line is mapped onto itself.

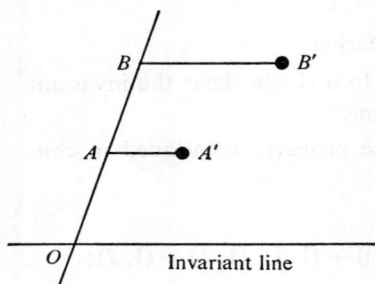

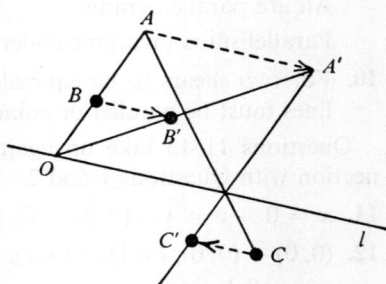

Invariant line

Fig. D

Fig. E

1.2 Shearing constructions

See Figure E. Join AB and extend it to meet l at O. O is invariant. Draw a line through B parallel to l to meet OA' at B'. A similar construction is shown for C'.

$$\frac{AA'}{BB'} = \frac{AO}{BO} = \frac{A'O}{B'O}.$$

Exercise B (p. 200)

1. See Figure F.

2. See Figure G. Construction lines are shown dotted. The arms of the 'A' are first extended to cut l. These points are then joined to V'. The remaining construction lines are drawn parallel to l.

3. VV' must be parallel to the invariant line. But the invariant line and VV' could be changed in direction relative to the letter A. See Figure H. Note again the use of the special points on the invariant line.

170

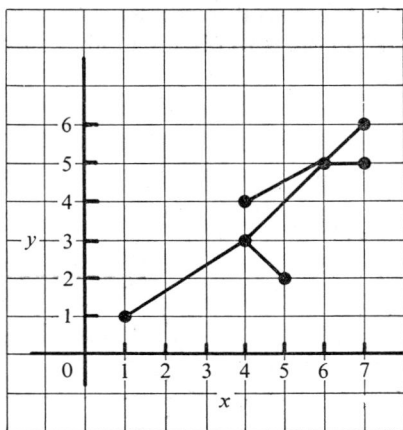

Fig. F

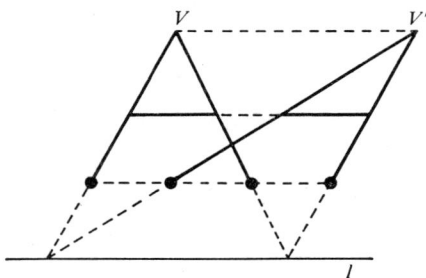

Fig. G

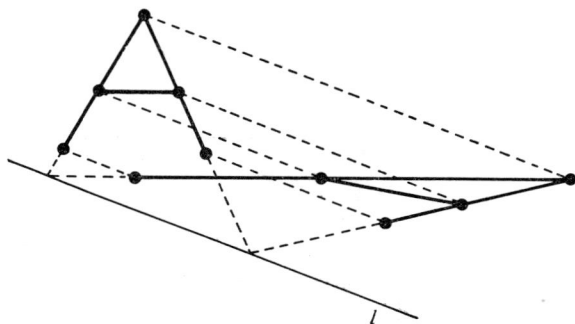

Fig. H

171

4. See Figure I. In this case it is necessary to join the ends of the arms of the '*W*' in order to obtain another special point on *l*.

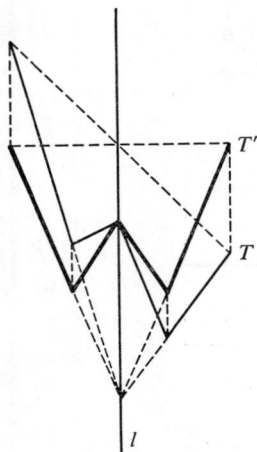

Fig. I

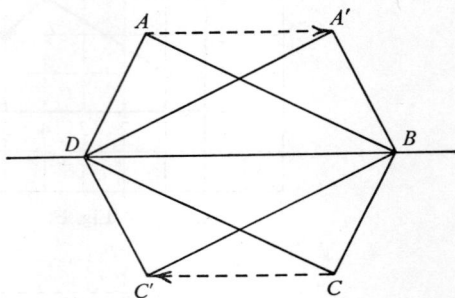

Fig. J

5. $ABCD \to A'BC'D$ with BD invariant (see Figure J).

6. See Figure K. Sheared circle is an ellipse with two lines of symmetry (OP' is not a line of symmetry).

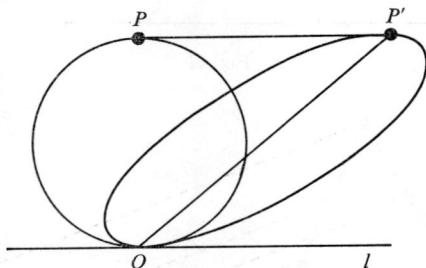

Fig. K

7. See Figure A.

8. This and Question 9 are more searching questions. See Figure L. When $P \to P'$ with *l* invariant, $A \to A'$; but for $P' \to P''$ with *m* invariant $A' \to A$. *A* is then a point fixed under the combination of shears, which is equivalent to a single shear with *n* invariant.

172

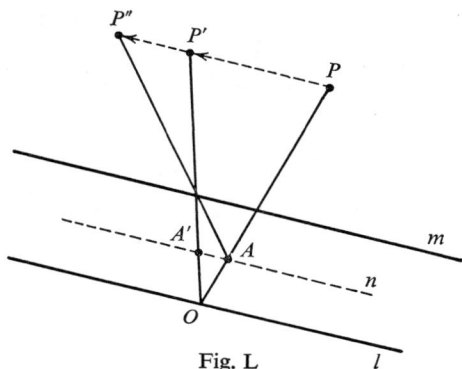

Fig. L

9. The two shears commute. Figure M illustrates the two shears combined in the opposite order. For $P \rightarrow P'$ with m invariant, $A \rightarrow A'$, and for $P' \rightarrow P''$ with l invariant, $A' \rightarrow A$. From the similarities of Figures L and M we can see that n is in the same position in each figure.

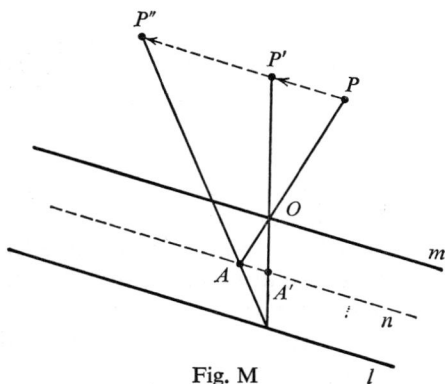

Fig. M

The results of Questions 8 and 9 demonstrate the similarity of shears to other transformations as far as their combination is concerned. Compare the result that the combination of two shears with invariant lines parallel is equivalent to a single shear, with the results

(i) the combination of two translations is equivalent to a single translation, and

(ii) the combination of two rotations is (apart from special cases) equivalent to a single rotation.

To see how reflection fits into this pattern we can introduce the idea of an 'oblique reflection'. In Figure N (i), A' is the image of A under oblique reflection in the line OX; $AM = MA'$ and AA' is parallel to a given line l.

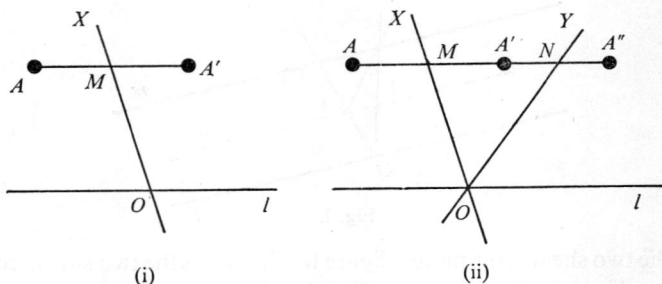

Fig. N

Figure N (ii) shows the combination of two oblique reflections and it is not difficult to see that these are equivalent to a shear.

$$AA'' = 2MN,$$

and therefore the distance moved by A is dependent only on its distance from l.

Thus the combination of two oblique reflections is a shear whose invariant line (l) passes through the intersection (O) of the two 'mirrors' (OX and OY) and is parallel to the direction of the reflection. This result compares closely with:

(i) the combination of two reflections in parallel mirrors is a translation through twice the distance between the mirrors and in a direction perpendicular to them;

(ii) the combination of two reflections in intersecting mirrors is a rotation about the point of intersection of the mirrors and through twice the angle between them.

If the two oblique reflections in Figure N (ii) are combined in the reverse order, then the direction of the shear is reversed.

2. AREA

The working model in Figure 12 can be usefully contrasted with the deformation of a Meccano parallelogram (mentioned in the chapter on Area in Book 1) which is, of course, not a shear.

174

This is the second time that the formulae for the area of a parallelogram and triangle have been stated. The concept of area should be now firmly established. Further work on areas, in connection with graphs, will be found in Book 5.

Exercise C (p. 203)

1. The area is equivalent to a rectangle 30 cm long and 7·5 cm wide (225 cm²).

   The transformation is not a shear as straight lines are not preserved; see, for example, the sides of the pile. However, like shearing, it preserves area and is a particular case of 'Cavalieri's Principle'.

2. Distances between sides are 8·10 and 10·8 cm; area is 97·2 cm². The mean of these values is likely to be the best estimate.

3. 20·7 cm². (Heights are 6·89, 5·90, 4·13 cm.)

4. 29·2 cm².   5. 67·7 cm².   6. 108 cm².

7. $x = 5$; rectangles are 10 cm × 2 cm and 4 cm × 5 cm.

8. $bp = cq$.

3. PYTHAGORAS'S THEOREM

This is just a brief mention of a topic dealt with at length in Book 2, Chapter 14.

An interesting method of building up Figure O by rotating the right-angled triangle BXV about the centre of square $BVST$ was given in Book 2 (p. 272).

$$AVWU \to AVSR \quad \text{with } AV \text{ invariant,}$$
$$ABCD \to ABTR \quad \text{with } AB \text{ invariant.}$$

Shearing $AVSR$ and $ABTR$ together, with VS and BT invariant respectively, we get square $BVST$.

To demonstrate that $BVST$ is a square we can use the method referred to above. For example, from the manner in which the figure was drawn it is clear that triangles VWS and SRT are congruent. We can map triangle VWS onto SRT by a rotation about the centre of the square $CRWX$; as VW is perpendicular to SR it follows, from the result that all lines rotate through the same angle, that $\angle VST = 90°$ and so on.

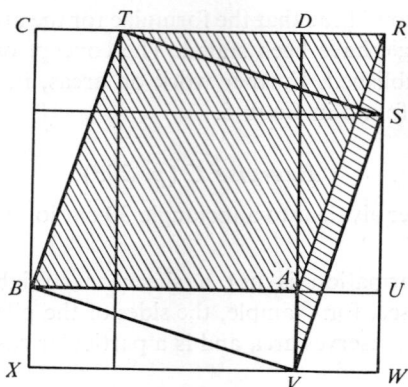

Fig. O

We have now shown that

> area of square $ABCD$ + area of square $AVWU$
> = area of square $BVST$,

that is, $x^2 + y^2 = z^2$.

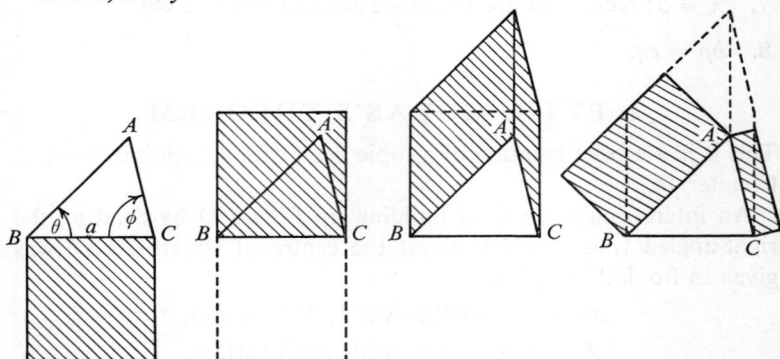

Fig. P

Figure P shows how a similar sequence of transformations can be applied to the square on the side BC of any triangle ABC. At each stage the previous stage is shown dotted.

The area of the two rectangles in the final figure is equal to the area of the square in the first figure.

It can easily be verified that the widths of the two rectangles are $a \cos \theta$ and $a \cos \phi$.

176

4. THE SHEARING MATRIX

This section explores the geometrical work covered in Section 1 in the context of matrices. We confine our attention to 2×2 matrices. Under these, $(0, 0)$ is an invariant point; all the possible shears we can investigate will, as a consequence, have their invariant lines through $(0, 0)$.

First of all, we consider shears with $y = 0$ and $x = 0$ as the invariant lines. This is done by finding what the elements of the matrix must be in order to map the unit square, for example, onto some given parallelogram. Then in Exercise D we deal also with matrices that describe other shears having lines through $(0, 0)$ invariant.

It is useful for the teacher to know what form a 2×2 matrix has to take in order to describe a shear.

The matrix can be conveniently written

$$\begin{pmatrix} 1+p & q \\ -p^2/q & 1-p \end{pmatrix} \quad (q \neq 0),$$

and the invariant line of the shear is $px+qy = 0$.

This result is obtained by considering the general matrix

$$\begin{pmatrix} a & b \\ c & d \end{pmatrix}.$$

For a shear the determinant is equal to 1 (see Section 5), that is $ad-bc = 1$.

Now let us suppose that a point (x, y) is invariant. Then

$$\begin{pmatrix} a & b \\ c & d \end{pmatrix} \begin{pmatrix} x \\ y \end{pmatrix} = \begin{pmatrix} x \\ y \end{pmatrix}$$

$$\Leftrightarrow \quad \begin{pmatrix} ax+by \\ cx+dy \end{pmatrix} = \begin{pmatrix} x \\ y \end{pmatrix}$$

$$\Leftrightarrow \quad \begin{matrix} (a-1)\,x+by = 0 \\ cx+(d-1)\,y = 0 \end{matrix} \Big\}.$$

The trivial solution of these equations is

$$x = y = 0,$$

but under a shear all the points of a line (the invariant line) are fixed and so these equations have non-trivial solutions.

Therefore, $$\frac{a-1}{c} = \frac{b}{d-1}.$$

This simplifies to $ad - bc + 1 = a + d$.

This combined with $ad - bc = 1$ gives two simple conditions that the matrix
$$\begin{pmatrix} a & b \\ c & d \end{pmatrix}$$

must obey:
$$ad - bc = 1,$$
$$a + d = 2.$$

The form of matrix already given can be deduced from these equations. The corresponding case in which $ad - bc = {}^{-}1$, $a + d = 0$ gives the matrix for an oblique reflection. (See p. 174.)

(a) In Figure 17 the invariant line is $y = 0$. As is stressed in the text, it is important to think in terms of the whole plane being mapped and to remember that the diagram shows only a representative section.

(b) $\begin{pmatrix} 1 & 0 \\ 2 & 1 \end{pmatrix} \begin{pmatrix} 0 & 1 & 1 & 0 \\ 0 & 0 & 1 & 1 \end{pmatrix}$
$$= \begin{pmatrix} 0 & 1 & 1 & 0 \\ 0 & 2 & 3 & 1 \end{pmatrix}.$$

See Figure Q.

$x = 0$ is invariant.

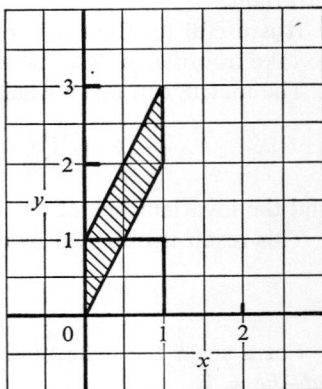

Fig. Q

Exercise D (p. 206)

1. See Figure R. Images shaded.

2. See Figure S. Image shaded. Object is a rhombus; image is a parallelogram.

   Area of rhombus is easily seen to be 4 units. Area of image is therefore also 4 units, as may be verified by enclosing the figure in a rectangle with sides parallel to $x = 0$ and $y = 0$.

3. For right-hand parallelogram
$$\begin{pmatrix} 1 & \frac{1}{2} \\ 0 & 1 \end{pmatrix}; \quad \text{left-hand} \quad \begin{pmatrix} 1 & {}^{-}2 \\ 0 & 1 \end{pmatrix}.$$

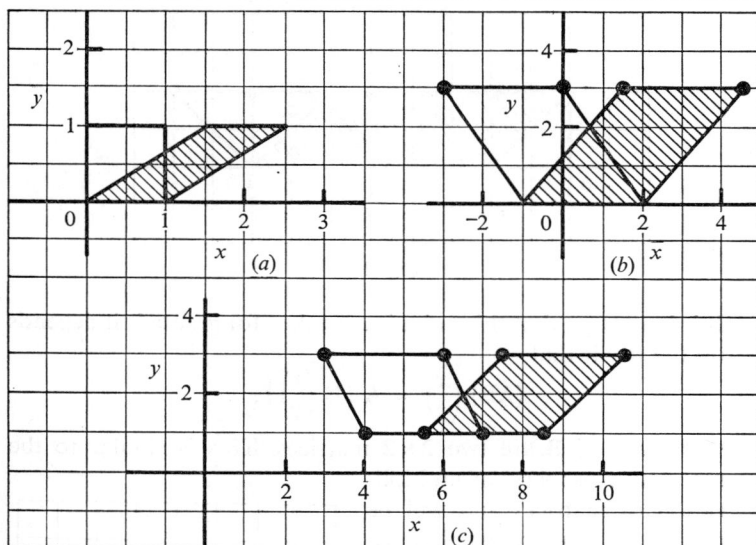

Fig. R

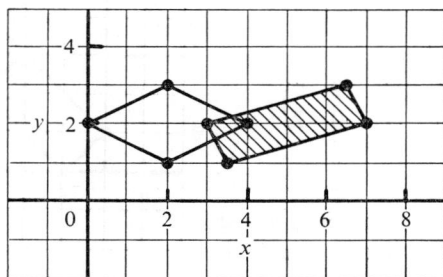

Fig. S

4. See Figure T. Rectangle dotted. First image in full outline. Second image shaded. The mapping of the rectangle onto the shaded parallelogram is described by

$$\begin{pmatrix} 1 & -1 \\ 0 & 1 \end{pmatrix}.$$

This can be derived from the product of

$$\begin{pmatrix} 1 & 1 \\ 0 & 1 \end{pmatrix} \text{ and } \begin{pmatrix} 1 & -2 \\ 0 & 1 \end{pmatrix}$$

in either order.

179

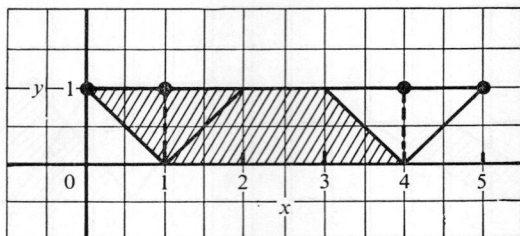

Fig. T

It is important that this point is not taken for granted; it depends on the result that

$$\textbf{(AB)} \begin{pmatrix} x \\ y \end{pmatrix} = \textbf{A} \left(\textbf{B} \begin{pmatrix} x \\ y \end{pmatrix} \right),$$

where **A** and **B** are two 2×2 matrices. This is similar to the associative property of multiplication of matrices and will be considered in more detail later.

5. $\begin{pmatrix} 1 & 0 \\ 2 & 1 \end{pmatrix}$.

6. See Figure U.

$$\begin{pmatrix} \frac{1}{2} & \frac{1}{2} \\ -\frac{1}{2} & \frac{3}{2} \end{pmatrix} \begin{pmatrix} -1 & -3 & -2 & 0 \\ 3 & 1 & 0 & 2 \end{pmatrix}$$
$$= \begin{pmatrix} 1 & -1 & -1 & 1 \\ 5 & 3 & 1 & 3 \end{pmatrix}.$$

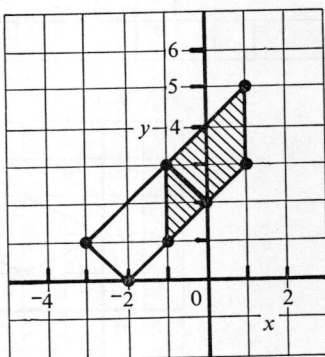

Fig. U

The transformation is a shear with invariant line $y = x$. This can be most easily found by considering where the sides of the parallelogram meet the corresponding sides of the rectangle, that is at $(-1, -1)$ and $(1, 1)$.

7. See Figure V.

$$\begin{pmatrix} 0 \cdot 6 & 0 \cdot 8 \\ -0 \cdot 2 & 1 \cdot 4 \end{pmatrix} \begin{pmatrix} 0 & 5 & 5 & 0 \\ 0 & 0 & 5 & 5 \end{pmatrix} = \begin{pmatrix} 0 & 3 & 7 & 4 \\ 0 & -1 & 6 & 7 \end{pmatrix}.$$

O and A are fixed points for the shear, A being where a side of the square intersects its image.

Invariant line is $y = \frac{1}{2}x$, shown dotted.

180

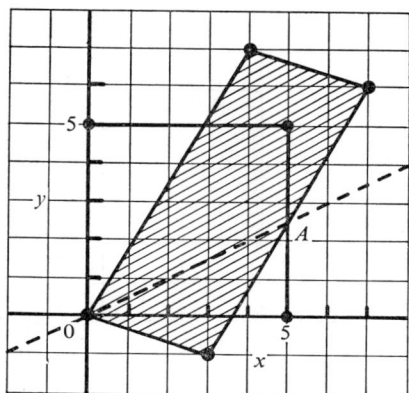

Fig. V

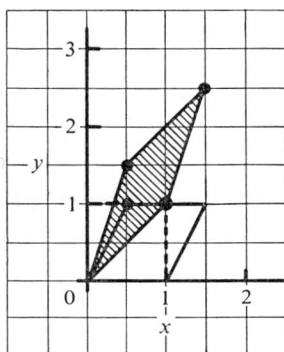

Fig. W

8. $\begin{pmatrix} 3 & 2 \\ -2 & -1 \end{pmatrix} \begin{pmatrix} 1 & 1 & -1 & -1 \\ 1 & -1 & -1 & 1 \end{pmatrix} = \begin{pmatrix} 5 & 1 & -5 & -1 \\ -3 & -1 & 3 & 1 \end{pmatrix}.$

Thus $(1, {}^{-}1)$ and $({}^{-}1, 1)$ are fixed points and the invariant line is $y = {}^{-}x$, or $x + y = 0$.

9. See Figure W. First image in outline and second shaded. The result is not a shear, and in this case the transformations do not commute.

Two shears described by 2×2 matrices are only equivalent to a single shear if the invariant lines coincide. This can be demonstrated by using the form of matrix mentioned at the beginning of this section. If the two matrices

$$\begin{pmatrix} 1+p & q \\ -p^2/q & 1-p \end{pmatrix} \text{ and } \begin{pmatrix} 1+r & s \\ -r^2/s & 1-r \end{pmatrix}$$

combine to give one of similar form, then $p/q = r/s$ which implies that the invariant lines $px + qy = 0$ and $rx + sy = 0$ coincide.

Questions 10–15 are on 'stretching' matrices.

10. See Figure X.

(a) $x = 0$ invariant. Lines parallel to $y = 0$ are also invariant but not pointwise.

(b) $y = 0$ invariant. Lines parallel to $x = 0$ are also invariant but not pointwise.

181

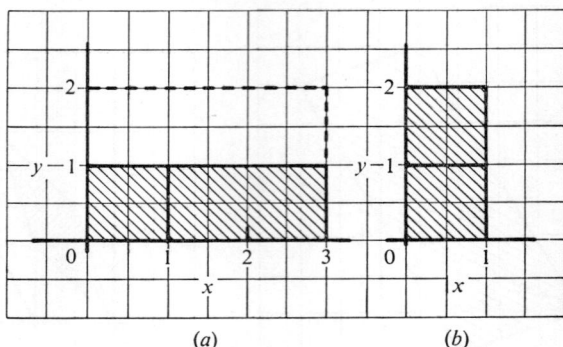

(a)   (b)

Fig. X

11. See Figure Y.

Invariant diameter AB.

12. See Figure X(a), dotted rectangle with vertices $(0, 0)$, $(3, 0)$, $(3, 2)$ and $(0, 2)$. Order does not matter:

$$\begin{pmatrix} 3 & 0 \\ 0 & 2 \end{pmatrix}.$$

Two 'two-way stretches' are equivalent to one two-way stretch

$$\begin{pmatrix} p & 0 \\ 0 & q \end{pmatrix} \begin{pmatrix} r & 0 \\ 0 & s \end{pmatrix} = \begin{pmatrix} pr & 0 \\ 0 & qs \end{pmatrix}.$$

An enlargement.

13. (a) $\begin{pmatrix} 2 & 0 \\ 0 & 2 \end{pmatrix}$, (b) $\begin{pmatrix} -1\frac{1}{2} & 0 \\ 0 & -1\frac{1}{2} \end{pmatrix}.$

14. $y = x$ is the invariant line.

If the matrix is $\begin{pmatrix} a & b \\ c & d \end{pmatrix}$,

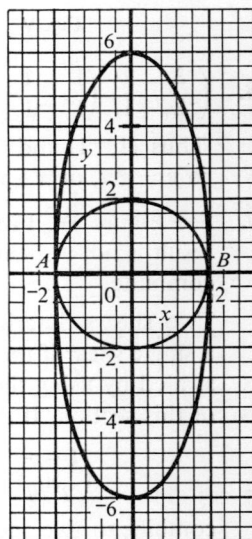

Fig. Y

then $\begin{pmatrix} a & b \\ c & d \end{pmatrix} \begin{pmatrix} 1 \\ 1 \end{pmatrix} = \begin{pmatrix} 1 \\ 1 \end{pmatrix}$ and $\begin{pmatrix} a & b \\ c & d \end{pmatrix} \begin{pmatrix} 1 \\ -1 \end{pmatrix} = \begin{pmatrix} 2 \\ -2 \end{pmatrix}.$

From these we deduce the required matrix

$$\begin{pmatrix} 1\frac{1}{2} & -\frac{1}{2} \\ -\frac{1}{2} & 1\frac{1}{2} \end{pmatrix}.$$

182

5. AREA AND MATRICES

We now move on to have a first look at the general affine transformation with (0, 0) as an invariant point. The first paragraph of
the section draws attention to the way in which our study of transformations is developing; the number of invariant properties is being
'eroded' away.

One can categorize different geometries by their invariant properties and by the transformations that leave these properties
invariant:

> demanding that lengths be preserved we obtain the geometry of
>   congruencies, sometimes called isometries;
> demanding that angles be preserved we obtain the geometry of
>   similarities;
> demanding that parallels be preserved we obtain affine geometry;
>   and so on.

Under rotations, reflections and translations, the invariants are
shape, length and area. Neither enlargement nor shearing preserves
length but the former preserves shape and the latter area. The general
affine transformation preserves none of these three properties but the
following, mentioned in connection with shearing, are still preserved:

(i) parallelism,
(ii) straightness,
(iii) ratios along straight lines.

An interesting and novel approach to the general affine transformation is found in *A Path to Modern Mathematics*, by W. W.
Sawyer.

Transformations in which (0, 0) is not invariant are described by
a mapping of the form

$$\begin{pmatrix} x \\ y \end{pmatrix} \rightarrow \begin{pmatrix} a & b \\ c & d \end{pmatrix} \begin{pmatrix} x \\ y \end{pmatrix} + \begin{pmatrix} p \\ q \end{pmatrix}.$$

This can be expressed alternatively by

$$\begin{pmatrix} x \\ y \\ 1 \end{pmatrix} \rightarrow \begin{pmatrix} a & b & p \\ c & d & q \\ 0 & 0 & 1 \end{pmatrix} \begin{pmatrix} x \\ y \\ 1 \end{pmatrix}.$$

Transformations of this kind will be considered at a later stage.

The primary purpose of this section is to induce a familiarity with the determinant of a 2×2 matrix by considering it as an area scale factor.

(a)

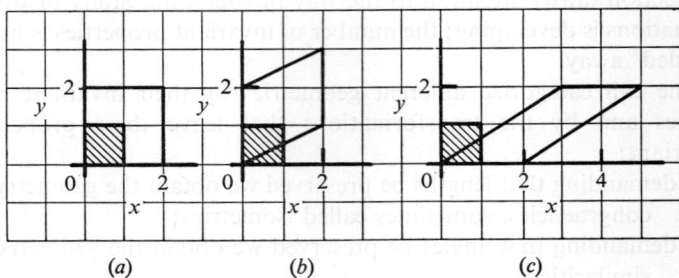

Fig. Z

Each image in Figure Z has an area of four units.

(b) Areas of the images in Figure AA are 9, 6, 5 and 5 units.

(c) The area scale factor '$ad - bc$' is now apparent. Pupils need very little prompting to spot the pattern.

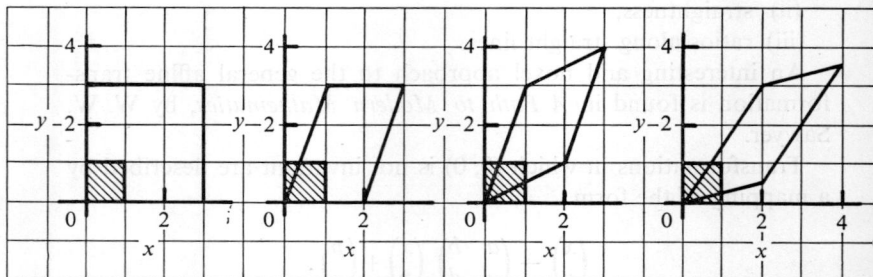

Fig. AA

Exercise E (p. 210)

1. See Figure BB.

   Areas (a) 8, (b) 10, (c) 12.

184

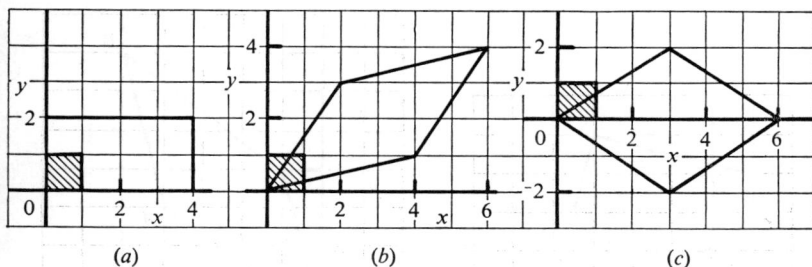

(a)   (b)   (c)

Fig. BB

2. A popular example showing the overall effect of the transformation. See Figure CC.

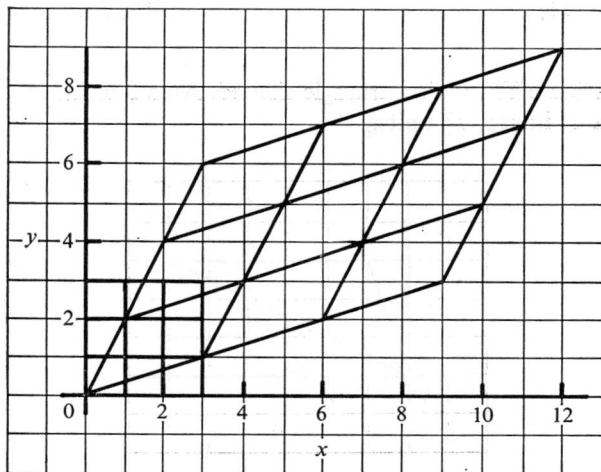

Fig. CC

3. Similar to Question 2.

4. See Figure DD. Image a square, area 17 units (using '$ad-bc$'). Length of side $\sqrt{17}$. In this transformation shape is preserved; it can be regarded as a combination of an enlargement and a rotation (a *spiral-similarity*).

5. See Figure EE. Area 13 units. $OA = CB = 5$ units. Distance between OA and BC, 2·6 units.

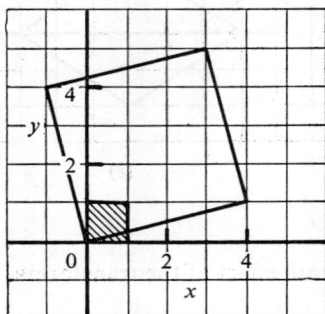

Fig. DD

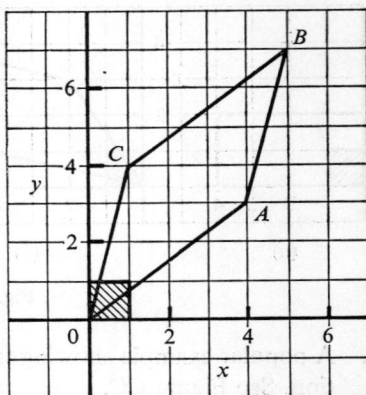

Fig. EE

6. See Figure FF. Object triangle shaded. Area 3 units.
    Area of image, $7\frac{1}{2}$ units.

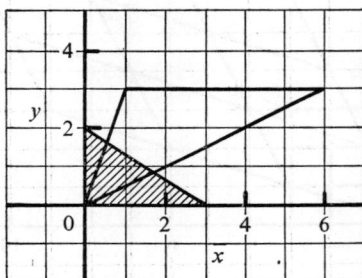

Fig. FF

7. $$\begin{pmatrix} 0.3 & -0.1 \\ 0.1 & 0.3 \end{pmatrix} \begin{pmatrix} 4 & 10 & 11 & 5 \\ 2 & 0 & 3 & 5 \end{pmatrix} = \begin{pmatrix} 1 & 3 & 3 & 1 \\ 1 & 1 & 2 & 2 \end{pmatrix}.$$

    See Figure GG. Image shaded. Area of image 2 units.
    Area scale factor

    $$(0.3 \times 0.3) - (-0.1 \times 0.1) = 0.1.$$

    Area of object 20 units.

186

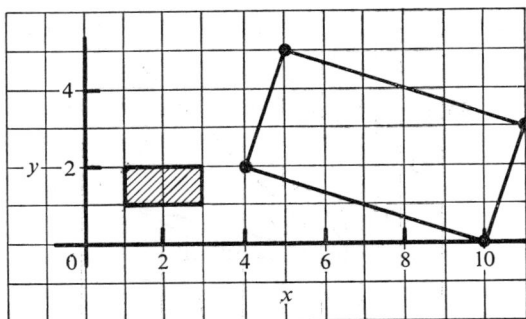

Fig. GG

8. (a) $\begin{pmatrix} h & 0 \\ 0 & h \end{pmatrix}$, area scale factor h^2,

(b) $\begin{pmatrix} h & 0 \\ 0 & k \end{pmatrix}$, area scale factor hk.

9. Coordinates of A' given by the first column of the matrix and of C' by the second column of the matrix.

$$\begin{pmatrix} 4 & 2 \\ 1 & 5 \end{pmatrix}.$$

10. (a) $(h+u, k+v)$; $\begin{pmatrix} h & u \\ k & v \end{pmatrix}$; $(hv-uk)$ units.

(b) (i) $15\frac{1}{2}$ units, (ii) $5\frac{1}{2}$ units, (iii) $9\frac{1}{2}$ units.

This question is based on the expression $\frac{1}{2}(x_1 y_2 - x_2 y_1)$ for the area of a triangle with vertices $(0, 0)$, (x_1, y_1) and (x_2, y_2). Here it is found by seeing that the area of the triangle is half that of the parallelogram.

11. See Figure HH. The effect of interchanging the rows of the matrix is to produce a mirror image in $y = x$.

Area is 2 units in each case. The negative sign appears because the sense of the figure is changed under the transformation; while $OABC$ is an anticlockwise movement round the unit square, $OA''B''C''$ is clockwise round the image. The result of interchanging the columns may also be investigated. Here the image is unaltered but its sense is reversed.

12. $\begin{pmatrix} a & b \\ c & d \end{pmatrix} \begin{pmatrix} 0 \\ 0 \end{pmatrix} = \begin{pmatrix} 0 \\ 0 \end{pmatrix}.$

13-2

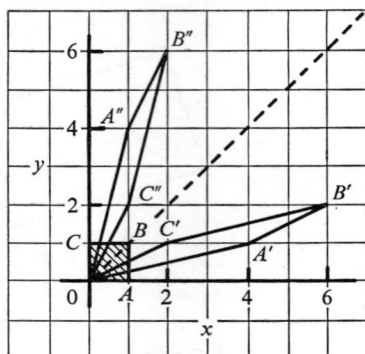

Fig. HH

6. SHEARING IN THREE DIMENSIONS

We now return to the purely geometric aspects of shearing, this time to extend the work in Book 2 on volume. As with area, the volume concept should now be firmly established.

This section can conveniently be taken separately from the remainder of the chapter.

In Figure 24, faces *ABCD*, *EFGH*, *BGHA*, and *CFED* are rectangles. Other faces are parallelograms. In Figure 26, *ABCD* and *EFGH* are rectangles. A cut parallel to these faces would result in a rectangle.

6.2 (*a*) This and the corresponding model outlined in Question 2 of Exercise F are very illuminating and each pupil should make one.

(*b*) *ABML*, *BCNM* and *ACNL* are parallelograms.

Triangles *ABL* and *MBL* are half of parallelogram *ABML*. Tetrahedra *ABCL* and *LMNC* have equal bases (triangles *ABC* and *LMN*) and equal heights since *ABC* and *LMN* are in parallel planes. This implies that their volumes are equal.

Exercise F (p. 216)

1. The tetrahedra *ABFC* and *AEFC* have equal bases *ABF* and *AEF*, and the same height *BC*. Tetrahedra *ABFC* and *ADCE* have equal bases *ABC* and *ADC*, and equal heights *BF* and *AE*. The three tetrahedra therefore have equal volumes. The pieces of cake may be auctioned at the conclusion of this example!

188

2. The volume of each is $\frac{1}{3} \times (3 \times 6 \times 9)$ cm³
$$= 54 \text{ cm}^3.$$

3. If the six pyramids are folded outwards leaving a cubical space inside, the resulting solid is a rhombic dodecahedron (see Book 2, p. 193).

4. 288.

With the 12, 5 and 3 cm edges along the 36, 60 and 54 cm edges of the box respectively.

5. $\frac{1}{3}$ m.   **6.** 24200 cm³.

7. 27·5 m³.   **8.** $6·87 \times 10^5$ l.

9. $3·32 \times 10^4$ cm³; 5200 cm³.

10. (*a*) 32·3 cm²;   (*b*) 149·3 cm³.

11. 13·86 cm³.   **12.** 10·3 cm³.   **13.** 3·64 cm.

14. (*a*) 99·2 cm²;   (*b*) 5·62 cm.

REVISION EXERCISES

SLIDE RULE SESSION NO. 5 (p. 219)
(See note on p. 57.)

1. 80·85; 80·8(5) ± 0·15.   **2.** 145·9; 145·9 ± 0·3.

3. 89·11; 89·1 ± 0·3.   **4.** 491·3; 491 ± 1.

5. 18·88; 18·88 ± 0·03.   **6.** 7·424; 7·42 ± 0·02.

7. 0·3958; 0·396 ± 0·001.   **8.** 7·867; 7·87 ± 0·002.

9. 1·7 (exact); 1·700 ± 0·003.   **10.** 0·018 44; 0·018 44 ± 0·000 03.

SLIDE RULE SESSION NO. 6 (p. 219)
(See note on p. 57.)

1. 7·162; 7·16 ± 0·02.   **2.** 273·9; 274 ± 1.

3. 6·968; 6·97 ± 0·02.   **4.** 22·91; 22·9 ± 0·1.

5. 24·28; 24·3 ± 0·1.   **6.** 1·003; 1·00 ± 0·02.

7. 7·239; 7·24 ± 0·04.   **8.** 156·1; 156·1 ± 0·4.

9. 0·527 (exact); 0·527 ± 0·001.

10. $2·8 \times 10^{10}$ (exact); $(2·8 ± 0·01) \times 10^{10}$.

M (p. 219)

1. $\frac{1}{2}$.   **2.** 45°.   **3.** $m = 5$.

4. $k = {}^{-}1$.   **5.** $^{-}2$.   **6.** 29.   **7.** ø.

8. $\mathscr{E}$.   **9.** $c = 9/T^2$.   **10.** $x = 11$.

N (p. 219)

1. 8 sq. units.   **2.** 2, 4·47, 4 units.   **3.** The inside of a square.

4. No. $x = 1 \Rightarrow x^2 = 1$, but $x^2 = 1 \Leftrightarrow x = 1$ or $^{-}1$.

5. The circle.   **6.** No.   **7.** $1\frac{1}{6}$.

8. $2x^2 - x + 7$.   **9.** 17_8.   **10.** 6 cm².

O (p. 220)

1. The angle of ascent must be greater than 5·7°.

Clearance is about 19 m.   **2.** About 4.00 a.m., 8.00 a.m.

3. $g^{-1}:x \to 2(x-1);\quad g^{-1}g^{-1}(2) = 2.$

$gg:x \to \frac{1}{4}(6+x);\quad gg(x) = 101 \Leftrightarrow x = 398$

4. (a) $^-2 < x < {}^-1;$ (b) $^-2 \leqslant x \leqslant 1;$

5.

×	P	Q
P	P	Q
Q	Q	P

P is the identity element.

6. $(X \cap Y') \cap Z.$

7. (a) $\{11, 13, 17, 19\};$ (b) $\{12, 15, 18\};$
(c) $\{16, 17, 18, 19\};$ (d) $\{11, 15\}.$
e.g. $A = \{10, 11, 12, 13, 14, 15\},\quad B = \{16, 17, 18, 19\}.$

8. (a) $v = 7t+1;$ (b) 8:64, i.e. 1:8; (c) 1:2.

P (p. 221)

1. $\sin A = \dfrac{-12}{13}.$

3. $X^2 = \begin{pmatrix} 1 & 2 \\ 0 & 1 \end{pmatrix},\quad Y^2 = \begin{pmatrix} 1 & 0 \\ 2 & 1 \end{pmatrix},\quad XY = \begin{pmatrix} 2 & 1 \\ 1 & 1 \end{pmatrix},\quad YX = \begin{pmatrix} 1 & 1 \\ 1 & 2 \end{pmatrix}.$

4. (a) $\{b_1, b_2, b_3\},\ \{b_2, b_3, b_4\},\ \{b_3, b_4, b_1\}\ \{b_4, b_1, b_2\};$
$\{g_1, g_2\},\ \{g_2, g_3\},\ \{g_3, g_1\}.$

(b) The probability that Bryan is not chosen is $\frac{1}{4}$; the probability that Grace is not chosen is $\frac{1}{3}$. The probability that neither is chosen is $\frac{1}{12}$.

The probability is $\frac{1}{2}$ that Bryan and Basil will both be chosen; it is $\frac{1}{3}$ that Gloria and Grace will both be chosen. The probability that all four are chosen is $\frac{1}{6}$.

5. $15+20 \cos 30° + 50 \cos 35° = 73$ kilometres.

6. On the pie chart each boy is represented by a $10°$ sector.

7. $x = 4$, so 11 suspects can be crossed from the list.

8. (a) $2x+3y \leqslant 25.$
(b) $x = 2, y = 7;\ x = 5, y = 5;\ x = 8, y = 3;\ x = 11, y = 1.$
(c) 24p.

Q (p. 221)

1. (a) 12·6 cm; (b) 8·4 cm.

2. £88; £32 less.

3. (a) No; (b) $x < {}^-4$; (c) $x > {}^-4\frac{1}{2}$;

5. 7.   6. (a) 4 times; (b) 8 times.

7. $(3 \cos \theta°, 3 \sin \theta°)$.

θ:	30	45	60	90	120	135	180
x:	2·60	2·12	1·5	0	${}^-1\cdot5$	${}^-2\cdot12$	${}^-3$
y:	1·5	2·12	2·60	3	2·60	2·12	0

8. (e) $n = 2^{\frac{1}{2}t}$.

R (p. 222)

1. (a) $\mathscr{E}$; (b) ø; (c) ø.

2. (c) About $(0\cdot15, {}^-2\cdot2)$.

3. 90p size is best buy, followed by 60p size.

4. The images can be mapped onto one another by rotations about the vertices of the triangle.

5. Course $198\frac{1}{2}°$; 63 min.

6. (a) $\angle XAB$; (b) $\angle XQB$; (c) $\angle XQP$.

   If the book were not opened at right-angles, (c) would still be correct.

7.

	Greatest	Least
$n(A \cup B)$	900	500
$n(A \cap B)$	400	0

   If $n(A \cap C) = 200$, then $200 \leqslant n(C) \leqslant 700$.

8. Not more than 53 m. At least 10 m more cable will be required.

13

STATISTICS

The chapter on Statistics in Book 2 was concerned mainly with displaying information by means of bar charts, pie charts, pictograms and frequency diagrams.

In this chapter frequency diagrams are discussed in greater depth, and the information they contain is summarized by giving two statistics: (i) a measure of position (an 'average'), (ii) a measure of spread.

Statistics at this level should be a *practical* activity. As far as possible the examples used should refer to the class or be collected by them; some ideas are given in the text—heights, ages, shoe sizes, sentence lengths; other ideas can be based on the particular interests of the class, who will be keen to make suggestions. A couple of lessons spent collecting data will repay themselves in providing material that can be used throughout the chapter.

1. MISREPRESENTATION

This section is intended to revise some of the ideas met in the Book 2 chapter on statistics. It is important that students should become critical of the statistical advertisements with which they are bombarded on television and in newspapers; the ability to discriminate between informative and misleading uses of statistics is of more value than the ability to find the mean from a grouped frequency table.

Many misleading representations are due to the lack of a scale or a misplaced origin.

(*a*) No scale.

(*b*) Figure A shows the exaggeration caused by a misplaced origin.

(*c*) The misleading features of the Doggo advert are: (i) there is no scale (it is possible to *compare* the contents of Doggo with those of shin beef, but there is no mention of absolute values); (ii) the Doggo contents are in heavy black which gives a stronger visual impression than the light grey of the shin beef contents.

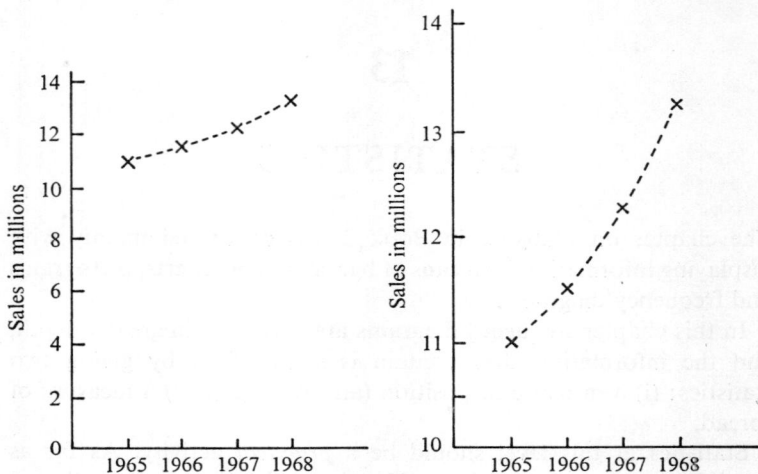

Fig. A

(d) The area property of pictograms is often mis-used. Although the heights are in the ratio 1:2, the areas are in the ratio 1:4. Three-dimensional money bags would introduce even greater distortion.

(e) It cannot be claimed that a non-linear scale is dishonest: the point here is that one can easily fail to notice it. A scale of this type is often used in economic applications where percentage changes are involved. The phrase 'logarithmic scale' need not be used, but the scale should be compared with that on a slide-rule: for example, the distance between £100 and £200 is the same as the distance between £200 and £400.

(f) Extrapolation is not always justified. Teams change when the players leave school and one cannot have more than 100% success!

It is a useful idea for the class to make collections of misleading statistical representations and display them on the classroom wall.

On the positive side it is worth making a collection of good, informative examples (see, for example, *The Times*, *Financial Times* and *Guardian*).

Further material can be found in:

> *Facts from Figures*, Moroney,
> *Use and Abuse of Statistics*, Reichmann,
> *How to Lie with Statistics*, Huff.

194

2. FREQUENCY FUNCTIONS

The term frequency *function* rather than frequency distribution is used in this chapter. The idea of a function has been met frequently and here we have an example of a non-algebraic function.

Suppose that in a test the marks of ten children are Anne 8, Barbara 9, Colin 6, Donald 7, Elizabeth 9, Frank 5, Geoff 7, Harold 10, Ian 8, Jean 8.

This describes a function that maps a set of people onto the set of numbers {5, 6, 7, 8, 9, 10}.

Note that the collection of numbers 8, 9, 6, 7, 9, 5, 7, 10, 8, 8 is *not* a set, because it contains repetitions; it is called the *population*.

It is possible to form another function from this information by mapping the elements of the population onto the number of times each element occurs. This is the frequency function (Figure B).

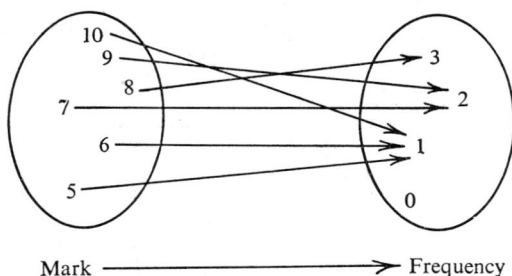

Fig. B

The frequency function can be represented by a graph as in Figure C.

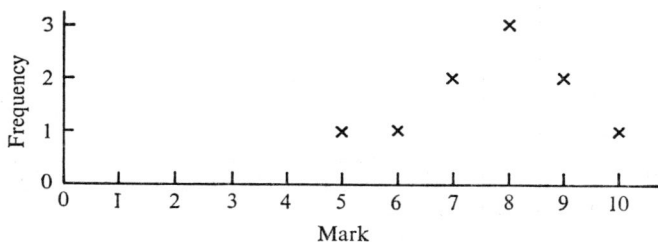

Fig. C

195

Usually, however, a column graph is used (Figure D).

This improves the visual effect and also introduces an idea which will be taken up later, namely the area property of the columns.

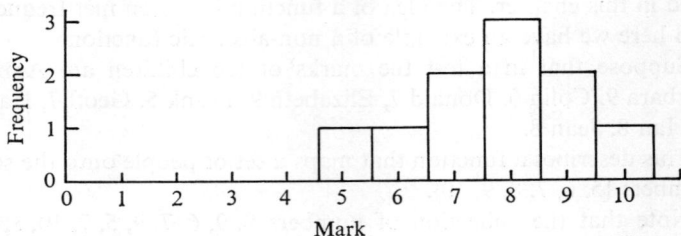

Fig. D

Note that a column graph is not a *histogram*. The term histogram is reserved for a frequency *density* diagram: to illustrate the difference consider the following example.

The table below gives the frequency of sentence lengths from a book using a random sample of 27 sentences:

Number of words	Frequency
1–10	2
11–20	5
21–30	9
31–40	6
41–50	3
51–90	1
91–130	1

The graph is shown in Figure E.

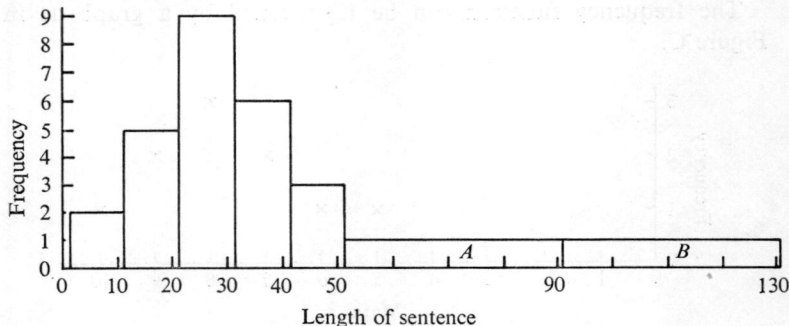

Fig. E

196

The removal of the bar at $90\frac{1}{2}$ would completely alter the representation: rectangle A indicates that there is one sentence of length between $50\frac{1}{2}$ and $90\frac{1}{2}$, rectangle B indicates that there is one sentence of length between $90\frac{1}{2}$ and $130\frac{1}{2}$. The combined rectangle without the bar would mean that there is *one* sentence of length between $50\frac{1}{2}$ and $130\frac{1}{2}$—and this is false.

This difficulty can be overcome by representing the frequency by the *area* of the rectangle, and not by the height. This gives the histogram in Figure F.

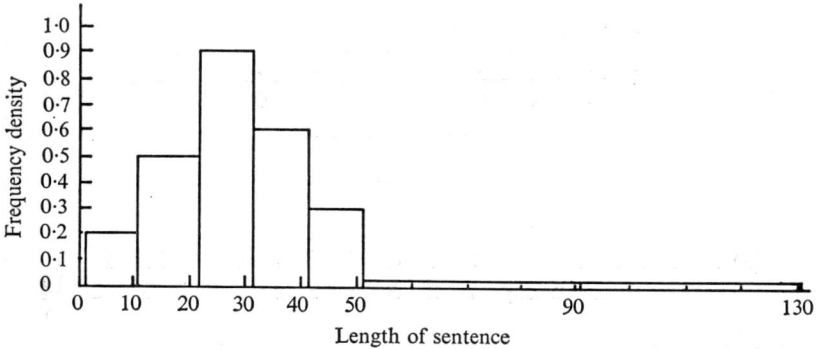

Fig. F

The scale up the page shows the frequency density.

Frequency = frequency density × length of interval. This corresponds to line density in physics where, for example, the mass of a length of a rod is given by

mass in kg = density in kg per m × length of rod in m.

Thus it is the area of the columns of a histogram that gives the frequency, while for a graph like Figure E it is the height.

If the lengths of the intervals are equal, then the frequency diagram and the histogram differ only in scales. If the lengths of the intervals vary, the graphs will have different shapes.

(*a*) The graph of this function (Figure G) has an early peak and a tail (it is called positively skew). Functions of this type are common —the frequency of scores in football matches is another example.

197

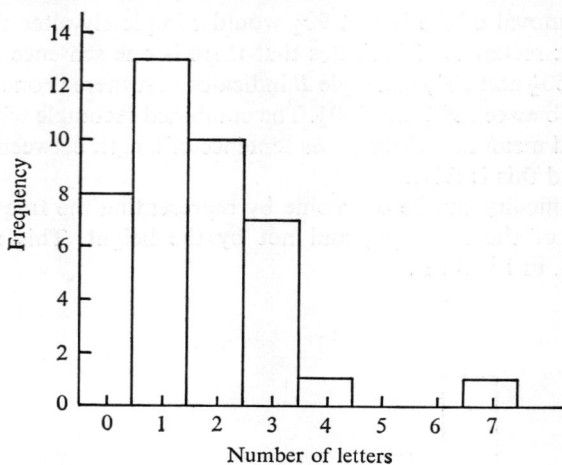

Fig. G

(b)

Possible scores	2	3	4	5	6	7	8	9	10	11	12
Expected frequency	1	2	3	4	5	6	5	4	3	2	1

See Figure H.

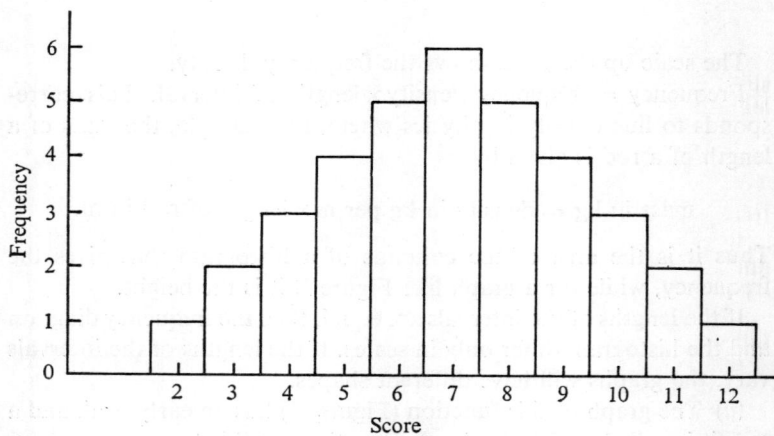

Fig. H

198

Pulse rates	Tally marks	Frequency
50 - 54	I	1
55 - 59	IIII	4
60 - 64	LHT I	6
65 - 69	LHT LHT	10
70 - 74	LHT LHT LHT III	18
75 - 79	LHT IIII	9
80 - 84	LHT II	7
85 - 89	III	3
90 - 94	II	2
	Total	60

See Figure I.

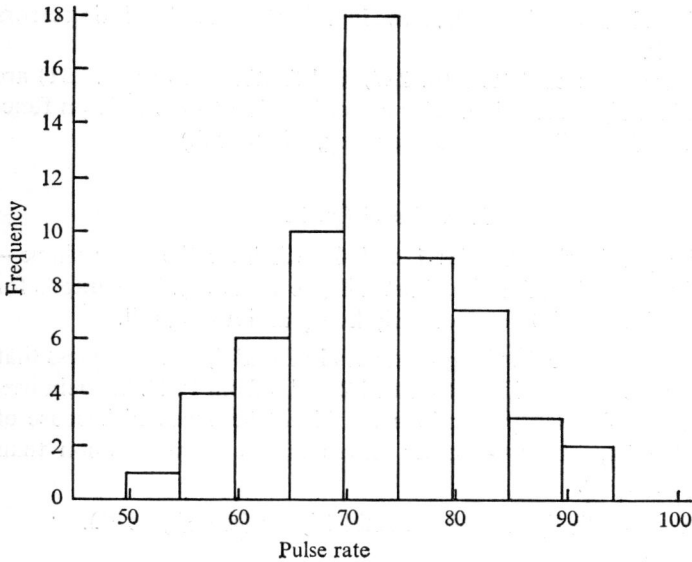

Fig. I

2.3. Normal frequency functions

The Normal function is often called the error function: it arose originally in errors in astronomical observations. It is common in a situation of this type where the population is equally distributed on each side of the mean. It is important in sampling: the means calculated from random samples tend to be Normally distributed even though the original population from which the samples are taken is not Normal.

The Normal frequency function is an example of a mathematical model: it gives a first approximation to many situations.

Another common mathematical model is the Poisson function which has an early hump and a short tail.

It is used to describe the distribution of rare events, for example, organisms in a blood sample, flaws in a sheet of metal, printing errors in a book.

The examples on letters (p. 227) and football scores (p. 231) are approximately Poissonian. (For a modification to the Poisson function to fit football scores see Moroney, Chapter 8.)

Exercise A (p. 230)

1. The graphs for samples 1 and 4 both have the same shape—a hump at 10–15 and a short tail (see Figure J). The graphs for samples 2 and 3 have an early hump and a long tail.

   Since there are few long sentences in 1 and 4, one can guess that they are from Enid Blyton, and 2 and 3 from P. G. Wodehouse. Normal frequency functions would not be expected because of lack of symmetry—shorter sentences are more common than longer ones.

2. It is more likely to be from Enid Blyton (see Figure K).

4. See Figure L.

5. The graph of the function

   $$\text{score} \rightarrow \text{expected frequency}$$

   is rectangular. The graph of the function

   $$\text{score} \rightarrow \text{experimental frequency}$$

   should approximate to it.

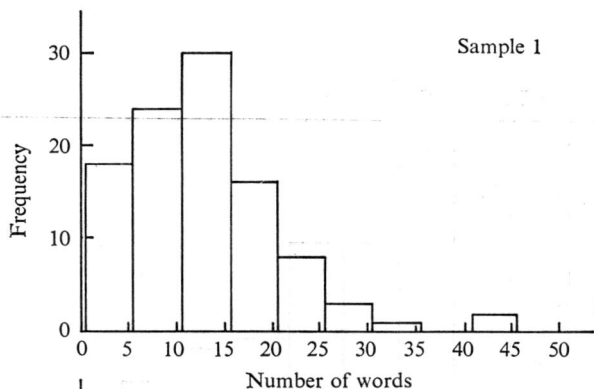

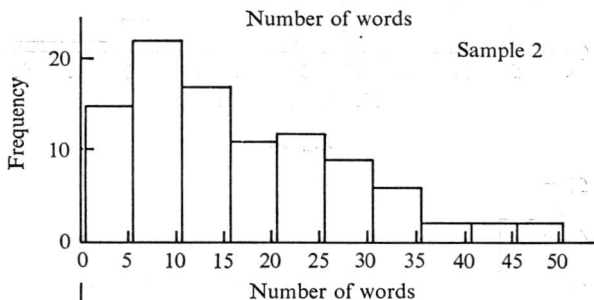

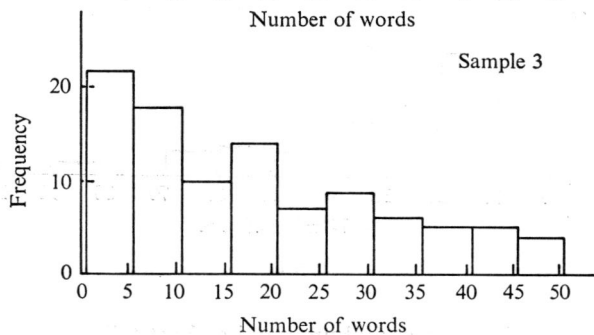

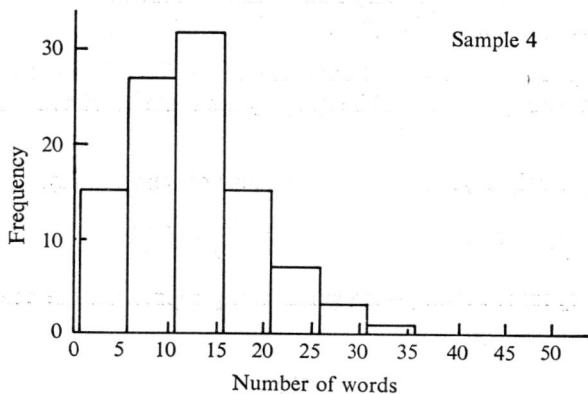

Fig. J

201

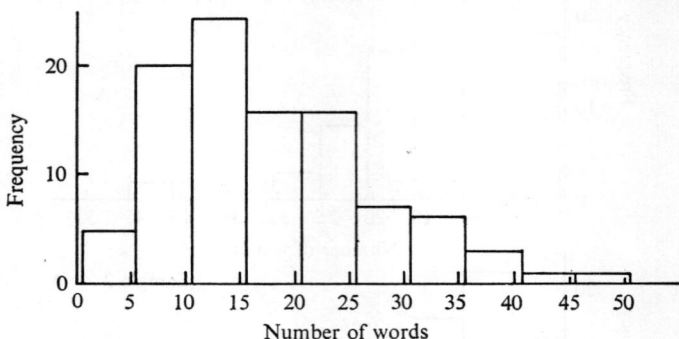

Fig. K

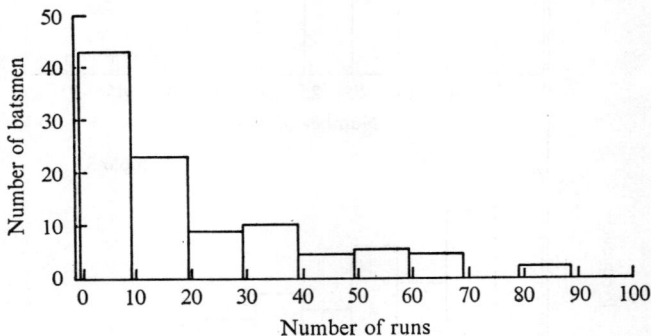

Fig. L

6. (a) and (c) have an early hump and a short tail.
    (b) is approximately symmetrical.

7. It depends on how the sample is chosen. The shape of the graph for a year group should be roughly the same as that for the whole school.

8. In general, days are either very clear or very cloudy.

9. (a) $\frac{53}{100} = 0.53$; (b) $\frac{32}{100} = 0.32$.

10. The sport is rowing—the small hump represents the coxes.

3. THE MEAN

The word 'average' is vague. The class will be familiar with it in the context of average ages, heights, cricket scores, etc. It must be pointed out that there are other types of average; the one which they know is called the arithmetic mean, or usually the mean. It can be misleading to quote an average without stating which one it is (see Exercise C, Question 4).

Here we are concerned mainly with finding the mean of a frequency function. It is important that this does not become a rote process: that it is realized why, in Section 3.1, for example, the clutch size is multiplied by the frequency (multiplication is repeated addition). For this reason the formal use of a working origin has been deferred until Book 4, although Questions 7 and 8 of Exercise B hint at the technique.

The fact needs making that from a grouped frequency table it is only possible to find an *approximate* mean. So often an answer is worked out to several decimal places in the hope of getting the exact answer! Exercise B, Question 5 emphasizes this point.

Mathematically the mean is the most useful measure of position—it corresponds to the centre of gravity in mechanics. It is the basis of most statistical work at a higher level.

The modal clutch size is 5.

The mean score is 25.

A shoe manufacturer would be interested in the mode.

3.1. Finding the mean from a frequency table

Numbers of letters	Frequency	Frequency × number of letters
0	8	0
1	13	13
2	10	20
3	7	21
4	1	4
5	0	0
6	0	0
7	1	7
	40	65

Mean number of letters $= \frac{65}{40} = 1\cdot625$.

14-2

Exercise B (p. 233)

It is far better to use information collected by the class than to have to say 'Turn to Exercise B and do Questions 2, 3 and 4'.

1. His mean score is 11.

2. (a) $\frac{136}{145} = 0.94$; (b) $\frac{171}{164} = 1.04$.

3. $\frac{797.5}{182} = 4.38$. 4. $\frac{375.5}{45} = 8.35$.

6. Sample 2, 16·44; sample 3, 18·00; sample 4, 12·25; sample 5, 17·55.

7. 13 yr. 5·9 mth.

   The easy method is to ignore the 13 years and just use the months, $1 \times 4 + 3 \times 7 + 5 \times 5 + \ldots + 11 \times 6$ and so on.

8. The mean time is $15 + \frac{2500}{500}$ hundredths of a second, i.e. $\frac{1}{5}$ s.

10. Both players have the same average, 10 runs per wicket.

4. THE MEDIAN

(a) The mean is £20.

   Since so many people hold £10 it is not fair to advertise the average as £20.

   The mean takes into account every element of the population. This is usually desirable, but there may be occasions when it is a disadvantage, as in this example, and Question 4 of Exercise C.

   The median has the advantage of not being affected by the dwarfs and giants. It also has the merit of easy calculation.

   In general the median is useful as a measure of position when there is a large population in which the middle elements are close together.

   (b) The heights in ascending order are

135, 155, 157, 157, 160, 160, 160, 163, 165, 165, 178.

160 is the median.

   (c) For 5 elements in ascending order the median is the 3rd. For 4 elements, the median is the 2·5th, which is meaningless: in practice we would take it to be the mean of the 2nd and 3rd values.

   For N elements the median is the $\frac{1}{2}(N+1)$th.

5. SPREAD

Two populations may have the same 'average' but differ considerably in the way the elements cluster around the mean. Thus it is necessary to give not only a measure of position but also a measure of spread.

This section is intended as a stage *A* approach. The range suggests itself naturally; the inter-quartile range is a reasonable refinement of it.

These two measures are easily calculated but they can be misleading. A measure of spread which takes into account every element is developed in the Advanced Mathematics books.

(*a*) The mean for each batsman is 50.

A's range is 114.

(*b*) The range of the heights is 43 cm.

(*c*) The scores in ascending order are

A	1	2	3	(6)	15	18	40	42	50	77	88	(94)	97	102	113
B	18	27	36	(40)	40	46	49	51	51	55	57	(61)	68	71	80

The inter-quartile ranges are 88 and 21 respectively.

6. CUMULATIVE FREQUENCY

The cumulative frequency curve provides a simple graphical method of finding the median and the inter-quartile range when the information is grouped.

In drawing up the table it is advisable to put in an extra column headed 'Not more than ...'. This helps to emphasize that the points are plotted at the *ends* of the intervals.

It is usual to join the points with a curve.

(*a*) Each number in the cumulative frequency column is best found by adding the appropriate frequency to the previous cumulative frequency.

The 50th and 51st are both in the 5 group.

(*b*) The areas of each portion of the frequency diagram are equal. (As was mentioned on p. 197 the area property belongs to histograms; it applies here because the class intervals happen to be equal.)

On a diagram of this size, and with a large population, it is sufficient to read off at the 25th and 75th positions.

Exercise C (p. 238)

1. The rainfalls in ascending order are

61   64   66   65   ⑥⑨   74   81   84   87   89   89   ⑨⑦   99   107   112

The inter-quartile range is $97 - 69 = 28$.

3.

	Cumulative frequency
Not more than 30 g	14
Not more than 60 g	37
Not more than 90 g	45
Not more than 120 g	49
Not more than 150 g	50

The median group is 30–60 g.

From the cumulative frequency curve (Figure M) the median is 45 g.

The mean is 48 g. The interquartile range is 36 g.

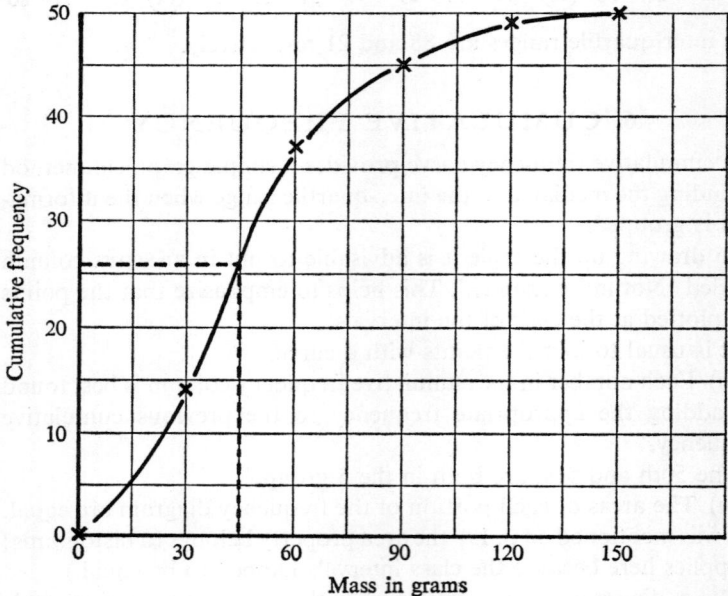

Mass in grams

Fig. M

4. The mean is £925.

The median is £680 (Figure N). It is difficult to read off to this accuracy. Assuming the graph is linear between (500, 0) and (700, 110) the median can be calculated using similarity.

Note that the curve begins at (500, 0), not at (0, 0).

(*a*) The shop steward would quote the median in order to make the average as low as possible.

(*b*) The managing director would quote the mean because it is higher than the median.

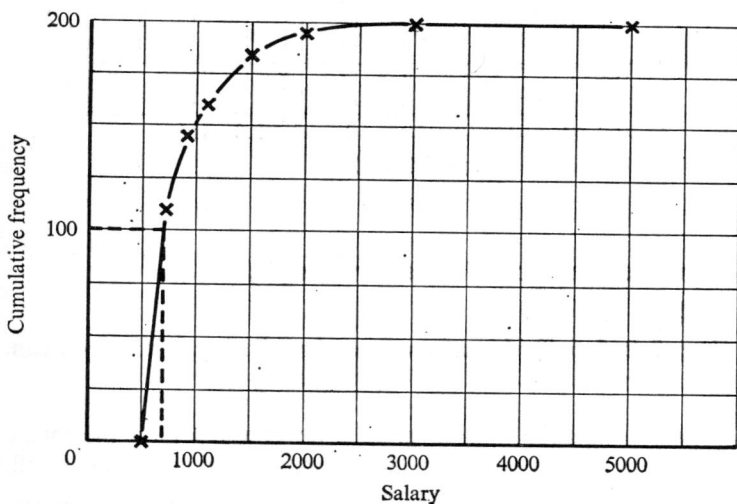

Fig. N

5. (*a*) The median is 82 km/h (Figure O).
(*b*) The inter-quartile range is 22 km/h.

Note that the cumulative frequency is plotted at 35; 45, etc.

6. (*a*) 10%;   (*b*) 8%;   (*c*) 45%.

7. (*a*) The answer expected here is that the shape is roughly symmetrical. Consider, however, the population 2, 2, 6, 9, 11. The median and mean are both 6, but the graph of the frequency function is not symmetrical.

(*b*) The graph has a late hump.

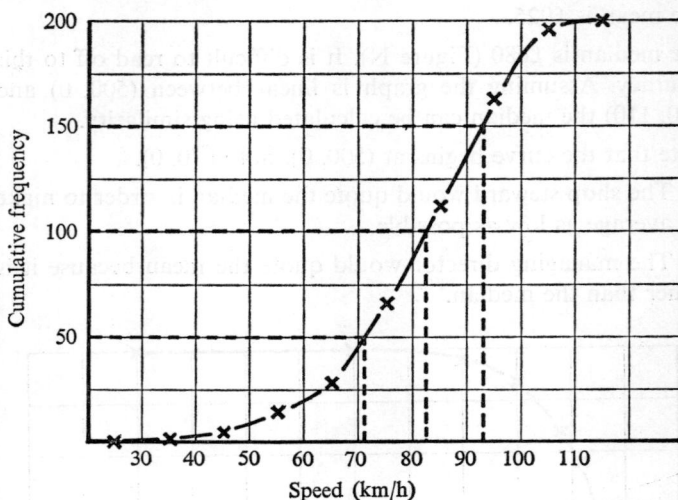

Fig. O

8. There are many possible sets, for example,

(a) {1, 2, 3, 8, 11};

(b) {⁻5, 2, 5, 6, 7} (the class may need reminding that integers can be negative).

9. In most cases the median gives a lower value than the mean because there are usually a large number of days with a small number of boys absent, and only a few days with many absences during epidemics.

10. The first brand will have a long tail of bad tyres which more than compensates for the chance of a really good one. There is no information about the spread of the second brand.

If you were insured against early failure, you would probably choose the first brand.

11. This point gives the mode of the population.

14

COMPUTERS AND
PROGRAMMING

There is no doubt that computers are having an increasing influence on the lives of everyone and that, in the future, more and more people will find themselves using computers either directly or indirectly. The object of this chapter is to provide a nucleus of ideas concerning computers and their uses on which teachers and pupils can build. The main topic of the chapter is computer programming, for it is our belief that the best way to understand how a computer processes data is to prepare one's own programs no matter how simple. It is our hope that most teachers of mathematics will, in time, take a short course on computer programming so that they will more readily appreciate the impact of computers on present-day mathematics.

Recently some members of The British Computer Society formed The Computer Education Group whose primary aim is 'To spread knowledge in the field of computing in education'. One of the ways they propose to do this is to issue a regular bulletin. Further information can be obtained from

> The Secretary,
> British Computer Society,
> Staffordshire College of Technology,
> Beaconside,
> Staffordshire.

School membership entitles the school to copies of the bulletin, and is a worthwhile investment.

There are many books continually being published on computers but most of these are too specialized. Two books giving a good overall picture are

> *Electronic Computers*, by S. H. Hollingdale and G. C. Tootill,
> *Digital Computers*, by J. P. Marchant and D. Peggy.

1. HIGH SPEED DIGITAL COMPUTERS

This section attempts to describe the main components of a computer and their various functions, showing how these may be compared to the different processes involved when a desk calculator is used. The great advantages that a computer has over a desk calculator are:

(*a*) its fantastic speed, and

(*b*) the fact that it can store a set of instructions and be left to work by itself.

The exercise at the end of this section is intended to give some ideas for research on the part of the pupils and many interesting projects have been carried out by classes taught by the authors. It is not intended that such projects should be completed before the rest of the chapter is attempted. The projects could run concurrently and might possibly be spread out over a term.

Most computer manufacturers will gladly send on request free literature, and often films, about their machines and their uses, while newspapers and magazines frequently have articles on recent developments. If a visit to a computer installation can be arranged so much the better, although normally there is very little to see and some of the demonstration programs are rather contrived. In some schools the senior boys have built simple computers and it is a good idea to let them talk about these to the junior forms (see *We Built Our Own Computers*).

One does not have to know how a car works in order to drive it and similarly most users of computers need have no idea of what goes on 'under the bonnet', although it is probably true to say that most boys are interested in this technical side. The following sections are concerned with 'driving' and the engineering aspects can be forgotten. A knowledge of the 'hardware', however, makes sense of restrictions which might otherwise appear to be quite arbitrary.

Exercise A (p. 247)

5. (*a*) 10010; (*b*) 11111010; (*c*) 100; (*d*) 11.

2. PROGRAMMING

Computers are sometimes described as 'brains' but this is very misleading and it might be more helpful to think of a computer as a well-trained monkey equipped with a desk calculator. The monkey is trained to respond to a symbol by carrying out a specific operation on the desk calculator, no more, and no less.

Consider the calculation

$$\frac{(2\cdot7 \times 3\cdot4) + (5\cdot8 \times 9\cdot7)}{6\cdot5}$$

and imagine that you want the class to do this without writing any of the numbers down and without their seeing the complete problem. They are only to do what you tell them—they are to be the computers.

You would need to give a set of instructions such as:

> Multiply 2·7 by 3·4
> Write down the product
> Multiply 5·8 by 9·7
> Write down the product
> Add together the two numbers written down
> Divide the sum by 6·5
> Write down the quotient.

If these instructions were carried out correctly, each member of the class would have the same answer written down. This set of instructions is a program. However, it is a program that only fits this one calculation and when using a computer it is usual to devise a program having more general application. Suppose, for example, that you wish the class to compute $(ab + cd)/e$, where a, b, c, d and e are any five numbers. The following program, which does not refer to the specific values taken by these variables would work for all sets of numbers:

> Write the numbers in order one below the other
> Multiply together the numbers on the 1st and 2nd lines
> Write down the product on the 6th line
> Multiply together the numbers on the 3rd and 4th lines
> Write down the product on the 7th line
> Add together the numbers on lines 6 and 7

Write the result on the 8th line
Divide the number on line 8 by the number on line 5
Write the quotient on line 9.

This is now very close to the kind of program introduced in this section. The above set of instructions has broken down the computation into a sequence of steps which concern *at most two numbers at a time*. No matter how complicated a computation is we cannot deal with more than two numbers at a time, and a computer is just as limited.

To give this set of instructions to a computer we have to translate them into the computer's own language. Every new computer has its own language but in principle all computer languages have much in common and attempts are being made to construct a language (for example, Algol) which can be understood by all computers. The language for direct communication with a computer (machine language) is very fundamental and breaks down every calculation into such small steps that it would take the average person far too long to write any program. To overcome this computer manufacturers produce autocodes. These are coded languages which bear a strong resemblance to mathematics as we would normally write it. They are, therefore, easy to learn and greatly facilitate the writing of programs. Supplementing each autocode is a super-program which acts as a dictionary or interpreter conversant with the machine language of the computer, and this when fed into the computer is able to translate the autocode into machine code.

To carry out a computation with a computer the program has first to be written in autocode and then transferred to paper tape or punched cards. The computer is then fed with the 'interpreter' and it copies this information into its stores. The autocode program is then fed in and copied into further stores. At this stage no computation is carried out. All that has happened is that the program of instructions has been put into the computer in a form which it can use. When this stage is completed, the press of a switch will set the machine to work following the instructions in the order in which they were stored.

Simon is a hypothetical computer although its autocode, Simpol, bears resemblance to some of the earlier commercial codes. More sophisticated codes, such as Algol, so resemble normal mathematical writing that they give little indication of how a computer actually sets about its work.

Exercise B (p. 250)

1. Only the input instructions have to be altered.
In practice the program would not contain an instruction such as

$$\text{Input } 7\!\cdot\!6 \text{ to } S_1$$

but rather $\qquad$ Input to S_1.

The numbers such as 7·6 would be punched on a tape and read, in order, off the tape by the computer in response to an input instruction. In this way the program can be used for different sets of numbers.

$$
\begin{aligned}
&\text{Input} \quad 326\!\cdot\!7 \text{ to } S_1 \\
&\text{Input} \quad 68\!\cdot\!73 \text{ to } S_2 \\
&\text{Input} \quad 29\!\cdot\!35 \text{ to } S_3 \\
&\text{Input} \quad 0\!\cdot\!0876 \text{ to } S_4 \\
&\text{Replace } S_5 \text{ by } S_1 \div S_2 \\
&\text{Replace } S_6 \text{ by } S_3 \div S_4 \\
&\text{Replace } S_7 \text{ by } S_5 + S_6 \\
&\text{Output the number in } S_7.
\end{aligned}
$$

2. (a) $485\,(28\!\cdot\!3 - 19\!\cdot\!7)$; $\qquad$ (b) $\dfrac{36\!\cdot\!2 + 18\!\cdot\!9}{21\!\cdot\!4 - 14\!\cdot\!7}$;
(c) $(93\!\cdot\!5 + 37\!\cdot\!4 - 86\!\cdot\!3)^2$.

If required, these computations could be carried out with the aid of a slide rule. The above answers are, however, those expected.

3. Possible programs are as follows although these are not unique. (It is a good idea to copy pupils' programs on the board for comparison and discussion.)

(N.B. In the programs which follow, the words 'input' and 'replace' are left out when two or more consecutive instructions are of the same kind. This convention might well be adopted by the pupils to avoid tedious repetition. The purpose of the words is to emphasize what the instruction does, but they are not copied when the code is transferred to tape.)

(a) Input $\quad 3\!\cdot\!6 \text{ to } S_1$
$\qquad 6\!\cdot\!2 \text{ to } S_2$
$\qquad 2\!\cdot\!8 \text{ to } S_3$
$\qquad 0\!\cdot\!94 \text{ to } S_4$

213

Replace S_5 by $S_1 \times S_2$
S_6 by $S_3 \div S_4$
S_7 by $S_5 + S_6$
Output the number in S_7.

(b) Input   12·6 to S_1
4·7 to S_2
6·2 to S_3
13·9 to S_4

Replace S_5 by $S_2 \times S_3$
S_6 by $S_5 \div S_4$
S_7 by $S_1 - S_6$
Output the number in S_7

(c) Input   6·7 to S_1
Replace S_2 by $S_1 \times S_1$
S_3 by $S_2 \times S_2$
S_4 by $S_3 \times S_1$
Output the number in S_4.

(d) Input   65·1 to S_1
23·7 to S_2
218 to S_3
189 to S_4

Replace S_5 by $S_3 \div S_4$
S_6 by $S_2 \div S_5$
S_7 by $S_1 \div S_6$
Output the number in S_7.

These programs can be used to test pupils' understanding of brackets and indices. Other examples can easily be made up if it is felt necessary.

4.   (a) 4 stores.

Economizing on stores becomes very important with large programs, since one must ensure that one has sufficient stores in the computer to cope with all the program. It is useful to think of each small program as being part of a longer program and then the need for economy becomes more obvious.

(b) Input   2·3 to S_1
3·6 to S_2
4·2 to S_3
5·1 to S_4
2·9 to S_5
5 to S_6

Replace S_1 by S_1+S_2
S_1 by S_1+S_3
S_1 by S_1+S_4
S_1 by S_1+S_5
S_1 by $S_1 \div S_6$

Output the number in S_1.

(c) Dry checking a program is usually done using simple data to check that the logical structure is right.

5.   Input   4·6 to S_1

Replace S_2 by $S_1 \times S_1$
~~S_2 by $S_2 * S_1$~~
S_2 by $S_2 \times S_1$
S_2 by S_2+S_1

Output the number in S_2.

6.   Program computes 765^2+286^2.

A program to compute $(765+286)^2$ is:

Input   765 to S_1
286 to S_2

Replace S_1 by S_1+S_2
S_1 by $S_1 \times S_1$

Output the number in S_1.

3. PROGRAMS FOR FORMULAE

From programming particular calculations the pupil is now encouraged to see that, apart from the input instructions, a program is quite general in that the instructions refer only to addresses of stores (sometimes the word *location* is used) and not specific numbers. Programming a formula such as $V = \pi r^2 h$, for example, illuminates what is meant by this notation by forcing the pupil to consider how he would compute it. Pupils can presumably multiply together two

215

numbers so that if, as in this example, they can break down the problem into a succession of products of two numbers, then theoretically they can compute V when the occasion arises.

(a) Only the input instruction needs to be altered.

Nothing so far has been said about the form in which numbers are stored by a computer. The stores of a computer are often arranged to store a number in three parts as for example;

(i) a digit 0 or 1 depending on whether the number is positive or negative;

(ii) a number, A, satisfying $1 \leqslant A < 10$ and given to, say, 9 significant figures;

(iii) a number, N, corresponding to an integral index of 10 between 0 and 99 followed by the digit 0 or 1 indicating whether the index is positive or negative.

Thus the number $-568 \cdot 01342$ would be stored as

$$1|5\ 6\ 8\ 0\ 1\ 3\ 4\ 2\ 0|0\ 2|0$$

$$\underset{\text{of } A}{\text{sign}} \qquad A \qquad N \quad \underset{\text{of } N}{\text{sign}}$$

because $\qquad -568 \cdot 01342 = (^-)\ 5 \cdot 6801342 \times 10^2.$

The number $0 \cdot 0000472$ would be stored as

$$0|4\ 7\ 2\ 0\ 0\ 0\ 0\ 0\ 0|0\ 5|1$$

because $\qquad 0 \cdot 0000472 = (+)\ 4 \cdot 72 \times 10^{-5}.$

This is an oversimplification of the situation because all numbers are in fact stored in binary form but the above scheme covers the main features. The number of digits used to store a number (13 above) will always be the same for a given computer and this number is known as the *word length* for the computer. A typical length is 32 binary digits.

(b) 254 cm^3.

Exercise C (p. 252)

1.   (a) Input x to S_1
        Replace S_1 by $S_1 \times S_1$
                   S_1 by $S_1 \times S_1$
                   S_1 by $S_1 \times S_1$
        Output the number in S_1.

    (b) Any power of the form 2^n where n is a counting number.

(c) Input x to S_1

Replace S_2 by $S_1 \times S_1$ x^2

          S_2 by $S_2 \times S_2$ x^4

          S_1 by $S_1 \times S_2$ x^5 S_2 by $S_1 \times S_2$ x^5

          S_2 by $S_2 \times S_2$ x^8 alternatively S_2 by $S_2 \times S_2$ x^{10}

          S_2 by $S_2 \times S_2$ x^{16} S_2 by $S_2 \times S_2$ x^{20}

          S_2 by $S_2 \times S_1$ x^{21} S_2 by $S_2 \times S_1$ x^{21}

Output the number in S_2.   Output the number in S_2.

It will be noticed by most pupils that the same instruction is repeated several times over. This situation often arises in programming and by using a new kind of instruction the program can be considerably shortened. In general, the smaller the number of instructions the less time is taken to run the program and the less storage space is required.

The above programs are useful in revising laws of indices and questions like (c) give plenty of scope for ingenuity.

2.   (a) Input R_1 to S_1

               R_2 to S_2

Replace S_3 by $S_1 \times S_2$

          S_1 by $S_1 + S_2$

          S_1 by $S_3 \div S_1$

Output the number in S_1.

(b) 1·5.

Note that this program can also be used to work out f, the focal length of a lens, from the formula $f = uv/(u+v)$, if u and v are used for the input data.

3.   (a) Input π to S_1

               l to S_2

               R to S_3

               r to S_4

Replace S_1 by $S_1 \times S_2$

          S_2 by $S_3 + S_4$

          S_1 by $S_1 \times S_2$

          S_2 by $S_3 - S_4$

          S_1 by $S_1 \times S_2$

Output the number in S_1.

(b) 44.

4. (a) $T = xA + yB + zC + tD$;

(b) $P = \dfrac{xA + yB + zC + tD}{x + y + z + t}$;

(c) Input x to S_1
               y to S_2
               z to S_3
               t to S_4
               A to S_5
               B to S_6
               C to S_7
               D to S_8

Replace S_5 by $S_1 \times S_5$ xA
              S_6 by $S_2 \times S_6$ yB
              S_7 by $S_3 \times S_7$ zC
              S_8 by $S_4 \times S_8$ tD
              S_5 by $S_5 + S_6$ $xA + yB$
              S_5 by $S_5 + S_7$ $(xA + yB) + zC$
              S_5 by $S_5 \times S_8$ $(xA + yB + zC) + tD$
              S_1 by $S_1 + S_2$ $x + y$
              S_1 by $S_1 + S_3$ $(x + y) + z$
              S_1 by $S_1 + S_4$ $(x + y + z) + t$
              S_1 by $S_5 \div S_1$ P

Output the number in S_1.

(d) $P = 28$;

(e) (i) 18 had less than the average,
     (ii) 12 had more than the average.

5. (a) Input x to S_1
               p to S_2
               q to S_3
               r to S_4

Replace S_2 by $S_1 + S_2$ $x + p$
              S_2 by $S_1 \times S_2$ $x(x + p)$
              S_2 by $S_2 + S_3$ $x(x + p) + q$
              S_2 by $S_1 \times S_2$ $x[x(x + p) + q]$
              S_2 by $S_2 + S_4$ $x[x(x + p) + q] + r$.

Output the number in S_2.

This program computes the value of y as

$$y = x[x(x+p)+q]+r$$

using a method known as nested multiplication.

It is not anticipated that the pupils will do it this way but a discussion of this method can be profitable.

(b) 59·1

6. (a) Take $a = 2, b = 1, c = 7, p = 5, q = {}^-3, r = 1$ and substitute.

(b) Input a to S_1
           b to S_2
           c to S_3
           p to S_4
           q to S_5
           r to S_6

Replace S_7 by $S_1 \times S_5$ aq
           S_8 by $S_4 \times S_2$ pb
           S_7 by $S_7 - S_8$ $aq - pb$
           S_5 by $S_3 \times S_5$ cq
           S_2 by $S_6 \times S_2$ rb
           S_5 by $S_5 - S_2$ $cq - rb$
           S_5 by $S_5 \div S_7$ x
           S_1 by $S_1 \times S_6$ ar
           S_4 by $S_4 \times S_3$ pc
           S_1 by $S_1 - S_4$ $ar - pc$
           S_1 by $S_1 \div S_7$ y

Output the number in S_5
Output the number in S_1.

(d) When $aq = pb$. The lines are then parallel (or coincident).

7. (a) $y_1 = 3·5$.

(b) Input N to S_1
           x to S_2

Replace S_3 by $S_2 \times S_2$
           S_3 by $S_3 + S_1$
           S_2 by $S_2 + S_2$
           S_2 by $S_3 \div S_2$

Output the number in S_2.

(c) $y_2 = 3·464$, $y_3 = 3·4641$.

Testing the accuracy of a solution is an important part of programming and this is usually built in as an integral part of a program In this example the best test of accuracy is to compare the square of a given approximation with 12.

$$3 \cdot 5^2 \quad = 12 \cdot 25 \qquad \Rightarrow |3 \cdot 5^2 \quad - 12| = 0 \cdot 25.$$
$$3 \cdot 464^2 = 11 \cdot 999296 \quad \Rightarrow |3 \cdot 464^2 - 12| \approx 0 \cdot 0007.$$
$$3 \cdot 4641^2 = 11 \cdot 99998881 \Rightarrow |3 \cdot 4641^2 - 12| \approx 0 \cdot 00001.$$

4. FLOW DIAGRAMS

Flow diagrams are really the first stage in the organization of a program and some teachers may prefer to teach them first. However, it is the authors' experience that the printed order is better, for it is only when attempting to construct more complicated programs directly in autocode that one realizes the need for flow diagrams.

The diagrams need not be connected with numerical work in the first instance, for it is the logical structure that is important at this stage.

The effect of these lines (loops) is to make the reader retrace a part of the diagram.

Exercise D (p. 255)

There is no point in attempting all this exercise but a selection should be made to give the class sufficient experience in the use of decision boxes and loops.

1. The ideas in the exercise can be covered by selecting from the various parts. There is plenty of scope here for imagination. Try to encourage the correct use of decision boxes.

2. A book for an *L* driver could consist almost entirely of flow diagrams: one for starting, one for overtaking, one for turning right and so on. This could make an interesting project.

3. 0, 1, 1, 2, 3, 5, 8, 13, 21, 34. The Fibonacci numbers.

4. This is the geometric construction for the harmonic mean.

   See Figure A. No matter where *V* is taken, the position of *D* should always be the same with $CD = 4$ cm.

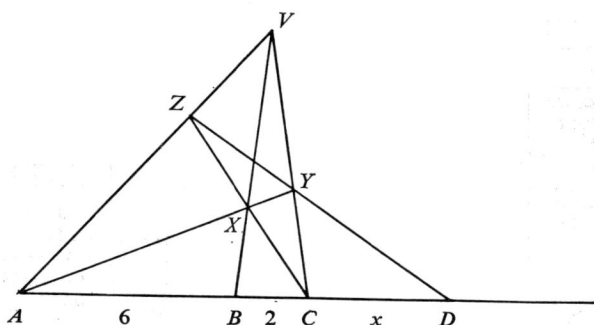

Fig. A

In general $\dfrac{AB}{CB}\cdot\dfrac{CD}{AD} = {}^-1,$

and in this case

$$\dfrac{6}{{}^-2}\cdot\dfrac{x}{8+x} = {}^-1, \quad \text{where} \quad CD = x.$$

Hence, $x = 4.$

5. (a)

X	Y
25	9
36	11
49	13
64	15
81	17
100	19
121	21
144	23
169	25
196	27

(b) (i) The square numbers from 25 to 196.

(ii) The odd numbers from 9 to 27.

This program is based on the identity.

$$(n+1)^2 = n^2+(2n-1)+2.$$

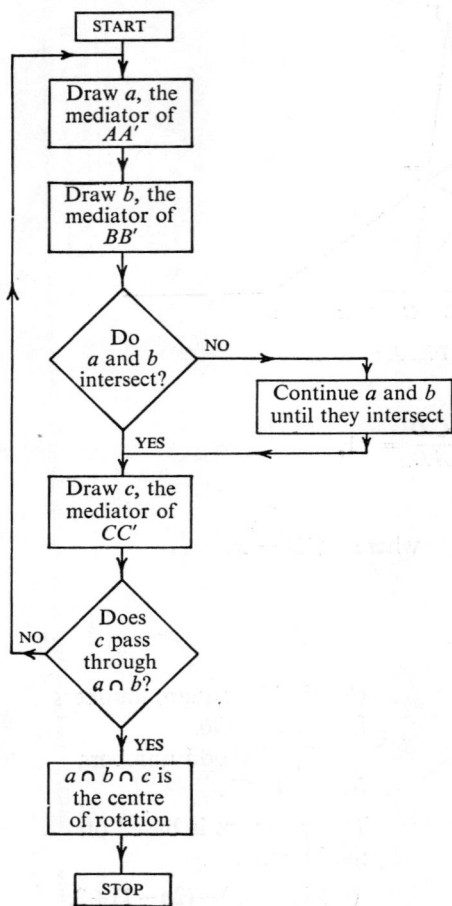

Fig. B

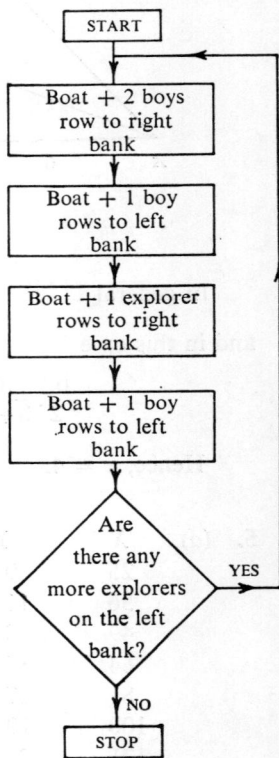

Fig. C

6. This is included to provide revision of the geometry (see Figure B).

7. See Figure C.

*8. This question and the next are quite difficult although a class discussion based on them would be valuable (see Figure D).

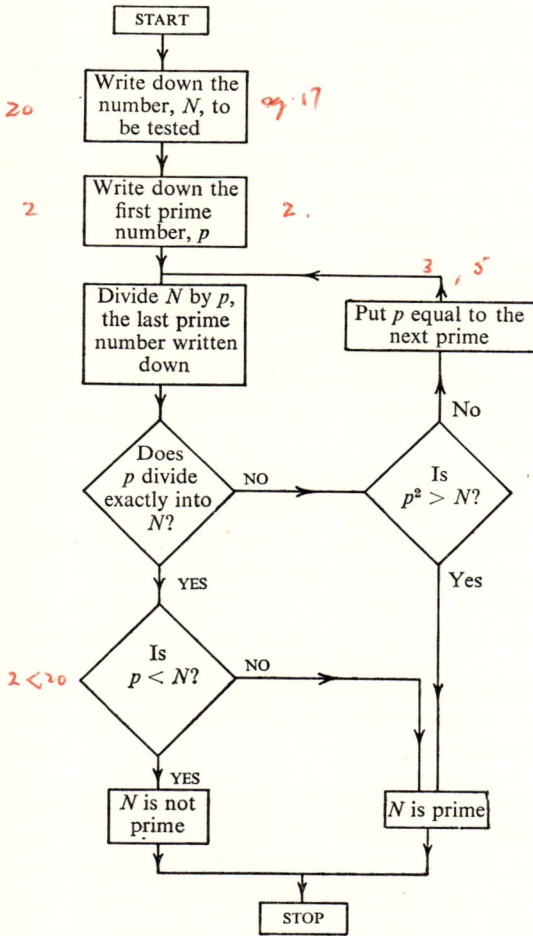

Fig. D

*9. The solution of this question is discussed at some length in the book *Some Lessons in Mathematics*. The book contains a chapter on numerical methods and flow charts that makes worthwhile reading.

5. REPETITION

An attempt to solve Example 5 using calculus will give $\sqrt{12}$ spans, an answer which is obviously meaningless. Here the number of spans must be integral and the number of different possibilities is so small that each can be considered in turn.

In many problems it is impossible, either because of the nature of the problem or restrictions on the time available, to find an exact answer. Instead, an answer is found to within reasonable limits of accuracy by using methods which give a sequence of approximations approaching the exact answer.

Example 6 is a good example of a numerical process consisting of a small number of steps that can be repeated over and over again so as to obtain an answer to the degree of accuracy required. Such a process (known as an *iterative* process) can be handled readily by a computer which will be able very quickly to run through the various stages many times.

Exercise E (p. 258)

There is a lot of disguised 'use of formulae' in this exercise. The questions are expected to be tackled by giving values to the independent variable and observing the changes in the dependent variable. A graph will often be helpful when discussing a solution.

1. $h(1) = 5000, h(2) = 8000, h(3) = 9000, h(4) = 8000, h(5) = 5000$. Note the assumption made about the symmetry properties of quadratic functions.

2. (a) $P(1) = 5250$, $P(2) = 18\,000$, $P(3) = 33\,750$, $P(4) = 48\,000$, $P(5) = 56\,250$, $P(6) = 54\,000$, $P(7) = 36\,750$.

 (b) 57. A graph here of $r \to P$ would be useful to illustrate how the power changes with the speed of the engine. Mechanical engineers try to design engines that give a good power output over a fairly wide range of speeds, rather than a very high output over a small range.

3. (a) $\sqrt{42} \approx 6\cdot48\,(1)$.

 (b) One obtains the negative number whose square is 42, i.e. $-\sqrt{42}$.

224

4.

x	2·0	2·2	2·4	2·6	2·8	3·0	2·5	2·45
y	8	7·93	7·90	7·91	7·94	8	7·90	7·90

Minimum $y = 7·90$ to 2 decimal places.

5. $P(2) = 16·3, P(3) = 18·7, P(4) = 19·8, P(5) = 20, P(6) = 19·8,$
$P(7) = 19·4.$

The motor with $R = 5$ gives the maximum power.

*6. This is rather a difficult question and demands a lot of computation.

(*a*) Length of tank: $12-2x$.
    Width of tank: $8-2x$.
    Depth of tank: x.

(*b*) The width of the tank is $8-2x$ and if $x = 4$ this becomes zero. If $x < 4$ the width becomes negative.

(*c*)

x	1	2	3	4	1·2	1·4	1·6	1·8	1·5	1·55
y	60	64	36	0	64·5	67·0	67·6	66·5	67·5	67·6

Max $V \approx 67·6$ m³.

7. $y_1 = 3·11, y_1^3 = 30·08.$

15

LOCI AND ENVELOPES

Pupils sometimes have difficulty with the pronunciation of the word locus. It may be helpful to note that the *Oxford English Dictionary* gives the pronunciation as 'low cuss', plural 'low sigh'!

Older textbooks give the word dynamic overtones, using such phrases as 'path traced out' and 'the point moves so that'. We prefer the static aspect and shall define the locus of P to be the set of points that P may occupy. It goes without saying that this has to be a well-defined set. This definition may be given geometrically, for example, 'the locus of a point P equidistant from fixed points A and B in a plane containing them', or, more shortly, $\{P: AP = BP, P \in \pi\}$ where π is a plane containing A and B. Alternatively the definition may be algebraic in terms of coordinates, for example $\{(x, y): 2x - 3y = 1\}$.

People with tortuous minds (usually boys) sometimes complain that the 'classroom is moving through space, sir, so the paper has moved too!' To such it is necessary to point out that we shall be concerned only with loci in relation to ourselves and not to celestial observers. In the first three sections we shall also limit ourselves to a plane, without specifically saying so on every occasion. Further examples may be found in *A Book of Curves*, by E. H. Lockwood, and in *Mathematical Models*, by H. M. Cundy and A. P. Rollett.

1. LOCUS

(*a*) The firework puzzle has necessarily to be answered in the text. The introduction is therefore best done on the blackboard without reference to books. The set p is the mediator of AB; $p \cap q$ is the single point at which this cuts the mediator of BC.

(*b*) It is better to shade in the required sets rather than to use the linear programming convention and shade out unwanted parts. The sets are shown in Figure A.

The set $p \cap q$ gives the possible positions for the tree.

The set $p \cup q$ comprises points which are either more than 10 m from the house or more than $7\frac{1}{2}$ m from the existing tree, or both. (i) The locus is indicated by the broken line in Figure A. (ii) This is the single point T.

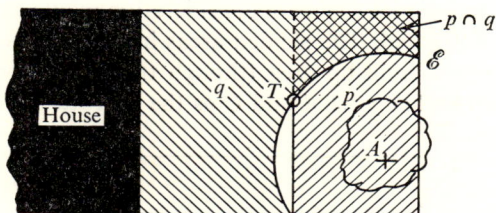

Fig. A

Exercise A (p. 263)

1. (a) Straight line;   (b) curved line (circle);
   (c) curved line or lines;   (d) region.

2. (a) A straight line lying equally between the two half-lines.

   (b) OY is a line of symmetry. Any point of OY is therefore equidistant from p and q. OY is the locus of a point equidistant from p and q. It is called the angle bisector since it divides $\angle POQ$ into two equal angles.

   (c) Draw the three angle bisectors (or two will do), and the point they have in common (the in-centre of the triangle) is as far as possible from the three roads.

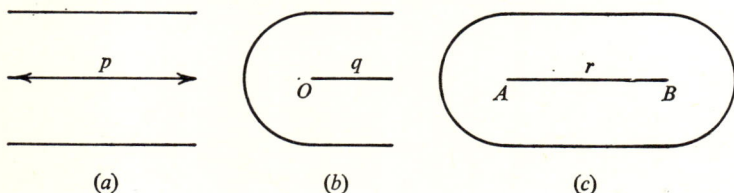

(a)   (b)   (c)

Fig. B

3. See Figure B.

   The point of this question is to make explicit the distinction between these three cases. It is also useful to point out that a line

227

segment has two 1-nodes (its end-points), a half-line has one
1-node and a line has none, although we have perforce to
illustrate it as though it had.

4. See Figure C. Transmitters at *B* and *C* give greatest coverage of
area. In practice the main consideration would be the number of
houses reached. The shaded areas in Figure 7 suggest that *C* is
the biggest built-up area (though the density would affect the
matter) and suggest *A* and *C* as the best sites.

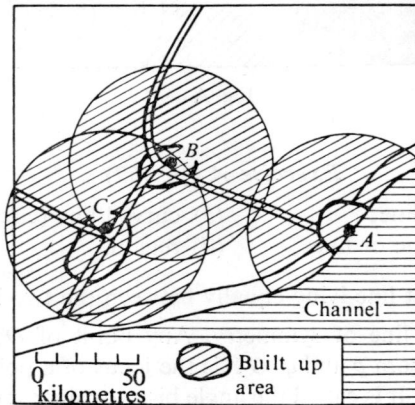

Fig. C

5. See Figure D.

$X \cap Y = \emptyset$. $X \cup Y$ is the set of points within the triangle which
are either nearer *B* than *C*, or nearer the side *AC* than *AB* or
(technically) both, although this is geometrically impossible.

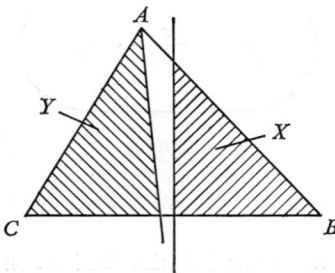

Fig. D

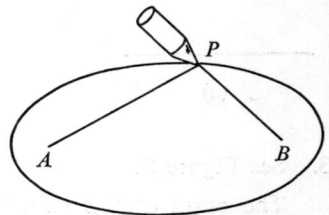

Fig. E

228

6. The distance from P to AB is 4 cm. The locus of P is a pair of straight lines parallel to AB and 4 cm distant from it.

7. See Figure E (not scale).

   AB is a line of symmetry, so is the mediator of AB.

8. $\{(r, \theta): r > 4, 0 < \theta < 90\}$.

2. INVESTIGATING LOCI

Most classes become very interested in double-ended searchlights. The subject is best introduced as a pure investigation; the unexpected nature of many of the loci provides its own motivation.

Although it is not difficult to draw the positions of the two beams at equal intervals of time using a protractor, the labour of drawing is minimized by using a simple aid and it is then easier to concentrate on the loci. The best method is to prepare a duplicated grid of radiating beams as shown in Figure F.

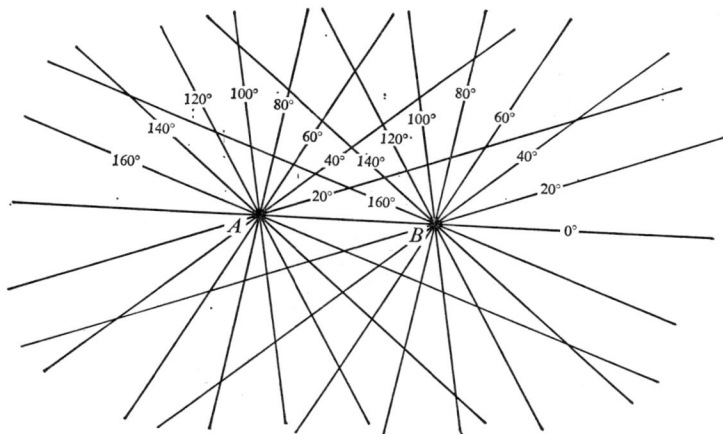

Fig. F

The number of beams drawn is not critical. Intervals of 30° are easy to construct, using compasses to mark off sets of six equal intervals at a time. Intervals of 20° (as in Figure F) give more polished loci and, if the teacher has time and patience, even closer grids may

229

be produced. We shall use 10° intervals in subsequent figures. The difficulty of distinguishing between one beam and the next sets an upper limit. The beams are marked in degrees, as shown, but it should be noted that only the numbers are used as coordinates (i.e. the degree signs are omitted).

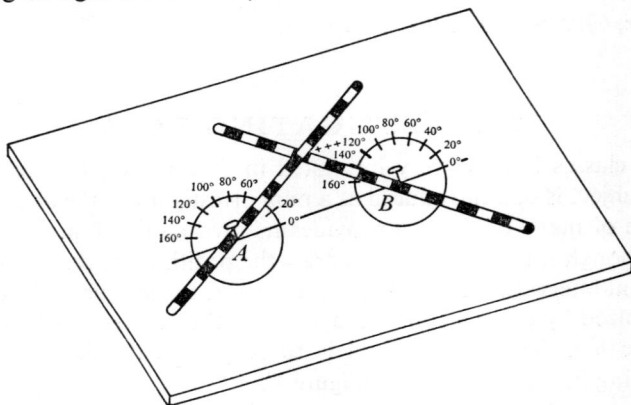

(i)

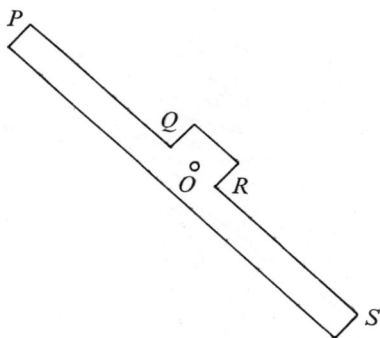

(ii)

Fig. G

For demonstration purposes a simple aid using milk straws is illustrated in Figure G(i). Milk straws may be joined by crumpling the end of one and pushing it inside another. It is fairly easy to slide one over the other in most (but not all!) position of the straws. The loci produced are not very accurate since the straws hide the graduated circle and the point of intersection has to be marked by lifting the pairs of straws through a small distance.

An alternative to milk straws is illustrated in Figure G (ii). Two strips of card are cut to the shape shown and are pinned through the holes O to the centres A and B of the graduated circles. This is more accurate and may also be used for class work.

Note that the hole O has to lie on the straight edge $PQRS$.

More complicated devices can be made using 'Spirograph' parts or meccano and may involve various forms of gearing.

The points required in Figure 13 are $P(100, 140)$, $Q(50, 140)$ and $S(50, 18)$. A is the point $(\theta, 0)$ and B is the point $(0, \theta)$. The fact that in each case one coordinate can be chosen at will is unexpected. (θ, θ) does not define a point of the plane, it is a point 'at infinity'. The point $(0, 0)$ could be anywhere on the line through A and B. We no longer have a one-to-one correspondence between points and number-pairs and this is the reason why the system is less useful for general purposes than the Cartesian system in which every point has unique coordinates and every number-pair represents a unique point.

Plan number 1

When A is at $\theta°$, B is at $(\theta+60)°$. $(160, 220) = (160, 40)$. The arithmetic is clock arithmetic, mod 180. Some other points on the locus are $(60, 120)$, $(80, 140)$, etc., also $(120, 0)$, $(140, 20)$. See Figure H. The locus is a circle through A and B. See Exercise A Question 2 (a) and the chapter on the The Circle in Book 4.

Plan number 2

Some points are $(20, 40)$, $(40, 80)$, etc., also $(100, 20)$, $(120, 60)$, etc. The fact that this is arithmetic mod 180 will be obvious. The locus is a circle with centre B and radius BA, and is shown in Figure I. This locus is a good test of the accuracy of your grid as the intersections at the extreme right of the figure are formed at small angles and an error of a degree or so throws the points well off the ideal circle. Some teachers will want to explain the reason for this particular locus. If P is any point of the locus, as shown in Figure J,

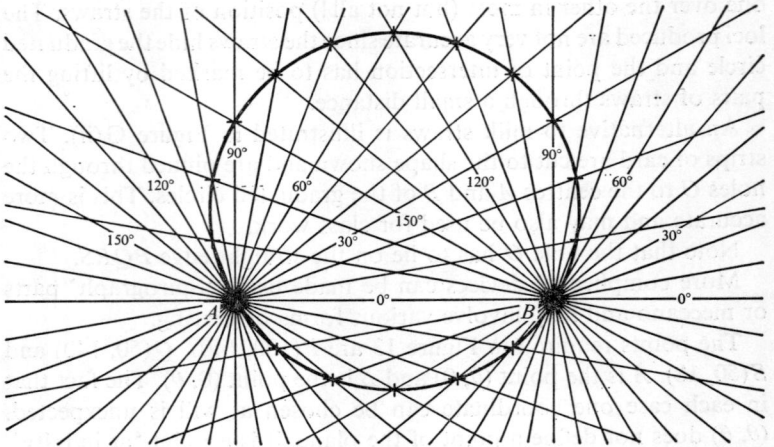

Fig. H

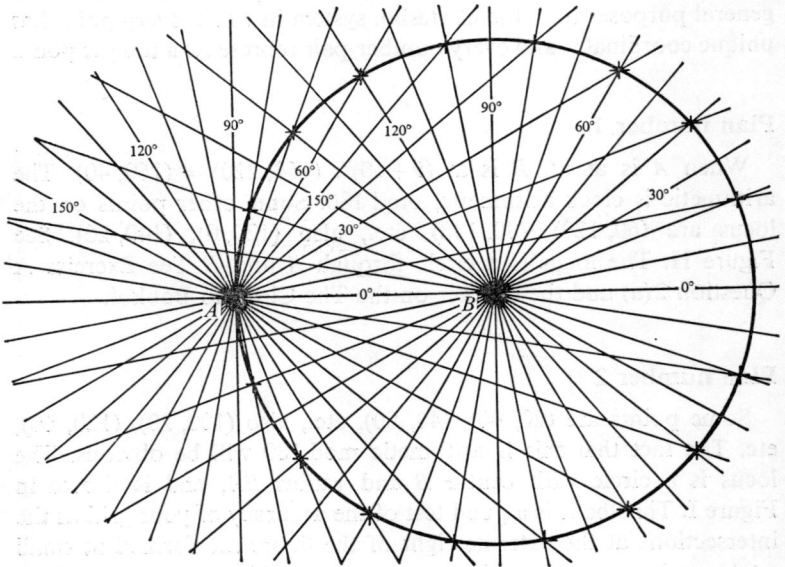

Fig. I

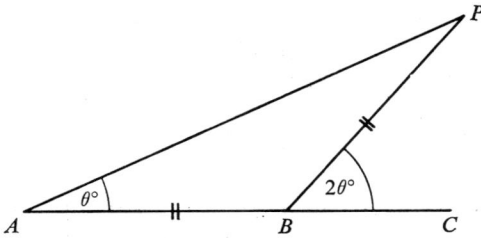

Fig. J

$\angle PBC = 2\theta°$ and $\angle PAC = \theta° \Rightarrow \angle APB = \theta°$, i.e. $BA = BP$ so that BP is of constant length and the locus of P is the circle with centre B and radius BP.

Plan number 3

From the symmetry of the plan it should be evident that the locus is the mediator of AB. Some points are (20, 160), (40, 140), ..., also (160, 20), (140, 40), etc. The relation is that the sum of the coordinates is 180 and the function is $\theta \to 180 - \theta$ (see Figure K).

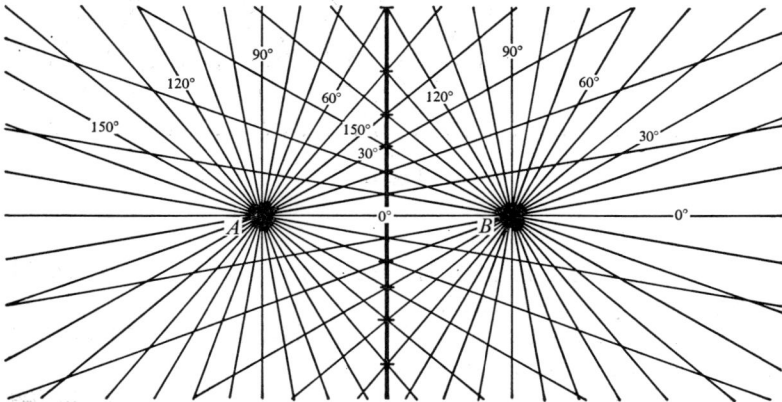

Fig. K

Plan number 4

Further points given will probably be of the type (50, 150) or possibly (150, 50). The relation is that the sum of the coordinates is

16   233   STG

20 (not 200, since we are working mod 180). We now see that points hitherto unsuspected such as (5, 15) are on the locus (see the chain-dotted line in Figure L). *A* and *B* also lie on it. The curve is a rectangular hyperbola with asymptotes in the 10° and 100° directions since (10, 10) and (100, 100) lie on it.

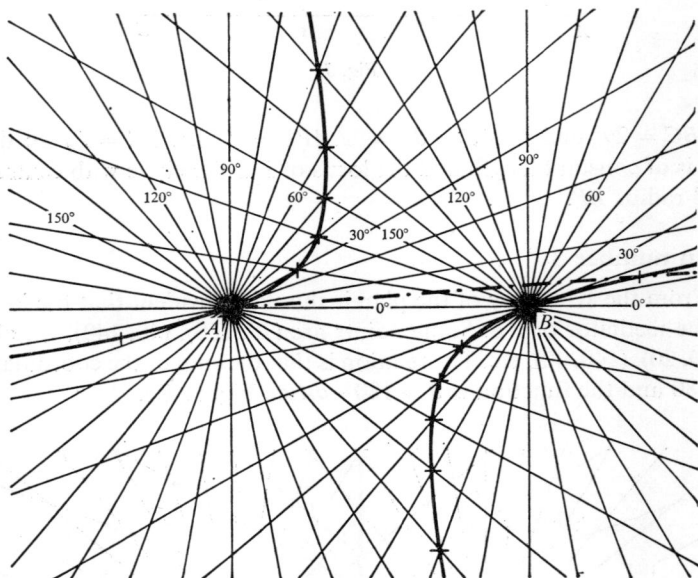

Fig. L

Provided a linear relation is chosen a reasonable locus should ensue under 'plan number 5'.

The coordinate system is itself of great interest and the following may serve as a stimulus for further work.

(*a*) Are there any number pairs that do not specify points in the system?

(*b*) What can be said about the points (θ, ϕ) and (ϕ, θ)?

(*c*) Describe the set $\{(\theta, \phi): \theta > \phi\}$.

(*d*) If θ denotes the first coordinate and ϕ the second, investigate loci expressed in relation form, in particular $\theta = 0$ and $\phi = 0$,

θ = constant and ϕ = constant. Rewrite the functions in the text in the form of relations.

(e) Is there a simple relation that gives a spiral locus?

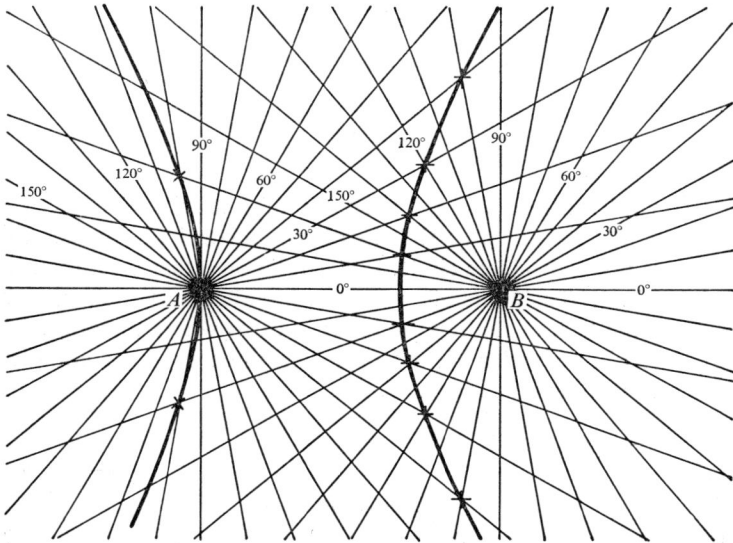

Fig. M

Exercise B (p. 267)

1. The locus is bow-shaped as shown in Figure M. It is not too easy to see the function in this case. It is plainly expressible as $\theta \to {}^{-}2\theta$, but negative angles are not acceptable. A few specimen points, e.g. (10, 160), (20, 140), (30, 120), ... lead to $\theta \to 180 - 2\theta$ and the other sequence (170, 20), (160, 40), (150, 60), ... leads to $\theta \to 360 - 2\theta$ which, we then realize, are equivalent (mod 180).

2. (a) The resulting locus should appear as in Figure N. To test it, draw the mediators of several chords and see whether they concur. If so, test the remaining points with compasses. The locus should be an arc of a circle through A and B, since this is the well-

16-2

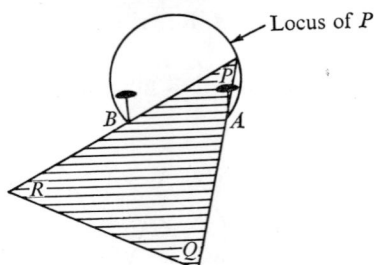

Fig. N

known 'Constant Angle' property of a circle. The locus is essentially the same as that in plan number 1 above, but this line is not a complete circle. If P can lie on either side, then the locus has AB as a line of symmetry. Members of the class might share the task of finding the locus in cases where the angle P is acute, obtuse and a right-angle. The three types of complete locus are shown in Figure O.

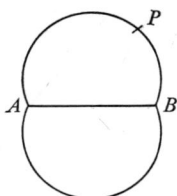

(i) Acute angle at P (ii) Obtuse angle at P (iii) Right-angle at P

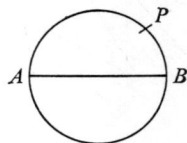

Fig. O

(b) The locus should be the arc of an ellipse between P_1 and P_2 (Figure P). Testing should quickly convince pupils that this is not part of a circle. The complete locus is also shown in Figure P. It comprises two ellipses whose lines of symmetry bisect the angles between m and n. The lines m and n are lines of symmetry for the locus as a whole.

3. See Figure Q.

4. See Figure R. It is a parabola, cf. Question 3.

236

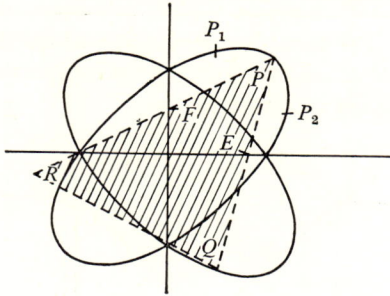

Fig. P

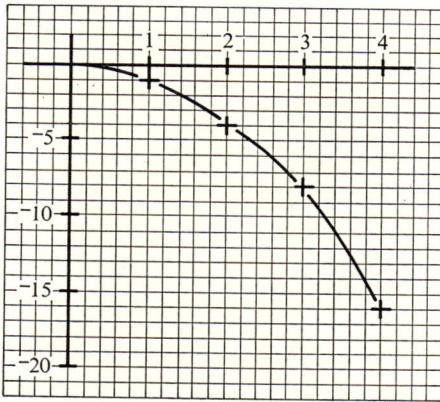

Fig. Q

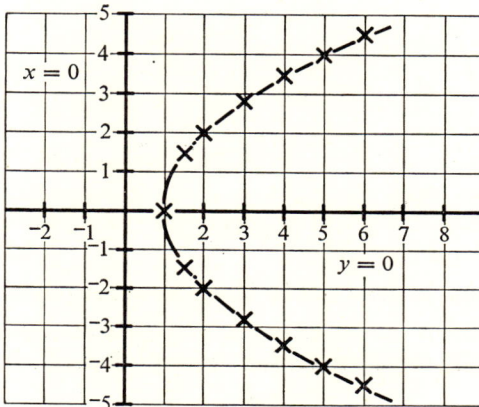

Fig. R

237

5. See Figure S. The locus is a succession of quadrants of circles, their centres, S, R' and Q', being the points on the ground about which the packing case rotates.

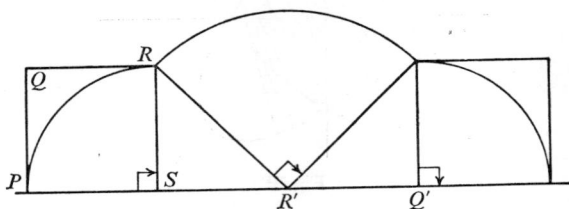

Fig. S

6. See Figure T. It is an ellipse.

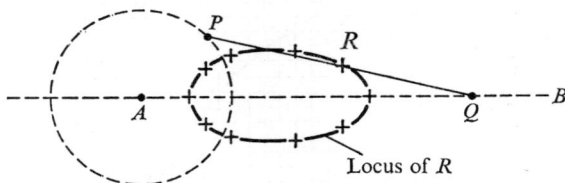

Fig. T

7. See Figure U. The locus is theoretically an enlargement (centre B, scale factor $\frac{1}{2}$) of the circle with centre A and hence is itself a circle.

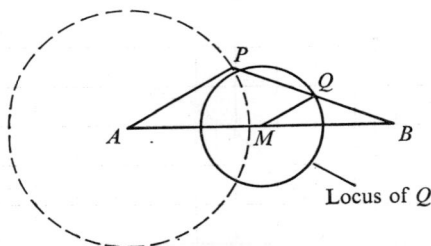

Fig. U

8. (*a*) All the differences will be found to be roughly 4.

(*b*) The locus is the set of points that are 4 cm further from F' than from F, or 4 cm further from F than F'. It is a two-branched curve, the opposite parts of the 'cross' go off to infinity along the same line—called an asymptote—however there will not be enough of the curve drawn to make this very clear.

(*c*) The difference would be the same at all points on the hyperbola. The locus would be a similar hyperbola. The mediator of *FF'*, a very specialized case of the hyperbola in which the two branches coincide. One extra station.

9, 10. *The Ellipse.*

The scales have been so chosen that the three ellipses should have the same dimensions. An ellipse may be tested by holding the figure in a plane not at 90° to the direction of vision and adjusting (with the other eye closed) to see whether it appears to be a circle. This relies on the fact that an ellipse is an orthogonal projection of a circle and vice versa.

11. $PM = 10 \cos \theta°$, $PN = 6 \sin \theta°$; these are double the ones in Figure 23.

3. ENVELOPES

The way in which a set of lines 'form' a curve is far less obvious than the way in which a set of points do but, aesthetically speaking, envelopes are more fun than loci and call for patience and care rather than any artistic skill. The cardioid in Figure 25 is a splendid example of the exciting results that can be obtained and is intended as hors d'oeuvre.

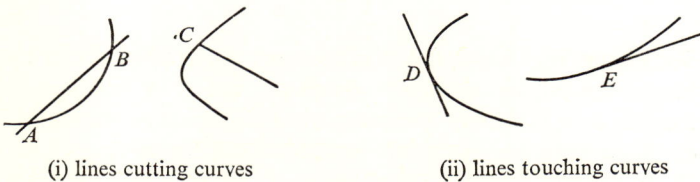

(i) lines cutting curves   (ii) lines touching curves

Fig. V

(*a*) The lengths of the lines are equal; they all touch the smaller circle. A discussion of tangency is postponed until a chapter in Book 4, but it would be well at this stage to clarify the conventional uses of the words 'cut' and 'touch' and these are illustrated in Figure V. The lines 0 → 9, 1 → 10, etc., would envelop a smaller circle; the lines 0 → 12, 1 → 13, etc., envelop a single point.

(*b*) Filter papers are very suitable for this example. The lines envelop an ellipse.

(*c*) Pin-board is specially useful for demonstration purposes.

Exercise C (p. 273)

1. The envelope is a circle centre A, radius $4 (= 8 \sin 30°)$ cm, the line l is always at a fixed distance from A which explains why the locus is a circle.

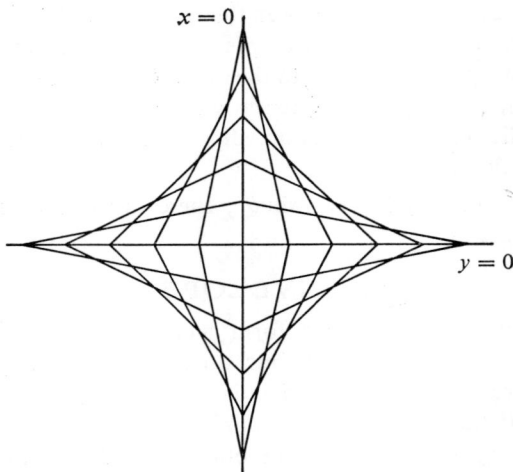

$x = 0$

$y = 0$

Fig. W

2. See Figure W. Only a few positions are required to give a clear impression of the complete envelope, but it is worth taking trouble to make them symmetrical. This envelope must not be confused with the parabolic arcs obtained by joining $(1, 0)$ to $(0, 8)$, then $(2, 0)$ to $(0, 7)$, $(3, 0)$ to $(0, 6)$, etc. The illustration of the use of a pin-board, Figure 28, contains two of these parabolic arcs.

3. Half the envelope is shown in Figure X. The remainder can be obtained by reflection in $x = 0$. It is an ellipse.

4. The envelope is shown in Figure Y. It is not necessary to take negative values of h and k in order to see that the envelope consists of the single point $(6, 0)$.

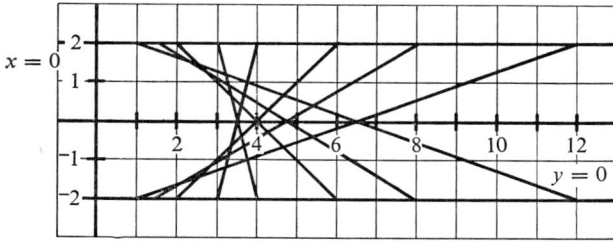

Fig. X

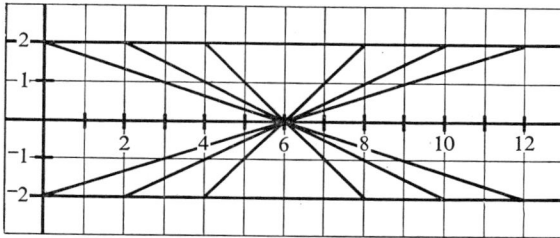

Fig. Y

5. See Figure Z.

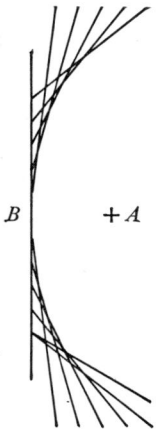

Fig. Z

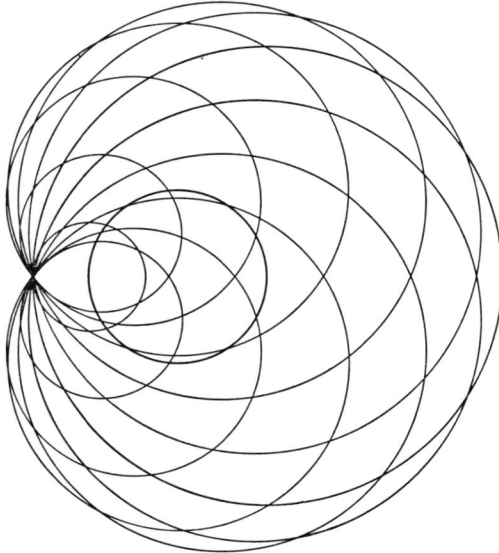

Fig. AA

6. See Figure AA. This is a limaçon, it has a 'hollow' middle most easily seen if the base circle is drawn in pencil and is finally rubbed out. The cardioid is a special case of the limaçon.

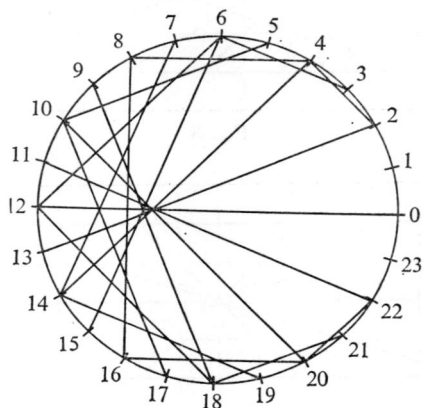

Fig. BB

7. See Figure BB. The 24 points are easily marked by measuring off the radius 6 times round the circle, then bisecting an arc and repeating, etc. Better envelopes may be drawn by taking more points. A 36-point envelope, using the protractor to find the points, gives good results. Note that the arithmetic must have an even modulus otherwise the process does not terminate after one circuit of the domain. The envelope is a cardioid.

8. See Figure CC. The envelope is a parabola. The same result can be obtained more simply by marking equal intervals on *l* and *l'* but the result is rather more obvious.

9. See Figure DD. The envelope is called a *nephroid*. It is like a ball of wool tied round the middle or like a kidney.

10. The locus is again a nephroid, whose other name is a two-cusped epicycloid.

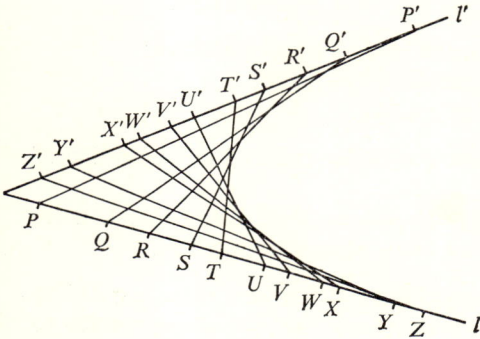

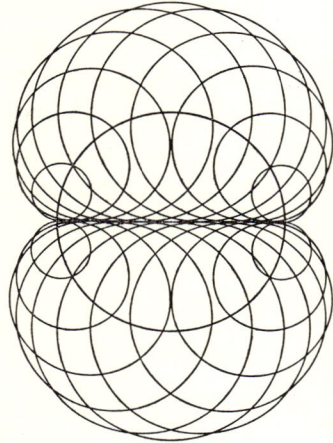

Fig. CC   Fig. DD

4. LOCI IN THREE DIMENSIONS

(*a*) An infinity of mediators, they form a plane. The universal set $\mathscr{E}$ is now the whole of space.

(*b*) The set of points P equidistant from A, B and C;

$$\pi_1 = \{P: BP = CP\};$$

and

$$\pi_2 = \{P: AP = CP\};$$

$$\pi_1 \cap \pi_2 = \{P: AP = BP = CP\}$$

and this is also the line p. Any point on it is equidistant from A, B and C.

(*c*) O lies on the mediators of the sides of the triangle (i.e. at the circumcentre); π_1 is at right-angles to BC and hence to the shaded plane; π_2 is at right-angles to AC and hence to the shaded plane, therefore, $\pi_1 \cap \pi_2$, i.e. p, is at right-angles to the shaded plane. If the planes are thought of as leaves of a book, any plane in the position of another leaf will contain p, in particular the plane $\{P: AP = BP\}$. An infinity of spheres can be drawn to pass through A, B and C. Their centres will lie on p.

Exercise D (p. 275)

1. (a) A sphere radius 1, centre A;
   (b) half of space, on the far side of π_2 in Figure 34.

2. (a) Treating it as a point, the locus would be a circle;
   (b) it lies on part of the surface of a sphere;
   (c) it lies on the surface of a cone.

3. (a) The surface of an infinite cylinder radius 1 m whose line of symmetry is l;
   (b) The surface of a torpedo shaped solid formed of a finite cylinder with hemispherical ends, each of radius 1 m.

4. A set of four parallel straight lines, two in one plane parallel to π and 2 cm away, and the other two in the other plane parallel to π and 2 cm away; each line is 3 cm away from l and is parallel to it.

5. X is the surface of a cylinder perpendicular to the paper of radius 10 cm and with c as a line of symmetry, $\pi \cap X$ is a circle in the plane of the paper, with centre where c cuts the plane and radius 10 cm. If c makes an acute angle with π, then $\pi \cap X$ is an ellipse in the plane of the paper.

6. (a) Two planes parallel to π and 4 cm away on either side;
   (b) a sphere of radius 5 cm and centre A;
   (c) a pair of circles, radius 3 cm in the planes mentioned in (a) above.

7. See Figure EE.

   The locus is part of a helix; familiar examples are springs, worm gears, bolts, etc.

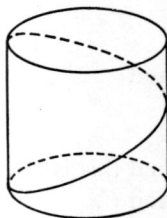

Fig. EE

8. (a) The surface of the cigar-shaped solid formed by rotating the ellipse $\{P: PA+PB = 6\}$ which would be obtained as a two-dimensional locus in the shaded plane;
   (b) the part of space lying outside this solid;
   (c) the sphere obtained by rotating the circle $\{P: PA = 2PB\}$ which would be obtained as the two-dimensional locus in the shaded plane.

10. Using the idea of Question 8 we can see that the three basically different envelopes are those shown in Figure FF. The curved parts of the envelopes resemble those of Figure 36(*b*).

(i) (ii) (iii)

Fig. FF

PUZZLE CORNER

1. See Figure A.

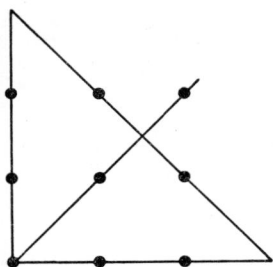

Fig. A

2. See Figure B.

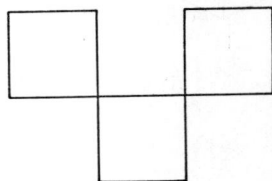

Fig. B

3.

Start	*H*	*T*	*H*	*T*	*H*	*T*	*H*	*T*	.	.
Move 1	*H*	.	.	*T*	*H*	*T*	*H*	*T*	*T*	*H*
Move 2	*H*	*H*	*T*	*T*	.	.	*H*	*T*	*T*	*H*
Move 3	*H*	*H*	*T*	*T*	*T*	*T*	*H*	.	.	*H*
Move 4	.	.	*T*	*T*	*T*	*T*	*H*	*H*	*H*	*H*

4. Two complete revolutions. It helps to see this by considering the half-way position (Figure C). The arc of the shaded semi-circle of *B* will have rolled along the arc of the shaded semi-circle of *A*, and point *P* will again be at the top. Thus *B* has made one complete revolution.

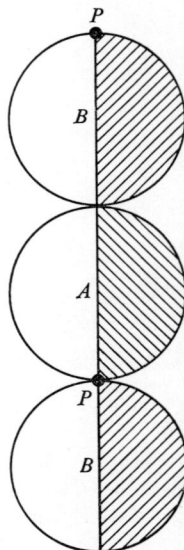

Fig. C

5. There are many possibilities, e.g.

AH	*KS*	*QD*	*JC*
JD	*QC*	*KH*	*AS*
KC	*AD*	*JS*	*QH*
QS	*JH*	*AC*	*KD*

Arrangements of this type are called Euler Squares. For a simpler problem see Chapter 1, Exercise D, Question 5. The original problem solved by Euler (of Koenigsberg Bridge fame) was '36 officers of 6 different ranks and from 6 different regiments have to stand in a square so that each orthogonal contains 6 officers from different regiments and of different ranks'.

See *Mathematical Recreations*, M. Kraitchik.

6. 2180 − 2199.

7. Use the method of repeated bisection.

Since $2^{20} = 1,048,576$, 20 questions of the form:

'Is your number less than or equal to 2^{19}?'

'Is your number less than or equal to 2^{18}?', etc.,

will solve the problem.

For example, suppose the number thought of is 10. The 16th question will be 'Is your number less than or equal to 2^4?' The answer is 'Yes'.

'Is your number less than or equal to 2^3?' 'No.'

'Is your number less than or equal to 12?' 'Yes'.

'Is your number less than or equal to 10?' 'Yes'.

'Is your number less than or equal to 9?' 'No'.

'Your number is 10'.

8. $53\frac{1}{2}$p made up of 4×10p, 1×5p, 4×2p and $1 \times \frac{1}{2}$p.

9. 100 kilometres.

The trains meet after each has travelled 50 kilometres, i.e. after 1h. Since Frank was travelling at 100 km/h he will have gone 100 kilometres.

10. A solid of constant breadth will not only serve as a wheel but will also roll round a square. One possibility is a figure consisting of an equilateral triangle with arcs described from the opposite corners (Figure D). This needs modifying in order to give it cutting edges (Figure E).

11. Macartney had the better bowling average for the first and second innings, but Noble had the better for the match as a whole. Macartney took a total of 6 wickets for 49, giving an average of $8\frac{1}{6}$. Noble took a total of 7 wickets for 53, giving an average of $7\frac{4}{7}$.

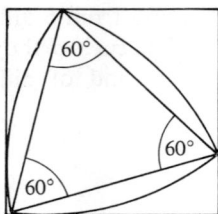

Fig. D

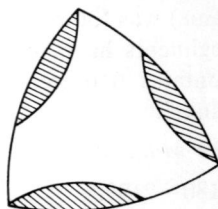

Fig. E

12. Fold the right-hand half under the left-hand half as in Figure F(i) and then fold the bottom half under as in Figure F(ii).

Insert fingers inside and tuck 4 and 5 between 6 and 3. Fold 1 and 2 under.

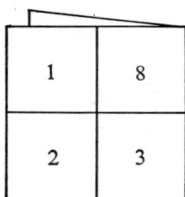

(i)

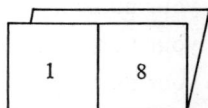

(ii)

Fig. F

13. See Figure G.

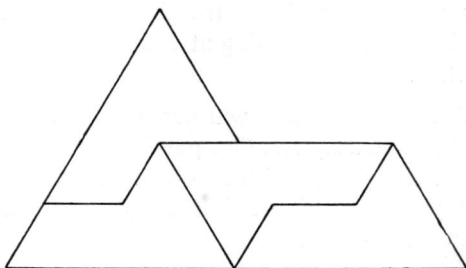

Fig. G

14. No, there is the same amount of wine in the water as there is water in the wine.

Since the quantities of liquid in the glasses are the same at the end as at the beginning the amount of wine in the first glass must just compensate for the amount of water which has been lost from the first glass. See *Prelude to Mathematics*, W. W. Sawyer, p. 28.

15. The time was $3.16\frac{4}{11}$ p.m.

The hands are together at 12 o'clock. They will next be together a little after 1.5 p.m. Suppose the time is then $1.x$ p.m. Since the minute hand moves 12 times as fast as the hour hand

$$x = 5 + \frac{x}{12}.$$

Hence, $x = 5\frac{5}{11}$.

The time is then $1.5\frac{5}{11}$ p.m.

After another 1 h $5\frac{5}{11}$ min the hands will again be together. Repeating this, gives the answer $3.16\frac{4}{11}$ p.m.

16.
```
   9,567
   1,085
  ------
  10,652
  ------
```

M must be 1 (since the sum of S and M, even with a carry from the previous column, cannot reach the 20's). Since $S + M$, possibly with 1 carried over, is a 2-digit number, S is either 8 or 9. This means that O must be 0 (it cannot be 1 since $M = 1$). If S is 8, there must be a carry from $E + O$. Hence there must also be a carry from the previous column, and then $N = 0$. But we already have $O = 0$. Hence S is not 8, and must therefore be 9.

Now $E + 1 = N$ and $N + R + $ possibly $1 = E + 10$

$$\Rightarrow R + \text{possibly } 1 = 9.$$

But $S = 9$. Hence $R = 8$.

Since N is 1 greater than E, there must be a carry from $D + E$. This means that $D + E \geqslant 12$ (since $Y \neq 0$ or 1). The only possibilities are $7 + 6$ or $7 + 5$. But $N = E + 1$, so $E = 5$, $N = 6$ and $D = 7$.

17. The pieces do not fit together exactly. The parallelogram, shown exaggerated in Figure H, makes up the extra square centimetre. The angle $x°$ can be calculated easily (by the teacher).

$$\tan y° = \tfrac{3}{8}; \quad \tan z° = \tfrac{5}{2};$$

$$y = 20·6 \quad z = 68·2;$$

$$x = 90 - 20·6 - 68·2 = 1·2.$$

Squares of other dimensions can be obtained by using numbers of the Fibonacci sequence

$$0, 1, 1, 2, 3, 5, 8, 13, 21, 34, 55, 89, ...$$

For any three consecutive numbers the product of the first and last numbers is the square of the middle number plus or minus one.

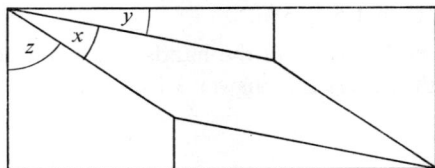

Fig. H

18. 31 regions.

This is a good example of the dangers of inductive thought. It can be shown that the number of regions for n points is

$$^nC_2 + {}^nC_4 + 1 = \frac{n(n-1)}{1.2} + \frac{n(n-1)(n-2)(n-3)}{1.2.3.4} + 1.$$

It is a coincidence that this gives powers of 2 for $n = 2, 3, 4, 5$. (It also gives a power of 2, 256, for $n = 10$.)

19.

Number of discs	Number of moves
1	1
2	3
3	7
4	15
5	31
.	.
.	.
.	.
Guess n	$2^n - 1$

250

By looking at the pattern, a reasonable guess is that for n discs $2^n - 1$ moves are required. This can be proved by the method of mathematical induction, and provides a good example for use at the sixth-form level.

The end of the world is not yet imminent since $2^{64} - 1$ moves are needed, and at one move per second this will take about 582,000,000,000 years.

20. Since the square of the 3-digit number TWO is a 5-digit number, and these numbers begin with the same digit, this means that $T = 1$ and $W \leqslant 4$.

Since the last digit E of the product is not O, it follows that $O \neq 1$ or 5 or 6.

Trial and error, looking for a square ending in two equal digits gives
$$138 \times 138 = 19,044.$$

21. Yes, there would be enough space, and he does not even have to crawl.

If R is the radius of the earth, C its circumference and h the height of the wire, all measurements being in metres, then
$$2\pi R = C$$
and
$$2\pi(R+h) = C+30.$$
Hence
$$h = \frac{30}{2\pi} \approx 4\cdot8 \text{ m.}$$

22. Number the coins 1, 2, 3, 4, 5, 6, 7, 8, 9. Split them into 3 sets 123, 456, 789.

The diagrams show the weighing plans.

(a) Two weighings

Compare two sets and so find the heaviest of the three sets. Within heaviest set, compare two coins to find the heaviest.

251

(b) Three weighings.

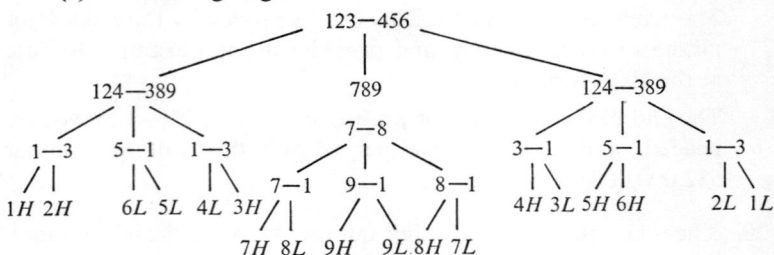

123—456

124—389   789   124—389

7—8

1—3   5—1   1—3   3—1   5—1   1—3

1H 2H   6L 5L   4L 3H   7—1   9—1   8—1   4H 3L 5H 6H   2L 1L

7H 8L   9H   9L 8H 7L

23. Call the 5 people *A*, *B*, *C*, *D* and *E*. *A* is allowed to cut off what he considers is one-fifth of the cake. If *B* thinks that this is too big, he is allowed to reduce it to what he thinks is one-fifth by cutting off a slice. If he does not think it is too big, he leaves it. *C*, *D* and *E* are now given similar options; the last one to touch the portion keeps it.

The remainder of the cake, together with the cut-off slices (if any), is then divided amongst the remaining four people by a similar procedure. And so on.

24. A maximum of 7 weighings is required. 2 objects require 1 weighing. 3 objects require 3 weighings. 4 objects require 5 weighings, since the last object must be weighed against the middle one of the first 3, and then against the first or third.

For 5 objects the procedure is: take 2 objects and compare them. Take another 2 and compare them. Weigh the heavier of the first pair against the heavier of the second.

Call these four objects *A*, *B*, *C*, *D*, where $A < B < C$ and $D < C$. Two weighings are now required to put *E* in the sequence *A*, *B*, *C*. Then at most 2 more weighings to insert *D*, since it is known that $D < C$.

25. The minimum number is 79.

There are a variety of methods: see a discussion of the 5-man problem in *More Mathematical Puzzles and Diversions*, by M. Gardner.

At this level a trial and error method is expected: suppose they finish up with 1 coconut each, then at the previous stage there must have been 4, and so on, working backwards.

26. Line the bags up. Take 1 coin from the first bag, 2 coins from the second, 3 from the third, etc. If the coins were genuine the weight should be

$$1+2+3+\ldots+12 = \tfrac{1}{2}\times 12\times 13 = 78 \text{ kg}.$$

The number of (50 g)s short of 78 kg gives the number of the forged bag.

27. The shortest time is 1·77 min.

Time (min)	Event
0·00–0·05	Put in A
0·05–0·10	Put in B
0·55–0·57	Turn A
0·60–0·65	Remove B
0·65–0·70	Put in C
1·07–1·12	Remove A
1·12–1·17	Put in B (second side)
1·20–1·22	Turn C
1·67–1·72	Remove B
1·72–1·77	Remove C

28. The motorist points to one road and asks 'If I asked you if this road leads to Exeter, would you say "Yes"?'. This will produce the right answer, even if the untruthful brother answers.

Another possible question is 'If I asked your brother whether this road leads to Exeter, would he say "Yes"?' This will always produce the wrong answer.

29. C's hat was blue.

At first sight this may seem indeterminate. It is best seen by writing out all the possibilities.

	A	B	C
1	B	R	R
	Yes	Yes	
2	R	B	R
	No	Yes	
3	R	R	B
	No	No	
4	B	B	R
	No	Yes	
5	B	R	B
	No	No	
6	R	B	B
	No	No	
7	B	B	B
	No	No	

In case 1, A sees two red (R) hats. Since there were only two reds altogether, he knows he must have a blue. B sees a red hat, and having heard A say 'Yes', knows that he must have a red.

In case 2, A sees a blue and a red, and has to say 'No'. B sees a red, and having heard A say 'No', realizes that he cannot have a red, for then A would have said 'Yes'. Hence he knows he must have a blue. Similar arguments apply to the other cases. The interesting point is that in the two cases where A says 'No' and B says 'Yes', C has a red hat, and in the four cases when A and B both say 'No', C has a blue.

30.

¹ 2	² 9	³ 1	⁴ 2
⁵ 3	8	⁶ 9	1
⁷ 6	⁸ 7	⁹ 4	9
¹⁰ 6	4	8	7

$8D \Rightarrow a$ is a square number,
$9D \Rightarrow 10 \leqslant 3a^2 \leqslant 99,$ $\Big\} \Rightarrow a = 4.$

$2D \Rightarrow 10 \leqslant 2b^2 \leqslant 99 \Rightarrow b \in \{3, 4, 5, 6, 7\}.$

$5A$ and $2D \Rightarrow c$ is odd, and $c \leqslant 33.$

$4D \Rightarrow 10 < c \leqslant 21.$

$8D \Rightarrow b$ is odd. Hence $b \in \{3, 5, 7\}.$

$9A \Rightarrow c \leqslant 13.$ Hence $c \in \{11, 13\}.$

Trial gives $c = 13, \quad b = 7.$

REVISION EXERCISES

SLIDE RULE SESSION NO. 7 (p. 282)

(See note on p. 57.)

1. 3.499; 3.50 ± 0.01.
2. 7.666; 7.67 ± 0.03.
3. 6.0025; 6.00 ± 0.02.
4. 9.872; 9.87 ± 0.03.
5. 0.06798; 0.0680 ± 0.0002.
6. 1.333; 1.333 ± 0.003.
7. 1.198; 1.198 ± 0.003.
8. 0.3025; 0.3025 ± 0.001.
9. 1.047; 1.047 ± 0.003.
10. 5.420; 5.42 ± 0.02.

SLIDE RULE SESSION NO. 8 (p. 282)

(See note on p. 57.)

1. 3.240; 3.24 ± 0.01.
2. 64.03; 64.0 ± 0.2.
3. 0.9899; 0.990 ± 0.003.
4. 0.3130; 0.313 ± 0.001.
5. 695.5; $695(.5) \pm 3$.
6. 0.001405; $(1.405 \pm 0.005) \, 10^{-3}$.
7. 172.1; 172 ± 1.
8. 32.72; 32.7 ± 2.
9. 1.145; $1.14(5) \pm 0.005$.
10. 407.7; 408 ± 1.

S (p. 282)

1. $p = 85$.
2. $n(X) = 16$.
3. $x = 5, y = 0$.
4. $\frac{2}{3}$.
5. 12.
6. $45°$.
7. $\frac{17}{36}$, for example.
8. 0.0735.

T (p. 282)

1. 10^{16}.
2. $7, 8$.
3. It is non-commutative.
4. Always.
5. 9.
6. $p^2 + 4pq + 4q^2$.
7. A kite, for example.
8. $1, 2, 3, 4, 10$, for example.

U (p. 283)

1. (a).
2. (c).
3. (c).
4. (a).
5. (b).
6. (a), (b).
7. (b).
8. (c).
9. (c).
10. (b).

V (p. 284)

1. (a) True;   (b) false;   (c) true;   (d) false.

2. (a) True;   (b) true;   (c) false;   (d) true.

3. (a) True;   (b) true;   (c) true;   (d) false.

4. (a) False;   (b) false;   (c) true;   (d) false.

5. (a) True;   (b) true;   (c) false;   (d) true.

6. (a) True;   (b) false;   (c) false;   (d) true;   (e) true.

7. (a) True;   (b) true;   (c) false;   (d) true.

8. (a) True;   (b) true;   (c) false;   (d) true;   (e) false.

9. (a) False;   (b) false;   (c) false;   (d) true;   (e) true.

10. (a) False;   (b) false;   (c) false;   (d) true;   (e) true.

W (p. 285)

1. (a) $\{-10, 10\}$;   (b) $\{3\}$;   (c) $(x: -5 < x < 5)$;   (d) ø.

2. The mean number of active machines each day is $8\frac{11}{51}$. 32 (31·7) days should be allowed, assuming similar conditions.

3. No (e.g. all quadrilaterals with right-angled vertices are not squares).

4. (a) $59·5 \leqslant l < 60·5$;   (b) false;   (c) 2647·75 cm².

5. The locus of P' is a line parallel to AB. C' is (0, 4), D' is (4, 2).

6. (a) $\angle AVC, \angle BVC$.
   (b) If M is the mid-point of AB, the plane of symmetry contains C, V and M.
   (c) $\angle x = \angle CMV$; $\angle y = \angle AVB$.

7. (a) A;   (b) 6·16 units.

8. (a) Regular tetrahedron;   (b) A;   (c) $4\sqrt{3}$ (= 6·9) cm².

X (p. 287)

1. (a) 53_6;   (b) $2n^2+3n$;   (c) n and $(2n+3)$.

2. (a) $0\cdot267$;   (b) $0\cdot027$;
  (c) $10x = 2\cdot6666...$, so $9x = 2\cdot4$. Hence $x = \frac{4}{15}$.

3. (b) $\angle ABC = 110°$;   (c) $240°$.

5. (a) A;   (b) Some dogs are not fat.

6. (a) A half-turn about the mid-point of CC';
  (b) They bisect one another.

7. (a) $\mathbf{MN} = \begin{pmatrix} 2 & ^-1 \\ 6 & 4 \end{pmatrix}$, $\mathbf{NM} = \begin{pmatrix} 5 & ^-3 \\ 3 & 1 \end{pmatrix}$. No.
  (b) $(1, 2)$.

8. Mean $= 26\cdot7$ days, median $= 26$ days, lower quartile $= 20$ days, upper quartile $= 33$ days. Inter-quartile range is 13 days.

Y (p. 288)

1. (b) $\sqrt{68} = 8\cdot25$ cm;   (c) $90°$.   (d) yes.
  (e) If O is the centre of the base, and M the mid-point of BC, the angle required is $\angle VMO$.
  (f) Yes!

2. $\sqrt{5} = 2\cdot24$.

3. $\mathbf{AE} = \begin{pmatrix} 8 \\ 6 \end{pmatrix}$. This vector is 10 units long.

4. The respective shares are 96, 72, 48, 24 sweets. Alan has $133\frac{1}{3}\%$ of Brian's share, Colin has $66\frac{2}{3}\%$, David has $33\frac{1}{3}\%$.

5. There are sixteen possible combinations.
  (a) $\frac{1}{16}$;   (b) $\frac{1}{4}$;   (c) 0.

7. $53\cdot5$ m; $0\cdot065$ cm².

8. 111.

REVISION EXERCISES

Z (p. 289)

1. $x \geqslant 10$.   2. 7.   3. (0, 0).

4. Between 90° and 180°.

5. y is proportional to x^2; the 48 should be 44.

6. Mean = 46·2 cm;   mode = 45 cm;   median = 45 cm;   lower quartile = 42 cm; upper quartile = 51 cm.

7. Profit = $3x/10$; price paid = $7x/10$.

8. 6·4.

BIBLIOGRAPHY

Archbold, J. W. *Algebra*. Pitman, 1961.

Battersby, J. *Mathematics and Management*. Penguin Books, 1967.

Berge, C. *The Theory of Graphs*. Methuen/Wiley, 1962.

Birkhoff, G. and Maclane, S. *A Survey of Modern Algebra*. Macmillan, 3rd ed. 1965.

Bolt, A. B. (*Ed.*). *We Built Our Own Computers*. Cambridge University Press, 1966.

Coulson, A. E. *An Introduction to Matrices*. Longmans, 1965.

Cundy, H. M. and Rollett, A. P. *Mathematical Models*. Oxford University Press, 2nd edition, 1961.

D'Arcy W. Thompson. *On Growth and Form*. Cambridge University Press, 1917 (First edition abridged by J. T. Bonner, 1961.)

Félix, L. *Modern Mathematics and the Teacher*. Cambridge University Press, 1966.

Fletcher, A. and Clarke, G. *Management and Mathematics*. Business Publ., 1964.

Fletcher, T. J. (*Ed.*) *Some Lessons in Mathematics*. Cambridge University Press, 1964.

Gardner, M. *More Mathematical Puzzles and Diversions*. Bell, 1961 and Penguin Books, 1965.

Gibson, G. R. and Mayatt, J. *First Stages in Matrices*. University of London Press, 1965.

Hogben, L. *Mathematics in the Making*. Macdonald, 1960.

Hollingdale, S. H. and Toothill, G. C. *Electronic Computers*. Penguin Books, 1965.

Huff, D. *How to Lie with Statistics*. Gollancz, 1954.

Jeger, M. *Transformation Geometry*. Allen and Unwin, 1966.

Kemeny, J. G., Snell, J. L. and Thompson, G. L. *An Introduction to Finite Mathematics*. Prentice Hall, 1957.

Kraitchik, M. *Mathematical Recreations*. Allen and Unwin, 1949.

Lockwood, E. H. *A Book of Curves*. Cambridge University Press, 1961.

Lockyer, K. G. *An Introduction to Critical Path Analysis*. Pitman, 1964.

Loveday, R. *Statistics, a First Course*. Cambridge University Press, 1958.

Mansfield, D. E. and Bruckheimer, M. *Background to Set and Group Theory*. Chatto and Windus, 1965.

Mansfield, D E. and Bruckheimer, M. *Mathematics, a New Approach*, vol. 4. Chatto and Windus, 1966.

Marchant, J. P. and Pegg, D. *Digital Computers*. Blackie, 1967.

Matthews, G. *Matrices 1*. Arnold, 1964.

Maxwell, E. A. *Algebraic Structure and Matrices*. Cambridge University Press, 1965.

Moroney, M. J. *Facts from Figures*. Penguin Books, 1958.

Ore, O. *Graphs and their Uses*. Random House, 1963.

BIBLIOGRAPHY

Pedoe, D. *The Gentle Art of Mathematics*. English Universities Press, 1958 and Penguin Books, 1963.

Reichmann, W. J. *The Use and Abuse of Statistics*. Methuen, 1961 and Penguin Books, 1964.

Rogers, F. E. *Topology and Matrices in the Solution of Networks*. Iliffe, 1965.

Rouse Ball, W. W. *Mathematical Recreations and Essays*. Macmillan, 1959.

Sawyer, W. W. *Mathematician's Delight*. Penguin Books, 1943.

Sawyer, W. W. *Prelude to Mathematics*. Penguin Books, 1955.

Sawyer, W. W. *Vision in Elementary Mathematics*. Penguin Books, 1964.

Sawyer, W. W. *A Path to Modern Mathematics*. Penguin Books, 1966.

Singh, J. *Mathematical Ideas*. Hutchinson, 1959.

Vajda, S. *An Introduction to Linear Programming and the Theory of Games*. Methuen/Wiley, 1961.

INDEX

261

INDEX